Merleau-Ponty

"This is the best introduction to Merleau-Ponty's work available. It provides a clear and lucid overview of the whole of Merleau-Ponty's thought, presenting the central ideas and themes of his writings in an accessible yet rigorous way. As such, it will be of interest to beginners and advanced scholars alike."

Mark Wrathall, University of California–Riverside, U.S.A.

"…a wonderful exposition of Merleau-Ponty's philosophy as a whole. It offers clear explanations of Merleau-Ponty's ideas and some of the most significant theories and movements that influenced him, and shows how his thinking developed across the course of his life. In addition, Carman has written with great panache."

Komarine Romdenh-Romluc, University of Nottingham, U.K.

"Carman's accounting is nuanced, closely argued, and exceptionally clear. His introduction covers the whole of Merleau-Ponty's considerable corpus, tracing its development and exhibiting its continued relevance for contemporary debates in phenomenology and psychology, philosophy of mind, and metaphysics. It will be enormously useful to teachers and students seeking an accessible introduction to Merleau-Ponty's writings."

Wayne Martin, University of Essex, U.K.

"This book is extremely well written—very clear and engaging—and, with regard to its representation of Merleau-Ponty's philosophy, the account is comprehensive and insightful. I would recommend this book as the first and main commentary for students to consult."

Sebastian Gardner, University College London, U.K.

Routledge Philosophers

Edited by Brian Leiter
University of Texas, Austin

Routledge Philosophers is a major series of introductions to the great Western philosophers. Each book places a major philosopher or thinker in historical context, explains and assesses their key arguments, and considers their legacy. Additional features include a chronology of major dates and events, chapter summaries, annotated suggestions for further reading and a glossary of technical terms.

An ideal starting point for those new to philosophy, they are also essential reading for those interested in the subject at any level.

Hobbes	A. P. Martinich
Leibniz	Nicholas Jolley
Locke	E. J. Lowe
Hegel	Frederick Beiser
Rousseau	Nicholas Dent
Schopenhauer	Julian Young
Freud	Jonathan Lear
Kant	Paul Guyer
Husserl	David Woodruff Smith
Darwin	Tim Lewens

Forthcoming:

Aristotle	Christopher Shields
Spinoza	Michael Della Rocca
Hume	Don Garrett
Fichte and Schelling	Sebastian Gardner
Rawls	Samuel Freeman
Heidegger	John Richardson

Taylor Carman

Merleau-Ponty

Routledge
Taylor & Francis Group

LONDON AND NEW YORK

First published 2008
by Routledge
2 Park Square, Milton Park, Abingdon, Oxon, OX14 4RN

Simultaneously published in the USA and Canada
by Routledge
270 Madison Ave, New York, NY 10016

Routledge is an imprint of the Taylor & Francis Group, an informa business

© 2008 Taylor Carman

Typeset in Joanna MT by Taylor & Francis Books
Printed and bound in Great Britain by TJ International Ltd, Padstow, Cornwall

British Library Cataloguing in Publication Data
A catalogue record for this book is available from the British Library

Library of Congress Cataloging in Publication Data
A catalog record for this book has been requested

ISBN 10: 0-415-33980-4 (hbk)
ISBN 10: 0-415-33981-2 (pbk)
ISBN 10: 0-203-46185-1 (ebk)

ISBN 13: 978-0-415-33980-3 (hbk)
ISBN 13: 978-0-415-33981-0 (pbk)
ISBN 13: 978-0-203-46185-3

For Caleb and Sophie

Acknowledgments viii
Abbreviations ix
Chronology x
Introduction 1

Life and Works   One   4

1. What Is Perception?   6
2. The View from Somewhere   8
3. Formative Influences   14
4. Language, Painting, and Politics   22
Summary   26
Further Reading   29

Intentionality and Perception   Two   30

1. What *Is* Intentionality?   30
2. Beyond the Phenomenological Reductions   37
3. What Perception Is *Not*   43
4. The Phenomenal Field   61
5. Molyneux's Problem   67
Summary   74
Further Reading   76

Body and World   Three   78

1. What the Body is *Not*   83
2. The Bodily Point of View   93
3. The Body Schema   102
4. Motor Intentionality   111
5. Flesh and Chiasm   120
Summary   132
Further Reading   134

Self and Others Four 135

1. Husserl and Sartre on Other Minds 137
2. Empathy and Solipsism 141
Summary 149
Further Reading 150

History and Politics Five 151

1. Perception of History 155
2. Liquidation of the Dialectic 166
Summary 177
Further Reading 179

Vision and Style Six 180

1. The Depth of the Visible 182
2. The Language of Art 194
3. Cézanne and His World 204
Summary 211
Further Reading 212

Legacy and Relevance Seven 213

1. Structuralism and the Habitus 214
2. Behaviorism, Cognitivism, and Artificial Intelligence 219
3. Embodied Cognition, Extended Mind, Enactivism 225
Summary 229
Further Reading 230

Glossary 231
Notes 234
Bibliography 248
Index 258

Acknowledgments

I am indebted to many friends and teachers who have helped me understand Merleau-Ponty and phenomenology. In addition to the participants in the annual meetings of the International Society for Phenomenological Studies, I especially want to thank Lydia Goehr, Sean Kelly, Komarine Romdenh-Romluc, Mark Wrathall, and two anonymous readers for Routledge who offered invaluable critical feedback on the manuscript. My greatest intellectual debt is, as always, to Bert Dreyfus.

I am grateful for support I received from Barnard College during a sabbatical leave in the fall of 2005. Thanks also to my editors, Brian Leiter and Tony Bruce, for their support and patience during the rather long time I have spent writing this book.

Abbreviations

HUSSERL

Id I   Ideen, Erstes Buch
Id II   Ideen, Zweites Buch
Id III   Ideen, Drittes Buch

MERLEAU-PONTY

AD   Les Aventures de la dialectique / Adventures of the Dialectic.

HT   Humanisme et terreur. Essai sur le problème communiste / Humanism and Terror: An Essay on the Communist Problem.

N   La Nature: Notes, Cours du Collège de France / Nature.

Œ   L'Œil et l'esprit / "Eye and Mind," in The Primacy of Perception / "Eye and Mind," in The Merleau-Ponty Aesthetics Reader.

PM   La Prose du monde / The Prose of the World.

PP   Phénoménologie de la perception / Phenomenology of Perception (1962) / Phenomenology of Perception (Routledge Classics Edition) (2002).

RC   Résumés de cours, Collège de France 1952–1960 / "Themes from the Lectures at the Collège de France, 1952–1960." In Praise of Philosophy and Other Essays.

S   Signes / Signs / The Merleau-Ponty Aesthetics Reader.

SC   La Structure du comportement / The Structure of Behavior.

SNS   Sens et non-sens / Sense and Non-Sense / The Merleau-Ponty Aesthetics Reader.

VI   Le Visible et l'invisible / The Visible and the Invisible

Chronology

1908	Born in Rochefort-sur-Mer, France.
1926–30	Attends the École Normale Supérieure, Paris.
1930–31	Military service.
1931–33	Teaches at lycée in Beauvais.
1933–34	Research scholarship from the Caisse Nationale des Sciences, Paris.
1934–35	Teaches at lycée in Chartres.
1935–39	Lecturer at the École Normale Supérieure; attends Aron Gurwitsch's lectures on Gestalt psychology.
1938	Submits *The Structure of Behavior* as thesis (*thèse complémentaire*).
1939–40	Mobilized and serves as lieutenant in the 5th Infantry Regiment and in the administrative staff of 59th Light Infantry Division.
1940–44	Teaches at the Lycée Carnot, Paris.
1942	*The Structure of Behavior* published.
1945	*Phenomenology of Perception* is published; Merleau-Ponty is awarded doctorate; co-founds, with Sartre and de Beauvoir, the journal *Les Temps modernes*.
1945–48	Appointed junior faculty (*maître de conférences*) and promoted to Professor of Philosophy at the University of Lyon.
1947	*Humanism and Terror* published.
1948	*Sense and Non-Sense* published.
1949–52	Professor of Child Psychology and Pedagogy at the Sorbonne University.
1952	Elected to Chair of Philosophy at the Collège de France.

1953   In *Praise of Philosophy* published; quarrels with Sartre; resigns from editorial board of *Les Temps modernes.*

1955   *Adventures of the Dialectic* published.

1960   *Signs* published.

1961   Dies of heart failure in Paris, 3 May.

1964   *The Visible and the Invisible* and "Eye and Mind" posthumously published.

1969   *The Prose of the World* posthumously published.

Introduction

Merleau-Ponty was one of the most interesting and original philosophers of the twentieth century. His most enduring contributions to philosophy belong to the theory—or rather, as the title of his magnum opus has it, the *phenomenology*—of perception. Although it is impossible to summarize his most significant and enduring insights in a few pages, four main points are worth highlighting at the outset.

First, Merleau-Ponty maintains that perception is not an event or state in the mind or brain, but an organism's entire bodily relation to its environment. Perception is, as psychologist J. J. Gibson puts it in *The Ecological Approach to Visual Perception*, an "ecological" phenomenon. The body consequently cannot be understood as a mere causal link in a chain of events that terminates in perceptual experience. Instead, it is constitutive of perception, which is the most basic— and in the end, inescapable—horizon of what Merleau-Ponty, following Heidegger, calls our "being in the world" (*être au monde*). Human existence thus differs profoundly from the existence of objects, for it consists not in our merely *occurring* among things, but in our actively and intelligently *inhabiting* an environment.

Second, precisely because it is a bodily phenomenon, perception is also essentially finite and perspectival: my body, Merleau-Ponty says, "is my point of view on the world" (PP 85/70/81). Though that might sound obvious, perceptual perspective is elusive and difficult to describe. It is neither symmetrical nor geometrical, for instance, but concretely anchored in the structures and capacities of the body. I can have a point of view on the world only by being in the world: I can perceive the environment only because I can inhabit it. Moreover, as Merleau-Ponty would say in his later works, my being in the world in turn depends on my being of the world: to see, I must also be visible; the world and I must be of the same "flesh" (chair):

> To say that the body is seeing, curiously, is to say nothing other than: it is visible. When I reflect on what I mean in saying that it is the body that sees, I find nothing other than: it is "from somewhere"...visible in the act of looking.
>
> (VI 327/273–74)

To understand perception as bodily being in the world is to pose a radical challenge to traditional distinctions between subject and object, inner and outer, mental and physical, mind and world. To say that our bodies, in at once seeing and being seen, must be of the same flesh as the world, is to cast doubt on the primacy of consciousness and the distinction between first- and third-person points of view, which Merleau-Ponty himself took for granted in Phenomenology of Perception. Prior even to having a perspective we can call our own, we are always already in a kind of unconscious communion with the world, which is necessarily a world of sense and sensibility, touch and tangibility, seeing and being seen. Perception is bodily, the body is perspectival, and perspective emerges —as if miraculously—out of the very stuff of the world: "my body sees only because it takes part in the visible where it opens forth" (VI 201/153–54).

Third, conceptual confusion about perception persists in part as the natural, perhaps inevitable, effect of a vital tendency at work in perception itself, namely our absorption in the world, our directedness toward objects, hence the systematic deflection of our attention away from our own experience. This is no mere accident, for "it is the essence of consciousness to forget its own phenomena" (PP

71/58/67); "perception masks itself to itself" (*VI* 266/213). Like a vortex, perception constantly pushes us out toward the world and away from itself, and so, as often happens in philosophy, we forget ourselves. Small wonder, then, that philosophers and psychologists have found perception so hard to describe or even think about clearly, for it is part of its very nature to deflect thought.

Finally, Merleau-Ponty undertakes an ambitious, though unsystematic and incomplete, program of extending his phenomenological insights beyond sense perception into a general account of the perspectival structure of *all* human experience and understanding. Perception is our most basic mode of being in the world, and the body is the ultimate and abiding subject of all perspectives available to us in principle. Bodily perspective grounds and informs culture, language, art, literature, history, science, and politics. Human conduct in all areas is marked, to a greater or lesser degree, by its bodily aspect, its perspectival orientation, and its inherent tendency toward self-deflection and self-forgetting.

For Merleau-Ponty, perception is essentially bodily, perspectival, self-deflecting, and in principle generalizable to all aspects of the human condition. These insights are the keys to making sense of his work as a whole. It is a body of work that goes beyond the problems of metaphysics, epistemology, and the theory of perception—the more or less specialized subdisciplines to which his chief philosophical contributions belong—to include psychology, biology, culture, language, painting, history, and politics. His published works cover a broad spectrum of disciplines and subjects, yet his ideas always hang together in a distinctive way, with abiding reference to the bodily, perceptual, and existential themes that originally inspired him.

One

Life and Works

Maurice Merleau-Ponty was born on March 14, 1908 in Rochefort-sur-Mer and raised by his mother in Paris after his father died in the First World War. He attended the Lycée Louis-le-Grand and then, from 1926 to 1930, the prestigious École Normale Supérieure, along with his friends Claude Lévi-Strauss and Simone de Beauvoir, and others he did knot know at the time, including Jean-Paul Sartre and Simone Weil. (Merleau-Ponty appears in Beauvoir's *Memoirs of a Dutiful Daughter* under both his real name and the pseudonym "Pradelle.")

Merleau-Ponty performed his initial military service in 1930–31, after which he was appointed professor of philosophy at the Lycée de Beauvais, where he taught until 1933. He was awarded a temporary grant the following year by the Caisse Nationale des Sciences, a government research fund subsumed in 1939 by the creation of the Caisse Nationale de la Recherche Scientifique (CNRS), and then taught in 1934–35 at the Lycée de Chartres. He returned to Paris as a lecturer (*agrégé-répétiteur*) at the École Normale Supérieure, where he taught from 1935 to 1939. During this period he attended Aron Gurwitsch's lectures on Gestalt psychology and in 1938 completed his first major philosophical work, *The Structure of Behavior*, which he submitted as his *thèse complémentaire* for the *doctorat d'état*, but which was not published until 1942. When war broke out, he was mobilized and served for a year as a lieutenant in the 5th Infantry Regiment and in the administrative staff of the 59th Light Infantry Division. From 1940 to 1944 he taught philosophy at the Lycée

Carnot and became active in the Resistance. He was granted the title of Docteur dès Lettres for the work that would be his magnum opus, *Phenomenology of Perception* (1945).

In 1945 Merleau-Ponty became a junior faculty member (*maître de conférences*) at the University of Lyon and was granted the title of professor in January 1948. In the fall of 1945 he co-founded, with Sartre and Beauvoir, the influential journal, *Les Temps modernes*, contributing articles of his own, some of which he later published under the titles *Humanism and Terror* (1947) and *Sense and Non-Sense* (1948). He held the chair in Psychology and Pedagogy at the Sorbonne from 1949 to 1952 and was then appointed to the prestigious Collège de France, occupying a position once held by Henri Bergson and similar to those later held by Roland Barthes, Raymond Aron, Michel Foucault, and Pierre Bourdieu. His inaugural lecture of 15 January 1953 was published under the title *In Praise of Philosophy*, and other lectures and notes from this period have appeared in print, some of them quite recently. The year 1953 also saw a bitter political and personal dispute with Sartre that led to Merleau-Ponty's resignation from the editorial board of *Les Temps modernes*. His critique of what he called Sartre's "ultrabolshevism" subsequently appeared in the volume *Adventures of the Dialectic* (1955), to which Sartre's own *Critique of Dialectical Reason* (1960) is in some ways a response. Finally, in 1960, Merleau-Ponty published a wide-ranging volume of philosophical and political essays under the title *Signs*. He died of a heart attack on May 3, 1961 at the age of 53.[1]

Such are the outward facts of Merleau-Ponty's life and career. In themselves, they are not especially relevant to his contributions to philosophy, for example his critique of intellectualism and empiricism, his notion of the bodily nature of perception, or his non-representational account of intentionality. Those central themes, belonging as they do to metaphysics, epistemology, and the philosophy of mind, bear little trace of Merleau-Ponty's personal relationships, his institutional affiliations, or his professional trajectory. Similarly, his work in aesthetics, especially concerning painting, and even more especially concerning Cézanne, has nothing much to do, as far as I can tell, with the external circumstances of his life. Like many philosophers—though unlike a distinguished few— Merleau-Ponty led a life not especially relevant to the inner logic and development of his ideas. Consequently, with the exception of Chapter 5, on history and politics, what follows makes virtually no reference to the biographical context of his work.

Things are very different, however, perhaps inevitably so, when it comes to Merleau-Ponty's political writings, which were bound up in complicated ways with his own life and with contemporary events: the rise of communism, the Moscow Trials, the Occupation and Liberation of France, the Cold War, the role of French intellectuals in modern public life, and his intellectual collaboration and friendship with Jean-Paul Sartre, which came to an end in 1953 over questions of politics. Chapter 5 therefore approaches Merleau-Ponty's political texts in a broader historical and personal context.

The present chapter is an attempt to articulate what I take to be the deep and important idea running throughout Merleau-Ponty's thought as a whole, a brief description of the main influences on his work— above all, the phenomenology of Husserl and Heidegger and Gestalt psychology—a preliminary account of his main phenomenological works, and finally a few remarks about how his writings on language, art, and politics fit into his larger, unfinished philosophical project.

1. WHAT *IS* PERCEPTION?

There is a difference between philosophical problems, puzzles, and mysteries or enigmas. Problems can be stated, solutions proposed, analyzed, accepted, rejected. Problems that cannot be adequately formulated are pseudoproblems or mere puzzles, sophisticated trick questions. Throughout much of the tradition, philosophers have seen their task as consisting in the formulation, examination, and solution of problems. When they become suspicious of those problems, they sometimes dismiss them as mere puzzles, pseudoproblems, illusions, conundrums.

Mysteries, or what Merleau-Ponty calls *enigmas*, are different. Like problems and puzzles, they take the canonical form of questions, yet they are better expressed simply by the words referring to them: *being, time, truth, knowledge, love, death*. Problems can be stated, we might say, whereas mysteries can only be named, gestured at, pondered. The paradigm form of philosophical inquiry into mysteries is thus the Socratic question, *What is X?* That there should be such a thing as justice or beauty or time or consciousness or truth or death can just seem incredible, even if we find it difficult to say why there ought *not* to be such a thing. Such phenomena are somehow intrinsically wondrous. At an extreme, that there *is* anything at all, rather than nothing, has struck some as primitively mysterious. It is tempting to say that what makes problems and puzzles *philosophical*, as opposed to merely technical or scientific, is precisely the whiff of mystery that lingers about them, the aura of wonder, as opposed to sheer conceptual opacity or complexity.

Merleau-Ponty's philosophical thought centers around one such mystery, a mystery that surfaces and resurfaces throughout his work, both implicitly and explicitly, whose full scope and consequences he thinks are as profound as they are elusive, but which, once expressed, can sound trivial. The mystery is, in a word, *perception*. What is so mysterious about perception? Not simply that it occurs, or that it has this or that qualitative feature, but that it discloses a world. Moreover, the world it discloses is one we can then think about, anticipate, remember, and ponder in all its mystery. In the preface to *Phenomenology of Perception* Merleau-Ponty thus writes, "the task of phenomenology is to reveal the mystery of the world and the mystery of reason" (PP xvi/xxi/xxiv).

Theories of perception date back to antiquity.[2] As a reminder of just how little about it is intuitively obvious, consider that many ancient theorists of vision, including Plato, Euclid, and Ptolemy, believed that our eyes actually *emit* light, which then supposedly combines with light coming from external objects, so that perception itself takes place outside us in the world where the two meet.

Aristotle rejected those "extramission" theories and hypothesized instead that objects reflect light, which then moves through a medium to our eyes. Others, including Democritus and Epicurus, supposed that copies or images of things literally move through space to our eyes, and versions of that idea survived into the seventeenth century. Leonardo da Vinci compared the eye to a *camera obscura* ("dark room") into which images are cast on a screen, and Johannes Kepler was the first to give an accurate account of the projection of what he called the optical *pictura* onto the surface of the retina. That picture in the eye, so it seemed, then had to be recorded or transformed into a more genuinely internal, subjective visual experience.

But how? For centuries, this inner-pictorial model of vision posed a number of serious problems. For example, experiments confirmed Kepler's claim that the crystalline lens inverts and reverses the image on the retinal surface. How then do we manage to see things right side up and right way around? Or do we? Moreover, most of us have two eyes, not just one, hence two retinal images. Why do we not always see double? Do we see with only one eye at a time? We will return to these problems briefly in the next two chapters. Suffice it here to say that the fact that they could have struck anyone as serious problems at all gives some indication of how deep the conceptual confusion about perception remained, even after many centuries of sophisticated empirical observation and reflection.

2. THE VIEW FROM SOMEWHERE

It is tempting to distinguish empirical questions concerning the mechanics and psychology of perception from *philosophical* questions concerning its essential nature, or the fundamental ways in which we understand it. And yet the mysteriousness of perception itself makes that distinction difficult to draw, for many substantive claims embedded in empirical theories of perception are themselves philosophically problematic. Still, there are clear cases at either end of the spectrum: recent neurological findings concerning the function of sensory mechanisms on the one side, perennial philosophical questions about perception on the other. Merleau-Ponty's phenomenology lies somewhere between the two. How, then, and to what extent is it *philosophical*?

Again, it is crucial to remember that what fascinates Merleau-Ponty about perception is the way in which it makes manifest a *world*. For it does so not just generically or abstractly, but by carving out a concretely shaped, distincitvely human perspective *within* the world it discloses: "perception is not born just anywhere," but "emerges in the recesses of a body" (*VI* 25/9). By manifesting itself in a body, perception establishes forms constitutive of all human experience and understanding, namely, finite perspectival orientation and a contrast between figure and background, focus and horizon. We have a perceptual perspective on the world, but we also have intellectual, social, personal, cultural, and historical perspectives, which are themselves no less anchored in our bodies than sense experience itself. Concrete finite perspective is essential to all aspects of our existence, Merleau-Ponty believes, and what makes any perspective concrete and finite is its rootedness in our bodily orientation and behavior.

What then *is* perspective? Rationalist philosophers like Leibniz, who conceive of our relation to the world as a cognitive or intellectual relation, as the relation of a thought to its object, have tended to imagine human knowledge as at best a finite approximation, indeed a pale reflection, of God's omniscience. God's perfect and unlimited knowledge of the universe, they supposed, is the proper standard against which to measure the scope and limits of what we can know. God's view is the ideal "view from nowhere." Our view, by contrast, is emphatically a view from *somewhere*, and is to that extent flawed and imperfect. And yet consider that the very idea of a view from nowhere is not just fanciful or extravagant, but incoherent. Taken literally, after all, a view from nowhere could not be a *view*. When I look at a house from different perspectives, Merleau-Ponty writes, "the house *itself* is none of these perspectives ... it is the house seen from nowhere. But what do these words mean? Isn't seeing always seeing from somewhere?" But how can we understand experience as both anchored in a point of view and yet open out onto the world, as opposed to trapped in the mind of the subject? As Merleau-Ponty says, "We must try to understand how vision can take place from somewhere without being enclosed in its perspective" (PP 81/67/78).

It is tempting to suppose that the world itself exists objectively (out there) and that we perceive and know it *through* or *by means of* subjective perspectives or inner experiences of some kind (in here). A perspective, of whatever sort, would then be a kind of extraneous superaddition to what there is, a mere instrument or medium, as Hegel put it, by means of which we grasp the world, or through which we discern it, however darkly.[3] Skeptical problems entailed by such metaphors have fueled modern epistemology, arguably at the expense of the mystery that inspired them in the first place, namely that it is a *world* that reveals itself to us. Hegel was one of the first to recommend dispensing with such representationalist images, and Merleau-Ponty follows him in wanting to overcome what they both regard as the crippling effects such models have on how we understand our place in the world.

The philosophical mystery that so impressed Merleau-Ponty and guided his work, then, has two sides—that we are *open onto* the world and that we are *embedded in* it. The first side of the mystery is the astonishing fact the world is disclosed to us at all, that our awareness reaches out into the midst of things other than ourselves, binding us to them in a way seemingly incomparable with the mute external relations in which mere objects blindly stand to one another. Perception is at once our "absolute proximity" to things and yet our "irremediable distance" from them (VI 23/8). How does vision, for example, manage to banish the darkness and density of brute physical reality, opening before us a visible milieu and rendering the world available for further exploration and discovery?

Perception, regarded in this deliberately naïve philosophical light, can seem like an ongoing mundane miracle; we take it for granted, yet it remains enigmatic.

The second side of the mystery is that we ourselves are neither angels nor machines, but living beings. We encounter the world neither as data-crunching information processors, nor as ghostly apparitions floating over the surface of things like a fog. Perceptual perspective is *bodily* perspective. We have a world only by having a body: "the body is our anchorage in the world" (PP 169/144/167); "The body is our general way of having a world" (PP 171/146/169). Of course, it is misleading to say that we "have" bodies, just as it would be misleading so say that we "have" minds or selves. Better, we *are* minds, selves, bodies.[4] It is equally misleading to say that we "have" a world, as if having a world were a kind of lucky accident, or as if it might turn out that we do not *really* have one, however much it *seems* as if we do. To say that we are bodily is to say that we *are* our bodies, just as saying that we are worldly is to say that worldliness is neither a property nor a relation, but constitutes our existence. For human beings, as Heidegger put it, *to be* is to be *in the world*.

Merleau-Ponty's thought is thus driven by the idea that perception and embodiment are not just problematic or puzzling, but mysterious or enigmatic. Like being and time, truth and knowledge, or love and death, embodiment and perception are not just problems (or puzzles) we might someday solve (or dissolve), but the *source* of problems and puzzles that arise once we try to reflect on them. Merleau-Ponty's phenomenology is therefore not just an analytical exercise aiming at the construction of an explanatory theory of perception or knowledge, but—more modestly, and yet more ambitiously—an effort to describe perception and the body in a radically new way, both to gain insight and to avoid the paradoxes and dead ends that plague traditional accounts of mind, body, and world.

The looming target of all Merleau-Ponty's efforts, his abiding philosophical *bête noire*, one might say, was and remained *rationalism*.

The term should be understood broadly to include not just the valorization and sublimation of *theôria* that has defined Western philosophy since Plato, but more specifically the *intellectualism* of Descartes and Kant, and of psychologists like Hermann von Helmholtz and Wilhelm Wundt. The most recent and still vital incarnation of rationalism, which Merleau-Ponty did not live to see, is *cognitivism*, which many philosophers, psychologists, and linguists take as definitive of the multifaceted discipline they now see as their shared domain, namely *cognitive science*.

Rationalism, intellectualism, and cognitivism are all different versions of a common underlying idea, namely, that *thought* constitutes our essential relation to the world; that insofar as our attitudes have content, they must be modes of *thinking*. Applied to sense experience, the idea, put crudely, is that perceiving is *a lot more like thinking* than people think it is. We will return to this idea in the next chapter, and throughout much of the rest of the book. Until then, consider two equally crude counterslogans, which might be said to capture the spirit of Merleau-Ponty's project.

First, perception is *not* a mode of thought, but is more basic; indeed, thought rests on and presupposes perception. Thinking subjects do not learn to attach their thoughts to a sensory world they encounter in the process of thinking; rather, perceiving agents must learn how to think about what they already see: "a child perceives before it thinks" (*VI* 27/11). Moreover, the intelligible world, being fundamentally fragmentary and abstract, stands out only against the stability and plenitude of a perceptual background:

> It is in its sense [*sens*] and intrinsic structure that the sensible world is "older" than the world of thought, for the former is visible and relatively continuous, and the latter, invisible and sparse [*lacunaire*], has its truth and seems to constitute a whole only on condition of being supported on the canonical structures of the other.
>
> (*VI* 28/12)

Second, in spite of the difference between the two, thinking is *a lot more like perceiving* than rationalists think it is. Why? Not because perception and judgment have the same kind of intentional content, which just happens to be coupled to different kinds of subjective attitudes in the two cases, but because thought and perception share many of the same underlying structural features. For example, thought, like perception, has a kind of perspectival orientation. We often try to approach a problem "from different angles" and sense that we've either grasped it or lost sight of it. When we think about something intently, we say we try to "get our minds around it." Similarly, thinking, like seeing, exhibits a fundamental figure/ground contrast. Even very abstract ideas confront me sometimes directly, at the "center" of my attention, and sometimes linger in the background or around the edges of my interests and concerns.

One could reply that these are mere metaphors, yet what really matters to phenomenology is whether such metaphors are *apt*, and to admit that they are is to admit that they capture something important about the experiential shape and contours of thinking, judging, assuming, wondering, and so on. Thoughts, though they may be in principle single and discrete, do not occur in a phenomenological vacuum; rather, I direct and focus my thoughts in a constantly shifting field of background assumptions, unfulfilled intentions, open questions, and competing considerations. Even when language expresses thoughts, it also makes the world intuitively present, not altogether unlike pictorial representations do: a writer does not manipulate symbols according to an algorithm, but sees through words to apprehend the world itself and render it visible, and in this sense, "his procedure is not very different from the painter's" (S 56/45/82). This is because thinking, judging, believing, remembering, imagining, expecting—all such attitudes, however abstract—are anchored in the body and so bear traces, if only faint ones, of the *situatedness* of perception: "The mind's eye, too, has its blind spot" (VI 55/33). Indeed, according to

Merleau-Ponty, all forms of human experience and understanding are grounded in and shaped by our finite bodily orientation in the world.

3. FORMATIVE INFLUENCES

1. Phenomenology

Merleau-Ponty was first and foremost a phenomenologist. Alongside pragmatism, logical positivism, and structuralism, phenomenology was among the dominant philosophical movements of the first two thirds of the twentieth century. Its founder was Edmund Husserl, and besides Merleau-Ponty its leading figures were Martin Heidegger, and Jean-Paul Sartre.

What is phenomenology? Simply put, it is an attempt to describe the basic structures of human experience and understanding from a concrete first-person point of view, in contrast to the reflective, third-person perspective that characterizes both scientific knowledge and received opinion. Phenomenology calls us to return, as Husserl put it, "to the things themselves." The "things" Husserl had in mind were not concrete external things (Dinge), but issues or matters (Sachen), the stuff—both form and content—of our experience and understanding as we live them, not as we have learned to conceive and describe them according to the categories of science and prejudices of common sense. Phenomenology urges us to resist the temptation to press our own experience into prefabricated conceptual boxes in the service of tradition or theory. Phenomenology is in this sense a descriptive rather than explanatory or deductive enterprise; it seeks to reveal the basic forms of experience and understanding as such, rather than construct hypotheses or draw inferences beyond their bounds.[5]

What are the phenomena, the "things themselves"? What is phenomenology a description of? Fundamentally, it is the study of what Husserl's teacher, Franz Brentano, called intentionality, that is, the directedness of experience, its of-ness or "aboutness." A perception or memory, for example, is not just a qualitative state of mind, but a perception or a memory of something. To think or dream is to think or dream *about* something. That may sound trivial, and yet, astonishingly, this seemingly obvious fact—that experience is of or *about* something—managed to fall through the cracks of traditional philosophical wisdom, thanks in part to the representationalism and the dualism of early modern thinkers like Descartes and Locke.

The Cartesian–Lockean conception of the mind—which still figures prominently in psychology and cognitive science today[6]—tries to give an account of perception, imagination, intellect, and the will in terms of the presence of "ideas" in the mind, or what Kant would later call "representations" (*Vorstellungen*). Ideas or representations were conceived as inner mental tokens, sometimes discursively on the model of thoughts, or the sentences expressing them, sometimes pictorially on analogy with images, or as Hume said, "impressions." But the "way of ideas," as Locke's version of the theory came to be known, was problematic from the outset. What *is* an idea? According to Locke, the term "serves best to stand for whatsoever is the Object of the Understanding when a Man thinks ... or whatever it is, which the Mind can be employ'd about in thinking." Locke seems to have considered the notion obvious and unproblematic: "I presume it will be easily granted me, that there are such *Ideas* in Men's Minds; every one is conscious of them in himself, and Men's Words and Actions will satisfy him, that they are in others."[7] Ideas are *objects* of consciousness; we are aware of them; they are what our attitudes are *about*. But of course this begs the question of intentionality, namely, how do we manage to be aware of anything? Simply positing ideas in the mind sheds no light on that question, for our awareness of our own ideas itself remains mysterious. Do we then need a further layer of ideas in order to be aware of the ideas that afford us an awareness of the external world? But this generates an infinite regress.

Perhaps Husserl's single greatest achievement was to insist on the uselessness of this theoretical framework in principle for shedding light on the problem of intentionality. For with or without ideas in the mind, the fact of intentionality remains, namely, that experience is *of* or *about* something; it has an *accusative* structure, which is to say *putative* (but not always actually existing) objects. Indeed, absent the hypothesis of inner mental representations, the problem of non-existent intentional objects becomes especially pressing. For that hypothesis seemed to explain how we can be aware of something that does not exist. When Macbeth hallucinates a dagger, there is no dagger before him, but surely, we suppose, there must be an idea or an image of a dagger in his mind, and *that* must be what he is conscious of in the hallucination. But again, this provides only the semblance of an explanation, for it tells us nothing about how Macbeth manages to be aware of the hallucinated image. Recognizing that the theory of inner mental tokens gets us nowhere, we must ask ourselves again how Macbeth can stand in an intentional relation *to the dagger*. But how is that possible? The dagger, after all, does not exist, and surely *relations* presuppose things related to one another.[8]

Husserl's solution to this problem is to distinguish between the *objects* and the *contents* of consciousness. There is a difference between the things we are aware of and the contents of our awareness of them. An intentional attitude is not itself strictly speaking a *relation* at all, but a mental act or state with *intrinsic* content. Perception is not *of* something, if the "of" in that formula indicates a causal relation to something in the external world; it is rather *as if* of something; it identifies or describes a merely putative object, whether such an object exists or not.

Husserl's distinction between the contents and the objects of consciousness parallels Frege's distinction between linguistic sense (*Sinn*) and reference (*Bedeutung*). To use Frege's own example, the expressions "Morning Star" and "Evening Star" have different senses, since they involve different descriptive contents and stand in different inferential relations to other terms, but they have one and the same referent, namely the planet Venus.[9] Similarly, for Husserl, my perception of an apple tree in a garden has what he calls a "perceptual sense" (*Wahrnehumungssinn*), namely the content of my perceptual experience, including not just what directly meets my eye, but also a vast background of assumptions, memories, associations, and anticipations that make my experience inexhaustibly rich. For example, I see the tree not just as a physical surface facing me, but as a three-dimensional object with back, sides and indefinitely many hidden features, which I can always examine further by looking more closely. Similarly, in addition to their apparent size, shape, and color, the trunk looks solid, the branches supple, the leaves smooth, the apples ripe. The fact that I have seen trees like this many times in the past also lends my perceptual experience a sense of familiarity that is part of my present consciousness.

This horizon of significance, which saturates every experience, distinguishing it from every other in its descriptive content, even when such experiences pick out one and the same object, is what Husserl calls the *noema* of an intentional attitude, as distinct from its *noesis*, that is, the concrete particular psychological episode that *has* or instantiates that content (Id I 182ff.). *Noesis* and *noema* are, respectively, the mental act and its content: the act of thinking and the thought as such, the act of judging and the judgment as such, the act of remembering and the memory as such. Similarly, on analogy with language, the *noesis* is to the *noema* roughly as a linguistic term is to its sense, and the noema is in turn distinct from the object of awareness just as the sense of a term is distinct from what it refers to (if anything).

The semantic basis of Husserl's concept of the *noema* has not always been obvious to scholars, though he makes the connection explicit in a number of texts. In *Ideas I*, for instance, he writes:

> Let us look exclusively at "mean" [*Bedeuten*] and "meaning"
> [*Bedeutung*]. Originally these words relate only to the linguistic
> sphere, to that of "expression" [*Ausdrücken*]. It is virtually
> unavoidable, however, and at the same time an important
> advance in knowledge, to broaden the meaning of these words,

> modifying them appropriately, so they may be applied ... to the
> entire noetic-noematic sphere; hence to all acts, whether they
> are interwoven with expressive acts or not.
>
> (*Id* I 256)

Similarly, in the third book of *Ideas*, Husserl sums up, "the *noema* in general is nothing other than the generalization of the idea of [linguistic] meaning [*Bedeutung*] to all act-domains" (*Id* III 89).[10]

Husserl's theory of intentionality thus stands as perhaps the supreme expression of the *semantic paradigm* in the philosophy of mind. Unlike empiricist versions of the theory of ideas, which construe mental representations on analogy with pictures or images, the semantic model conceives of mental content in general—not just the content of thought and judgment, but also that of perception, memory, and imagination—on analogy with linguistic meaning.[11]

Merleau-Ponty's conception of intentionality, stressing as it does the constitutive role of bodily skills and dispositions, amounts to a wholesale rejection of the semantic paradigm in the philosophy of mind. Like Husserl, Merleau-Ponty often uses the words "meaning" (*signification*) and "sense" (*sens*) in characterizing the content of experience, perceptual or otherwise. What he has in mind, however, is not linguistic meaning—that is, the semantic contents of subject terms, predicates, and propositions—but something more like the minimal intuitive coherence and perceptual significance the world arguably has even for nonlinguistic animals and pre-linguistic children. Language no doubt deepens and transforms our experience of the world, but in a way that must be understood as an expansion, refinement, and variation of the meanings we already find in things and situations and events, before we find them in words and sentences and verbal discourse. We will return to the emergence of culture and language, and its essential dependence on nature and perception, in Chapters 5 and 6.

More broadly speaking, Merleau-Ponty's departure from the semantic orientation of Husserl's phenomenology is part of a larger

effort to dispense with *representational* models of intentionality altogether. Perception is not mental representation, according to
Merleau-Ponty, but skillful bodily orientation and negotiation in
given circumstances. To perceive is not to have inner mental states,
but to know and find your way around in an environment. More
simply, to perceive is to have a body, and to have a body is to *inhabit*
a world. Merleau-Ponty therefore regards intentional attitudes not
as bundles of sensorimotor skills, describable in abstraction from
the worlds they disclose, but as modes of existence, ways of being
in the world. As we shall see, this way of understanding perception
and its philosophical significance has ontological as well as epistemological and methodological implications.

2. Gestalt psychology

The other major influence on Merleau-Ponty's thought was the
Berlin school of Gestalt psychology, which emerged in the 1910s
and 1920s. The central figures of the movement—Max Wertheimer,
Kurt Koffka, and Wolfgang Köhler—rejected the atomistic and
mechanistic assumptions that had dominated philosophy and psychology for centuries, arguing instead that sense experience has a
holistic and dynamic character in virtue of its intelligible form or
shape (*Gestalt*). Experience, they argued, does not accumulate piecemeal as the mere piling up or summation of discrete bits of
sensory input, but rests instead on meaningful configurations,
coherent chunks that admit of no further analytical dissection into
component parts. When I see a book on a table, I do not first
apprehend a shape, a color, or collection of particular sense data,
and only then stitch them together as a solid object with a hidden
middle and back sides; what I see is, at bottom, a figure on a
ground, and in this case a solid object in an environment. So too,
the mental operations that allow me to recognize the book are not
rigid causal processes that just happen to result in a standing belief,
but rather exercises of insight and intelligence that cannot be
reduced to strictly mechanical laws. Crudely put, contrary to still

sadly prevailing metaphor, our sense organs are not cameras and recording devices, and our minds are not calculators.

Merleau-Ponty learned about Gestalt psychology from Aron Gurwitsch's lectures at the Institut d'Histoire des Sciences in Paris in the 1930s. Gurwitsch was at that time combining a reading of Husserl's phenomenology with an active interest in the Gestalt school, a confluence of sources that would prove decisive for Merleau-Ponty's own subsequent work.[12] It was a natural connection to draw, for there are undeniable affinities between Husserl's theory of intentional content and the Gestalt concept of perceptual form. Moreover, phenomenology and Gestalt theory belonged to the same academic culture in Germany in the early decades of the century, one in which the relation between philosophy and psychology was, as it remains today, problematic and conflicted.[13]

The Gestalt theorists arguably did even more than Husserl to discredit the Cartesian-Lockean theory of ideas, in part because they based their case not just on intuitive insights and *a priori* considerations, but experimental evidence. Central to their program was a critique of the "constancy hypothesis," the assumption that sensory experience is at bottom a kind of mosaic of sensations, each correlated with a discrete stimulus. The Gestaltists tried to show that perception is, on the contrary, organized around configurations or ensembles of mutually reinforcing components, which often fail to correspond to stimuli in any direct or isomorphic way.[14] Meaningful forms or constellations of this kind, they argued, are the primitive elements in perception, and our perceptual grasp of them is neither a passive registration of meaningless input nor an unconscious act of judgment, but a kind of perceptual intelligence or insight that underlies both the application of concepts and inferential reasoning.

The holistic structure of experience, which is thus a function of neither sensation nor judgment, is especially striking in the context-sensitivity of perceptions of color and size constancy. People seem to remain the same size as they walk toward you or away from you. An unevenly illuminated wall looks to be a single uniform shade. What we see are not sensations or free-floating qualities, but things. Seeing isolated colors and shapes, like hearing mere sounds, is possible only (if at all) as a deliberate abstraction from ordinary perceptions of objects, events, places, obstacles, gaps, distances, and opportunities, as well as persons, doings, and situations. To suppose that we piece such things together from more primitive bits of sensory input is to mistake theoretical abstractions for concrete phenomena.

These ideas inspired Merleau-Ponty. Nevertheless, while acknowledging that the intelligible form of sense experience has philosophical implications, he thought the Gestaltists generally failed to appreciate them. There is, he insists, "an entire philosophy implicit in the critique of the 'constancy hypothesis'" (PP 62n/50n/58n)—but only implicit, for such a philosophy calls for a radical reconceptualization of perception as an aspect not just of this or that mental function or capacity, but of our entire existence. The Gestalt school tried to spell out general laws of perceptual form and envisioned an eventual reduction of those laws to causal mechanisms in the brain. Our relation to the world, however, like our relation to ourselves, is not just causal but intelligible, indeed practical, and Merleau-Ponty believed that no purely theoretical account of general laws could capture what we grasp intuitively and practically in our ordinary understanding.

Merleau-Ponty found some confirmation of his dissatisfaction with the psychological literature in the work of the neurologist Kurt Goldstein. In collaboration with the Gestalt theorist Adhémar Gelb, Goldstein conducted studies of aphasia in brain-damaged patients and thought deeply about the philosophical foundations of biological knowledge. Contrary to reductive impulses toward mechanism and modularity in the philosophy of psychology, Goldstein insisted that medicine and physiology be attentive to the unity of organisms and the global intermingling of their seemingly discrete organs and functions. Goldstein distanced himself from Gestalt theory,[15] but he shared with it an emphasis on the holistic character of experience and the idea that animals have a natural tendency to integrate their behaviors, minimize perceptual disturbances, and maintain a kind of equilibrium in their sensorimotor orientation. Even insects adjust their behaviors to their environments, and higher animals more obviously have an emerging *normative sense* of rightness and wrongness, however vague and inarticulate, when their actions are going right or wrong. A horse stumbles and catches itself to regain its balance, a cat recoils from a narrow passage it senses it cannot squeeze through, a bird cocks its head to hear better where the worms and insects are in the grass. Like us, more or less sentient and intelligent animals seem to have at least a primitive sense of where they *ought* to be and what they *ought* to do, not of course under any linguistically articulated description, but simply as somehow optimal or suboptimal, better or worse. This idea, common to Goldstein and the Gestaltists, that ordinary perception and behavior are always organized around a normative notion of rightness or equilibrium, is a crucially important insight at work in Merleau-Ponty's phenomenology.

4. LANGUAGE, PAINTING, AND POLITICS

Beyond his phenomenological account of the bodily nature of perception, Merleau-Ponty is best known for his writings dealing with the nature and conditions of linguistic meaning, the philosophical significance of art, especially painting, the problem of meaning in history, and the nature of political action and morality. I will return to these themes in more detail in the second half of this book, but it is worth saying something at the outset about the role of language, painting, and politics in Merleau-Ponty's thought. Merleau-Ponty was not strictly speaking a philosopher of language, an aesthetician, or a social or political theorist, at least not in the sense in which philosophers apply those labels nowadays. Instead, he approached a wide range of cultural practices in search of the general conditions of *meaning*—not just linguistic or conceptual meaning, which philosophers tend to focus on, but *significance* in the widest sense.

Like the English word "sense," the French *sens* can refer to sensation (as in "sense of smell"), skill (as in "sense of balance" or "sense of rhythm"), or intelligibility (as when something "makes sense"). Unlike the English word, however, it can also mean *direction* or *way*. This additional sense, so to speak, is metaphorically apt, for it is natural to think of *understanding* something as seeing or grasping where it's coming from, where it's going, what it's up to, as it were. As we have seen, Merleau-Ponty believes that perception and the body ground all forms of human understanding, hence all kinds of significance, however abstract. Reason and language are not unworldly miracles, transcending and floating free of the concrete environments available to our perceptual and bodily skills. Instead, they are grounded in more basic forms of intelligibility, intuitive forms of sense or direction, which we understand precisely by grasping, discerning, tracing, and following their lead.[16]

Merleau-Ponty's accounts of language, painting, and politics are not explanatory theories, but attempts to reveal the situational and perspectival character of understanding prior to its abstraction from its perceptual horizons, and so its potential misinterpretation of itself as pure, unconditioned, unsituated, and valid for all times and places. Merleau-Ponty's philosophical purpose is thus basically the same in his phenomenology of perception and in his reflections on language, art, and history, namely, to show that all forms of meaning are rooted in the bodily intelligibility of perception, and moreover that phenomenology can reveal the gradually differing intermediate forms we tend to lose sight of when we focus only on the extreme cases, or their distorted caricatures, for example brute sensation and abstract intellect.

Merleau-Ponty's reflections on art are concentrated in the essays "Cézanne's Doubt" (1945), "Indirect Language and the Voices of Silence" (1952), and "Eye and Mind" (1960). Merleau-Ponty nowhere formulates a theory of aesthetic experience or aesthetic properties, nor does he advance a general theory of art or art works pretending to apply generally across periods, traditions, materials, forms, and genres. Instead, he offers an interpretation of particular modern works of art, above all the paintings of Cézanne, both in order to understand them in their own right and to find in them hints of insights he articulates in his own phenomenological work.

Neither does Merleau-Ponty advance an explicit theory of language, though he has interesting things to say about the lived intelligibility of verbal expression and its relation to the formal intelligibility of linguistic structure—what the linguist Ferdinand de Saussure called *parole* (speech or speaking) and *langue* (language or language system), respectively.[17] Merleau-Ponty, for his part, draws a distinction within speech between the spontaneity of expression on the one hand, and established norms and conventions governing how we talk on the other—what he calls "authentic speech" and "secondary expression" (PP 207n/178n/207n), or "speaking speech" (*parole parlante*) and "spoken speech" (*parole parlée*) (PP 229/197/229), "speaking language" (*langage parlant*) and "spoken language" (*langage parlé*) (PM 17/10), even at one point "transcendental" and "empirical" speech (PP 448/390/454).[18] The latter, he argues, is parasitic on the former; linguistic forms and conventions are rooted in the ongoing articulation and rearticulation of new meanings. Primal expression can itself be articulate thanks only to the establishment of an institution or system of signs, yet what institutes any such system is the *act* of expression. As Wittgenstein put it, quoting Goethe's *Faust*, "In the beginning was the deed."[19]

More than just a philosopher and an academic, Merleau-Ponty was also an active public intellectual. His early essays on the Moscow Trials and "the communist problem," which first appeared in the pages of *Les Temps modernes* and were shortly thereafter published under the title *Humanism and Terror* (1947), amounted to a bold, but, as Merleau-Ponty himself later concluded, problematic effort to extend some of the basic insights of his phenomenology into the political sphere. He argued that history is meaningful in the way the perceptual world is meaningful, and more specifically that Marxism teaches us to see the gestalt or pattern inclining history from the inhumanity of contemporary life to socialism, the only "humanism" worthy of the name. By 1950, for a variety of theoretical and practical reasons, Merleau-Ponty had abandoned Marxism, and in 1953 he resigned from the editorial board of Les Temps modernes and broke off relations with Sartre. Thereafter, his political writing became more nuanced, but also more ambivalent. Adventures of the Dialectic (1955) is an account of what he now calls the "liquidation of the dialectic," the process by which Marxism in effect discredited itself by lapsing into an increasingly rigid deterministic theory of history on the one hand, and an increasingly dogmatic anticipation of spontaneous revolutionary change on the other.

Finally, it should be said that Merleau-Ponty can be difficult to read. Although he is less obscure than, say, Hegel or Heidegger, his prose lacks the clarity and plainness of the best philosophical writing in English, nor can it match the eloquence of Sartre, his nearest philosophical contemporary and rival. He occasionally relies on lush, sometimes hyperbolic formulations at the expense of conceptual precision, and he delivers few memorable bons mots or resonant slogans. Still, he writes with elegance and care, often dwelling at length on concrete examples to illustrate his point. Moreover, in spite of his avoidance of pithy, programmatic declarations, Merleau-Ponty has an uncanny ability to bring highly abstract philosophical ideas into sharp focus in a vivid and supple idiom. What is stylistically memorable about his books is not any particular phrase or sentence that might stand on its own, out of context, but the gradual unfolding and elaboration of an idea from paragraph to paragraph, page to page. Merleau-Ponty rarely asserts conclusions in discrete, conspicuous propositions. Instead, his approach is typicaly interrogative, suggestive, elliptical, conciliatory, yet persistent and unmistakable.

Substantively speaking, too, Merleau-Ponty cultivated a deliberately nonadversarial dialectical strategy that is likely to seem alien,

perhaps disconcerting, to anyone brought up on the explicit theoretical assertions and blunt argumentative techniques of contemporary analytic philosophy. He often avoids stating a thesis
directly by way of staking out his position over against competing
views, or he does so only obliquely, after extended preliminary
discussion, exploration, and imaginative contemplation of the
question at hand. More frequently—and more confusingly—he
tries to imagine himself into the competing perspectives of other
thinkers and ideas, borrowing their insights, appropriating their
terminology for his own purposes, and then making a clean break
by pronouncing a negative verdict in favor of his own, often radically opposed view. What might initially sound like a cautious
doubt, a tentative objection, or a subtle reformulation of another
thinker's ideas often proves on closer inspection to signal a fundamental disagreement, a deep shift in perspective, and in the end a
startlingly original insight of Merleau-Ponty's own.

SUMMARY

Merleau-Ponty's thought concerns *mysteries*, not problems or puzzles. The central mystery or enigma of his work is, in a word, *perception*, more precisely the capacity of perception to disclose a *world*.
A world is not just a collection of objects, but an environment or
situation we inhabit, in which we find ourselves having to cope
with possibilities and impossibilities, opportunities, obstacles—in
short, a space of *meaning*.

Merleau-Ponty's central philosophical idea is that perception is a
bodily phenomenon, not a mental event occurring at the end of a
chain of physical causes and effects, as Descartes supposed. It is the
body that perceives, not the mind. That is, we perceive not as subjects standing over against objects, but as bodily agents *in* and *of* the
world. Merleau-Ponty conceives of perception as an aspect of what
he calls, following Heidegger, our "being in the world" (*être au
monde*). The mystery of perception is thus the mystery that, in
addition to objects, there is also a *world*; that although we ourselves

are embedded in and part of it, the world itself is not utterly opaque and impenetrable, but open to us as a *field* of awareness and action.

Above all, Merleau-Ponty is critical of *rationalism*, the assimilation of experience to *thought*. In the late nineteenth and early twentieth centuries, rationalist theories of perception went under the banner of *intellectualism*, and more recently the reduction of intentionality to cognition, often construed as a kind of calculation or computation, is called *cognitivism*. Whereas rationalists maintain that experience is at bottom *thought-like*, Merleau-Ponty insists on the irreducible phenomenal difference between perception and thought and argues that cognition itself bears traces of some of the structural features of perceptual experience, in particular perspectival orientation and figure/ground contrast.

The two chief formative influences on Merleau-Ponty's work were phenomenology and Gestalt psychology. Phenomenology is an attempt to provide a concrete description of things philosophers often all too hastily try to explain (or explain away) abstractly. The central phenomenon of concern to phenomenologists is *intentionality* —the object-directedness, *of*-ness or "aboutness" of experience. Edmund Husserl, the founder of phenomenology, was the first to draw a rigorous distinction between the intentional *object* and the intentional *content*—what he called the *noema*—of an attitude, a distinction systematically obscured by talk of "ideas" or "representations," such as one finds in Descartes, Locke, Kant, and in contemporary cognitive science. Husserl's theory of intentionality is exemplary of the *semantic paradigm* in the philosophy of mind, for his notion of *noema* is a generalization of the concept of linguistic sense or meaning, in contrast to the referent of a term. As Frege argued, the sense of the expression "Morning Star" is different from the sense of the expression "Evening Star," though both terms refer to the same thing, namely the planet Venus.

In spite of his debt to Husserl, Merleau-Ponty's phenomenology poses a radical challenge to the semantic paradigm, for it calls into question not just the early modern "way of ideas," which likened mental contents to internal images or pictures of things, but *representationalism* more generally, according to which even our perceptual attitudes are directed to the world in virtue of descriptive conceptual content modeled on linguistic meaning.

The second most significant influence on Merleau-Ponty's phenomenology was Gestalt psychology, which emphasizes the *non-conceptual* or *prelogical* coherence of perceptual experience. According to Gestalt theory, perception is neither rational judgment nor the registration of meaningless sense data. Merleau-Ponty inherits from the Gestalt school a critique of the *constancy hypothesis*, the assumption of a one-to-one correspondence between sensory stimulus and perceptual content. The constancy hypothesis is the deep error common to both *empiricism* and *intellectualism*, according to which perception consists fundamentally in either sensation or judgment. A sensation is supposed to be the discrete effect of a sensory stimulus, yet what we experience in perception is not a fleeting mosaic of sensations, as empiricism suggests, but a stable and coherent *world*. Intellectualism recognizes the intelligibility of the perceived world and acknowledges that perception is not just a brute confrontation with sense data, yet it too takes the constancy hypothesis for granted by concluding that perceptual content must be supplied by a non sensory faculty, namely thought or judgment.

Merleau-Ponty is not remembered for any theoretical break-throughs in the philosophy of language, aesthetics, or political theory. Still, his reflections on language, painting, and politics are fascinating and original as extensions of his phenomenological insights into the bodily structure of perception. Linguistic, artistic, and political meaning are grounded in and akin to perceptual meaning, for they are at bottom finite, situated, and perspectival. Art expresses meaning not by articulating ideas or judgments, but, like facial expressions and handwriting, by manifesting recognizable stylized gestures. Language, too, is grounded in the spontaneous expressive capacities of embodied speakers. Merleau-Ponty initially maintained that Marxism revealed the same structures of meaning and direction in history and politics that phenomenology had discovered in perception. He abandoned that line of thought by 1950, however, as it became increasingly clear that Marxism had become ideologically stultifying and theoretically dead. He remained a leftist, broadly speaking, but his political orientation moved closer to liberalism in the 1950s.

FURTHER READING

Carman, T. "Husserl and Heidegger." A brief account of the philosophies of Husserl and Heidegger, as background for understanding Merleau-Ponty.

Dreyfus, H. and S. Todes. "The Three Worlds of Merleau-Ponty." A reply to Kullman and Taylor's review of *Phenomenology of Perception* (see below). Dreyfus and Todes argue that implicit in Merleau-Ponty's phenomenology is a threefold distinction among (1) a preobjective experience of the world, (2) experience of ordinary objects in what Husserl called the "lifeworld," and finally (3) the wholly objective, nonperspectival world described by the sciences.

Kullman, M. and C. Taylor. "The Pre-Objective World." A review of *Phenomenology of Perception*, including criticism of Merleau-Ponty's claim to be describing a level of experience that falls beneath the threshold of objectivity. Kullman and Taylor observe that Merleau-Ponty's phenomenology is not simply an epistemological theory, but an ontology of "being in the world" (*être au monde*).

Matthews, E. *The Philosophy of Merleau-Ponty*. A good general introduction to Merleau-Ponty.

Two

Intentionality and Perception

Merleau-Ponty's most important contribution to philosophy is his phenomenological account of perception and embodiment, which he argues are not mere *properties* of minds or subjects, but constitutive elements of our *being in the world*. Contrary to what philosophers have sometimes supposed, we have no clear notion of ourselves at all as mere souls or minds in abstraction from our bodies and perceptions. Indeed, Merleau-Ponty believes, there cannot be a mind or a subject without some form of bodily-perceptual orientation in a world. Being embodied and perceiving a world are part of what it is for us to exist at all.

Why does Merleau-Ponty suppose that phenomenology can help establish this kind of ontological claim concerning our *existence*? Isn't phenomenology just a description of experience, of subjective appearance as opposed to objective reality? How can the mere description of appearances demonstrate anything about the world itself and our place in it? To answer these questions, we need to know more about how Merleau-Ponty understood phenomenology, what he thought phenomenological descriptions are descriptions of, and more specifically what aspects of perception and embodiment he thought they could shed light on.

1. WHAT *IS* INTENTIONALITY?

As we have seen, what phenomenology attempts to describe is the *intentionality* of experience. The word "intentionality" derives from the Latin verb *intendo*, meaning to aim or point at, or to extend or stretch. As early as the third century BCE, the Greek Stoic Chrysippus used the word *enteinein* to refer to the extension of the visual cone from the eye to the thing seen. Saint Augustine later reiterated the Stoic theory of vision in Book 11 of *De Trinitate*, where *intentio* means something like thought or attention focused on or aimed at something.[1] Hence, as Elizabeth Anscombe observes, aiming one's mind at (*intendere animum in*) is like aiming one's bow at (*intendere arcum in*).[2] Similarly, even earlier, in the *Theaetetus* Plato has Socrates say that in false judgment, "like a bad archer, one shoots wide of the mark and misses."[3] There is a robust analogy, then, between *experiencing*—remembering, perceiving, imagining, or expecting—and *aiming* at something. Moreover, the analogy evidently seemed as compelling to ancient and medieval philosophers as it does to us.

The more relevant early history of the term *intentio* is to be found in the scholasticism of the later Middle Ages, by which time the concept had become interestingly ambiguous. The word entered into this later medieval tradition from a different path, from the Greek *noêma* via various Arabic commentaries on Aristotle. It meant simply "that which is immediately before the mind," but now, as al-Fārābī observed, "in two respects: in its relation to things outside the soul and in its relation to words."[4] Alongside but crucially distinct from the image of aiming or direction toward something in the world, intentions were now understood *semantically*, as the intelligible contents of linguistic expressions.

This semantic concept of intentionality came to dominate not only what Brentano called "descriptive psychology" and Husserl's phenomenology, but also later analytical philosophy of mind and cognitive science. And yet the analogy with aim and directedness persists. Why does that arguably more primitive image still seem so natural, so intuitively compelling and right? The affinity between intentional attitudes (seeing, believing, wanting, wishing, remembering, expecting) and concrete aiming relations, I want to suggest, is no accident, no arbitrary imposition of metaphor. Rather, it points up something deep and important about the ontological

structure of intentionality, something Merleau-Ponty's phenomenology makes explicit in its characterization of intentional content
not as representation, but as a kind of bodily "sense" or "direction" (*sens*) toward the world. Conceiving of intentionality as a kind
of *aiming at* something seems right and natural, not just because it's
a convenient heuristic, but because our bodily orientation and the
directedness of our actions in the world are what make intelligible
the very idea that perceptions, memories, judgments, expectations
and the like are *of* something, that they are not just states or properties of the mind, within the mind, but that they direct and con-
nect and bind us to the world itself.

That primitive image, however—the directedness and con-
nectedness of our attitudes to the world—becomes virtually unintelligible on the Cartesian–Lockean model of the mind, as it does
on all representationalist theories of mental content. By 1874,
when Brentano reintroduced the term "intentionality" into modern
philosophical jargon, the representationalist paradigm had reached
what was perhaps the height of its specious obviousness, and
Brentano evidently felt little need to justify it. Indeed, the locus
classicus of his account freely mixes the aiming or direction metaphor with talk of representational content as such:

> Every mental phenomenon is characterized by what the
> Scholastics of the Middle Ages called the intentional (or mental)
> inexistence of an object, and what we might call ... reference to a
> content, direction toward an object ... or immanent objectivity.[5]

Is the object of the attitude *out* in the world or *in* the mind? Crucially, notwithstanding his reliance of the image of directedness
toward something, Brentano goes on to say that intentionality "is
characteristic exclusively of mental phenomena. No physical phenomenon exhibits anything like it."[6] Intentional direction, for
Brentano, is thus more like the mere specification of a content or
meaning than any literal aiming or pointing at an object. Like the

ideas or representations of earlier theories of the mind, intentional content, in Brentano's view, is an intrinsic internal feature of mental states; it is nonrelational. And yet the relational metaphor of aiming or direction prevails in his final formulation, though he still describes the mind as somehow simply containing its own intentional objectivities.

The result is a curious hybrid of two very different conceptions of intentionality: according to one, intentionality is the directedness or extension of the mind outward toward things; according to the other, it is the containment of ideas or representations in the mind. "We can," Brentano writes, "define mental phenomena by saying that they are those phenomena which contain an object intentionally within themselves."[7] This definition is evidently a compromise between two theoretical impulses that pull in different directions: on the one hand, the image of the mind as aiming at or pointing to things in the world—which perhaps captures our most primitive intuitions concerning the world-orientedness of our attitudes—and on the other hand the conviction that intentionality can have nothing literally in common with pointing or direction relations manifest in the external world itself.

It is true, of course, that intentionality cannot be understood simply as a two-place pointing relation between minds and things. Perceptions and thoughts do not simply aim at things the way arrows and needles do. Following Brentano, it has therefore become customary to add that what intentional attitudes aim at need not actually exist in order for them to be aimed *as* if at them. The directedness of the attitudes swings free logically of the existence of their putative objects. There is something right about this, and indeed it is what lends representational theories of content their intuitive appeal, for of course we have no problem understanding that things need not be the way pictures or sentences portray them as being.

And yet emphasizing the fallibility of intentional attitudes obscures the fact that many of them *cannot* be detached from their objects, let alone from the world at large. As Merleau-Ponty says,

> Perception is precisely the kind of act for which there can be no
> question of distinguishing the act itself from the end to which it is
> directed. ... Perception and the perceived necessarily have the
> same existential modality. ... If I see an ashtray *in the full sense of
> the word "see,"* there must be an ashtray there ... To see is to see
> something.
>
> (*PP* 429/374/435–36)

Another way to put this is to say that our ordinary notion of *seeing* is
a success notion, for it logically requires that what I see *be there* to be
seen; otherwise, I am not really seeing it. I might have *thought* I saw
it, but if it wasn't there, I didn't.[8] So too with remembering, following, and ignoring: you can't remember something that didn't
happen; you can't follow someone who isn't out ahead of you, and you
can't ignore something that isn't there. Such actions and attitudes
are intentional, but not by being indifferent to the existence of their
objects. One might insist that in such cases you yourself are in the
same state whether or not the putative objective of your attitude exists.
But this is a philosopher's conceit and runs contrary to ordinary
language and common sense. On the contrary, your state of mind is
the state it is in virtue of the presence (or absence) of the object. If the
event did not really happen, for example, then your state is not one
of remembering, but of imagining. Such attitudes depend on their
objects in order to be the actions and attitudes they are.

Modern philosophers have been slow to acknowledge this
dependence of intentionality on the world, in part because it flies
in the face of the *internalism* they have inherited from Descartes and
the tradition, but also because the concept of intentionality itself
has drifted away from the notion of concrete world-directedness
toward a notion of abstract representational content in and of itself,
pure and cut off from the world. But what *is* pure, "worldless"
representational content?

As we have seen, early modern philosophers understood intentionality in terms of the possession of mental tokens called "ideas,"

which they conceived on analogy with either images or tactile impressions, the metaphor of "impressions" having survived from the Aristotelian tradition, according to which inner experiences were literally *impressed* upon the soul by external things, more precisely the forms of those things. By the nineteenth century the imagistic theory had given way to the *semantic paradigm*, according to which intentional content is a kind of *meaning* analogous to the *sense* of a phrase or proposition, in contrast to its *referent*. Hence Husserl's definition of the *noema* as "the generalization of the idea of [linguistic] meaning [*Bedeutung*] to all act-domains" (*Id III* 89).

Merleau-Ponty's phenomenology is an attempt to free perception from this semantic-representational paradigm by insisting on the *literal* rightness of our naïve understanding of intentionality as orientation in and directedness toward the world itself. That naïve notion is not just a vaguely suggestive metaphor, but literally right, for intentional states are realized in bodily attitudes situated in a concrete physical and social environment. We do not just "have"— grasp, possess, or contain—the contents of our perceptual experience. Instead, we are confronted with a surrounding situation— literally our *circumstances*—in which we see, think, remember, and anticipate. The idea of merely contemplating, entertaining, or grasping the contents of our experience in a kind of phenomenological vacuum is itself an abstraction arrived at precisely by ignoring the environmental contexts that always in one way or another, directly or indirectly, invite, provoke, support, or frustrate our attitudes. Merleau-Ponty wants to bring philosophical and psychological reflection back to that naïve understanding of perception not as merely having something "in your head," but as being oriented in a surrounding world. That phenomenological project, however, put Merleau-Ponty directly at odds with the basic assumptions and methods of Husserl's phenomenology.

For both Husserl and Merleau-Ponty, the point of a phenomenological study of perception is neither to discover the causal mechanisms that produce experience nor merely to clarify the

logic of ordinary or theoretical discourse about it. Instead, phenomenology calls us to return, as Husserl put it, "to the things
themselves" (*zu den Sachen selbst*). According to Merleau-Ponty, "It
tries to give a direct description of our experience as it is, without
taking account of its psychological origin and the causal explanations that the scientist, the historian, or the sociologist may be able
to provide" (PP i/vii/vii). Phenomenology urges us to resist the
temptation to assimilate our experience to familiar categories in
the service of a theory. Phenomenology is a descriptive, not an
explanatory enterprise. A phenomenology of perception is thus
an attempt to describe perceptual experience from a first-person
perspective, from the point of view of the experience being
described. About this Husserl and Merleau-Ponty agree.

Merleau-Ponty departs from Husserl, however, by insisting that
the purpose of a phenomenology of perception cannot be to
describe how some property or capacity internal to the subject
constitutes its relation to external objects, for that implies that the
subject's own internal states or properties can be conceptually
carved off from the wider context of its situatedness and embeddedness in the world. But can they be? If not, then a phenomenology of perception ought to try to describe the most primitive forms
of that situatedness and embeddedness, which we always necessarily presuppose whenever we regard our attitudes as directed at
objects by means of representations, whether pictorial or verbal or
otherwise mental. All thought, all knowledge, all kinds of pictorial
and linguistic representation—indeed, the very foregrounding of
objects against background settings and situations—presuppose more
basic modes of being in the world, above all bodily-situated perception. Alluding to Husserl's slogan, Merleau-Ponty writes:

> To return to the things themselves is to return to that world prior
> to knowledge of which knowledge always *speaks* and in relation
> to which every scientific determination is abstract, indicative
> [*signitive*], and dependent, like geography in relation to the

countryside in which we have learned beforehand what a forest, a
prairie, or a river is. ... The world is there before any analysis I
could carry out ... Perception is not a science of the world, it is not
even an act, a deliberate taking up of a position; it is the background
from which all acts stand out, and is presupposed by them.

(*PP* iii–v/ix–xi/ix–xi)

Merleau-Ponty's phenomenology is not a theory of mental representation, but a descriptive account of perception as a mode of
being in the world, an existential condition of the very possibility of
representations—imaginative, semantic, or otherwise cognitive—
intervening *between* ourselves and the world.

2. BEYOND THE PHENOMENOLOGICAL REDUCTIONS

In spite of his debt to Husserl, Merleau-Ponty's own phenomenological project turns out to be deeply antithetical to that of the
movement's founder. And yet throughout his lectures and published
works Merleau-Ponty seems to praise Husserl far more often than
he criticizes him. Why?

The reason has to do with the general hermeneutical and philosophical style of Merleau-Ponty's thought, his approach to textual
interpretation and critical reflection. Reading and understanding
another thinker, he believed, are not and should not be a matter of
isolating discrete propositions, identifying explicit theses, weighing
arguments for and against them, and then pronouncing judgment
on them. Philosophy is not a contest of competing hypotheses and
systematic constructions, but a cooperative endeavor of thinking
along with, following up, and expanding on what others have tried
to think and say in the past. In this spirit, in an essay of 1959 on
Husserl, evocatively entitled "The Philosopher and His Shadow,"
Merleau-Ponty writes,

Between an "objective" history of philosophy, which would rob the
great philosophers of what they have granted others to think, and

a meditation disguised as dialogue, in which we would ask the questions and give the answers, there must be a middle ground [*milieu*] where the philosopher of whom one speaks and the one speaking are present together, though it is impossible even in principle to decide at each instant what is owing to each.

(S 201–2/159)

This deliberately nonadversarial dialectical strategy made Merleau-Ponty an extremely sympathetic reader, not just of Husserl, but of all the historical and contemporary figures whose work he discusses. Citing Heidegger's remark that "the greater the work of a thinker ... the richer is that which is unthought in the work,"[9] Merleau-Ponty insists,

there is something unthought [*un impensé*] in Husserl, which is genuinely his own, yet which opens out onto something else. To think is not to possess the objects of thought, but to use them to circumscribe a domain for thinking, which we are thus not yet thinking.

(S 202/160)

Just as the perceived world includes "reflections, shadows, levels, horizons between things" over and beyond the things themselves,

so too the work and the thought of a philosopher are made of certain articulations between things said, with respect to which there is no dilemma between objective interpretation and arbitrariness, since they are not *objects* of thought, since, like shadows and reflections, they would be destroyed by being subjected to analytical observation or taken in isolation, and because one can find and be faithful to them only in thinking once again.

(S 202/160)

Needless to say, this attitude of interpretive charity and intellectual cooperation stands in stark contrast to the hypercompetitive adversarial style of much (thankfully, not *all*) philosophical discourse. Unfortunately, it can also be misleading when we try to untangle Merleau-Ponty's own ideas from those that influenced him, Husserl's especially.

One of the "unthought" shadows cast by Husserl's work, for example, has to do with the *phenomenological reductions*. The reductions constitute the essential conceptual resources of Husserl's project, and although Merleau-Ponty spent his career trying to interpret them in a congenial and fruitful way for his own purposes, the truth is that they are fundamentally incompatible with his own philosophical commitments, especially those he inherited from Heidegger. What are the phenomenological reductions?

Husserl's phenomenology hinges on two methodological devices: the *transcendental reduction* and the *eidetic reduction*. The transcendental reduction, or *epochê*, consists in directing one's attention away from the "transcendent" (perspectivally given) world back to the "immanent" (transparent) contents of consciousness. This reduction takes us back from the external world to the inner realm of consciousness, the domain of the mental. The eidetic reduction then distinguishes the *noema* from the *noesis* by pointing upward, as it were, away from the *real* (temporal, causal) properties of mental states and episodes toward their *ideal* (atemporal, normative) dimensions. This reduction moves us away from psychological reality toward atemporal conceptual and semantic content, from facts to essences.

What is striking in Merleau-Ponty's appropriation of Husserl is that although he frequently writes with some sympathy for both the transcendental and eidetic reductions, he nevertheless evidently regards them as paradoxical and self-defeating, hence strictly speaking impossible. His desire to find in both reductions something philosophically valuable therefore leads him to characterize them in ways that depart widely from Husserl's account.

First, consider the eidetic reduction, that is, the move from real psychological facts to ideal intentional essences, or more precisely semantic contents or meanings. As early as 1936, in a review of Sartre's *Imagination*, Merleau-Ponty criticizes Sartre for being "too quick to grant Husserl his distinction between hulê and morphê," or sensory material and intentional form.[10] A few years later, in the opening sentences of Phenomenology of Perception, he once again calls that distinction into question, but this time projecting his own ambivalence onto Husserl's phenomenology, which he describes as

> a philosophy that puts essences back into existence and does not suppose that one could comprehend man and the world except from the point of view of their "facticity." ... The need to proceed by way of essences does not mean that philosophy takes them as its object, but on the contrary that our existence is too firmly gripped [*prise*] in the world to be able to know itself as such at the moment of its involvement, and that it requires the field of ideality in order to know and prevail over its own facticity.
>
> (*PP* i, ix/vii, xiv–xv/vii, xvi)

Passages like these are curious hybrids of Husserlian and Heideggerian motifs. In one sense, it is precisely the point of the eidetic reduction to take essences as "objects"—not as substances, but as direct accusatives of intuitive insight, as themes of phenomenological study. Or consider the idea that phenomenology proceeds from a "facticity" in which human existence is unreflectively caught up, "too firmly gripped in the world to be able to know itself." That image is plainly a reflection of Heidegger's account of being-in-the-world (*In-der-Welt-sein*), not of the eidetic reduction, which Husserl for his part regarded as tricky in practice, but unproblematic in theory. The subsequent promise that we can nonetheless "know and prevail over" that facticity by means of a "field of ideality," by contrast, once again reiterates the Husserlian picture to which Heidegger's notion of worldliness stands as a radical challenge.

Merleau-Ponty's position is likewise ambivalent with regard to the transcendental reduction, or epochê, that is, the move from the external world to pure consciousness, or transcendental subjectivity. According to Husserl, this reduction rests on a "fundamental distinction among modes of being, the most cardinal that there is," namely, "between *consciousness* and *reality*" (Id I 77). For Husserl, "consciousness, regarded in its *'purity,'* amounts to a *self-contained context of being*, a context of *absolute being*, into which nothing can penetrate and from which nothing can escape" (Id I 93); consciousness and reality, immanence and transcendence, are separated by an "abyss" (Id I 93, 184).

In striking contrast, Merleau-Ponty describes the *epochê* as a kind of temporary, provisional, merely *gradual* loosening of our bond with the world, which can be neither dissolved in reflection nor fully apprehended in consciousness:

> The best formulation of the reduction is no doubt the one given by Eugen Fink, Husserl's assistant, when he spoke of "astonishment" in the face of the world. Reflection does not withdraw from the world toward the unity of consciousness as the foundation of the world, it steps back to see transcendencies rise up before it, it slackens the intentional threads that attach us to the world in order to make them apparent ... it reveals that world as strange and paradoxical. ... in order to see the world and grasp it as paradoxical, we must break with our familiar acceptance of it, and ... from this break we can learn nothing but the unmotivated upsurge of the world. *The greatest lesson of the reduction is the impossibility of a complete reduction.* ... If we were absolute spirit, the reduction would be unproblematic. But since on the contrary we are in the world, since even our reflections take place in the temporal flux they are trying to capture ... there is no thought that embraces all our thought.
>
> (*PP* viii–ix/xiii–xiv/xv, emphasis added)

In the 1959 essay, again, Merleau-Ponty nevertheless assures us, "We must not imagine Husserl embarrassed" by these inescapable constraints on reflection, for one of the "results" of his inquiry

is an understanding that the movement of return to ourselves ...
is as if torn [*déchiré*] by an inverse movement to which *it gives
rise*. ... It is thus not the unreflected that challenges reflection, it
is reflection that challenges itself, for its attempt to revive,
possess, internalize, or make immanent has meaning by
definition only with respect to an already given terminus that
withdraws into its transcendence beneath the very gaze that has
set out in search of it.

(*S* 204/161)

But this image of reflection pulling and tearing against itself in an
ultimately futile effort to free itself from the world is more much
Heideggerian in spirit than Husserlian; or rather, it is more original
to Merleau-Ponty himself than it is derivative of either of them.

What Merleau-Ponty inherited from Heidegger, and what he
could plausibly claim to be preserving through further original
elaboration of his own, is an idea that is anathema to Husserl,
namely, that our immersion in our environment, our being in the
world, renders impossible any reference to consciousness or subjectivity as an isolated or self-sufficient sphere or region of being.
Intentionality, for Heidegger, far from being separated from reality
by an "abyss," is worldly through and through: "the intentional
structure of comportments is not something immanent to the so-
called subject, which would first stand in need of transcendence."
Rather, "For Dasein there is no outside, which is why it is also
nonsensical to talk about an inside."[11]

Similarly, for Merleau-Ponty, perception is not an inner subjective
phenomenon, but a mode of existence, a manifestation of our
being in the world. Merleau-Ponty embraced this Heideggerian
theme wholeheartedly, but then projected it retrospectively back
onto Husserl's phenomenology. In trying to save Husserl from
himself, Merleau-Ponty in effect repudiates Husserl's central argument
that the notion of the *noema*—semantic content generalized, as
Husserl said, "to all act-domains"—can shed light on the most

basic forms of intentionality. Describing what he takes to be "an operant or latent intentionality ... more ancient than the intentionality of human *acts*," he writes:

> Here there is indeed still a grouping of intentional threads around certain nodes that order them, but the series of back-references [*Rückdeutungen*] that lead us ever deeper could never be completed in the intellectual possession of a *noema*.
>
> (S 209/165)

In stark contrast to Husserl's picture of consciousness and reality separated by an abyss, Merleau-Ponty struggles to articulate an account of "something between transcendent nature ... and the immanence of mind, its acts, and its *noema*" (S 209/165). Moreover, that in doing so he thereby in effect reads his own phenomenological insights back into Husserl, against Husserl, he virtually confesses: reading between the lines, in the shadows and reflections and horizons of Husserl's work, he says, "we can only ... formulate—at our own risk—the unthought we think we discern there" (S 209/165–66).

3. WHAT PERCEPTION IS *NOT*

If perception does not reside in "the immanence of mind," then, or "in the intellectual possession of a *noema*," where is it to be found? Merleau-Ponty's phenomenology is neither an empirical theory of sensory mechanisms nor the logical analysis of our concepts pertaining to perception, but instead a concrete description of what perception itself *is*, namely the phenomenal and motor aspect of our bodily being in the world.

The primitive contact we have with the world in perception is something we are intimately familiar with throughout our lives. But it is neither open to full public scrutiny nor completely hidden and ineffable. It is neither an object of natural scientific inquiry nor the concealed source of concepts we can only subsequently analyze adequately in the transparent medium of reflection, as Descartes supposed. It is neither of those things, and yet we all experience it, we know it already, we have a kind of primitive, intuitive understanding of it. Indeed, our perceptual inherence in the world is hard to think and talk about precisely because it is always already so pervasive and familiar to us. We often have to choose between two diverging paths in our language pertaining to perception. On the one hand, ordinary terms are expressive and evocative, but vague and unsystematic. On the other hand, the vocabulary of science, while precise, is technical and frequently obscures the experience and understanding that originally motivated it, from which it had to abstract, but to which (in this case at least) it must remain faithful as its standard of adequacy.

Merleau-Ponty is extremely sensitive to this dilemma between the concrete sloppiness of ordinary language and the abstract distortions of scientific jargon. The dilemma is particularly pressing when it comes to many of the basic words we use to describe our experience. Words like "sensation" and "judgment," for instance, have both common and technical meanings, yet the technical notions often have little to do with their common counterparts. "Sensation" in ordinary speech just means feeling and has broad reference beyond the purely "hyletic" (stuff-like) data that psychologists and philosophers sometimes try to isolate and distinguish from the intentional contents of judgments, beliefs, desires, and emotions. So too, in addition to its juridical sense, "judgment" usually refers to the kind of practical intelligence—or even "instinct"—that guides and informs our conduct, including our concrete application of abstract principles. A person can have good judgment or bad judgment, and this is obviously something different from what philosophers and psychologists often mean by "judgment," namely, the affirmation of a proposition or the mere discernment of a fact.

The (so-called) "Introduction" of Phenomenology of Perception, which is in fact its first substantive section following the brief programmatic

Preface, contains Merleau-Ponty's critique of traditional psychology and its uncritical reliance on abstract concepts such as sensation, association, memory, attention, and judgment. It is crucial to appreciate, however, that in criticizing such concepts, he is not denying that our mental life is indeed rich and complex in ways that virtually force us to avail ourselves of words like these in describing it. Indeed, as we shall see, Merleau-Ponty himself has many positive things to say about the perceptual phenomena that motivate ordinary talk of sensation, association, memory, attention, and judgment. For of course experience is rife with feeling, inwardly interwoven, haunted by the past, focused against a background, and intelligent. What Merleau-Ponty criticizes is not our pretheoretical understanding of what we ordinarily call "sensation" and "judgment," that is, but the technical redeployment of those terms in abstraction from what they are originally called upon to describe. In dismissing the psychological concepts of sensation and judgment, he is arguing that perception cannot be understood either as the passive registration of sense data or as free and spontaneous intellectual activity.

1. Sensation

The word "sensation," Merleau-Ponty observes, is perfectly at home in ordinary language, and the notion at first "seems immediate and obvious." Once uprooted and transplanted in the domain of psychological theory, however, it turns out, "nothing could in fact be more confused" (PP 9/3/3). Indeed, in theoretical contexts the concept of sensation systematically obscures our ordinary understanding of perceptual experience: "Once introduced, the notion of sensation distorts any analysis of perception" (PP 20/13/15). What is wrong with this ordinary notion once we enlist it in the service of a theory of perception?

The first point to observe is a purely phenomenological one, namely, that notwithstanding the ordinariness of the word "sensation," what we find in ordinary perceptual experience is not internal sensations, but external things: objects, people, places, events. The concept of sensation "corresponds to nothing in our experience" (PP 9/3/3–4). Nowhere in our perceptual awareness do we come across discrete qualitative bits of experience fully abstracted from the external, perceptually coherent environment. Occasionally we might see an afterimage or hear a ringing in our ears, but typically we see objects and hear noises made by things and events. This is in part just to say that perceptual experience is intentional, that it is of something, whereas impressions, sensations, and sense data are supposed to be the nonintentional stuff from which the mind somehow extracts or constructs an experience of something. The of in "sensation of pain" is evidently not the of in "sensation of red." In the latter we can draw a distinction between the red thing and our sensation of it, whereas a sensation of pain just is the pain. Moreover, even pains are not just detached feelings that we then associate with parts of our bodies; rather, my pain is my leg, my hand, my head hurting. Perception is essentially interwoven with the world we perceive, and each feature of the perceptual field is interwoven with others:

> Each part arouses the expectation of more than it contains, and this elementary perception is therefore already charged with a *meaning*. ... The perceptual "something" is always in the middle of something else, it always forms part of a "field." ... The pure impression is therefore not just undiscoverable, but imperceptible and thus inconceivable as a moment of perception.
>
> (*PP* 9–10/4/4)

The concept of sensation in philosophy and psychology thus finds virtually no support in our actual experience, however firmly planted the word may be in ordinary discourse. Merleau-Ponty also offers a phenomenological diagnosis of our tendency to recur to talk of sensations, as if they really did occur in the normal course of perception. When the concept arises, he suggests, "it is because instead of attending to the experience of perception, we overlook it in favor of the object perceived" (PP 10/4/4). We are naturally focused on or "at grips with" (*en prise sur*) the environment, so that when we turn our attention to perception itself, we tend to project onto it the qualities of the objects we perceive:

> we transpose these objects into consciousness. We commit what psychologists call the "experience error," which means that what we know to be in things themselves we immediately take to be in our consciousness of them. We make perception out of things perceived. And since perceived things themselves are obviously accessible only through perception, we end by understanding neither.
>
> (*PP* 11/5/5)[12]

The language of sensation is thus tainted by, and so parasitic on, the language with which we refer to the objects of perception: "When I say that I have before me a red patch, the meaning of the word 'patch' is provided by previous experiences that have taught me the use of the word" (PP 21/14/17).

Another error, Merleau-Ponty observes, is to suppose that objects are given to us in perception "fully developed and determinate" (PP 11/5/6). The two errors are distinct, but they go hand-in-hand, for the notion that things are given to us with perfectly crisp and sharply delineated features provides covert support to the idea that perception involves some kind of inner awareness of the determinate qualities of experience itself, qualities perhaps even incorrigibly present to the mind. But experience rarely exhibits such sharply defined features, and no analysis of perception into discrete attitudes with crisply defined contents intending isolated qualities can capture the peculiar "perceptual milieu" (PP 58/47/54), always at once a "behavioral milieu" (PP 94/79/91), in which things show up for us under meaningful aspects. Does the chair in the periphery of my visual field or at the edges of my attention appear to me

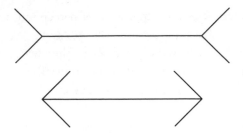

Figure 1: The Müller–Lyer illusion

as distinctly green or brown, or as larger or smaller than the filing cabinet, or as particularly well or ill placed in the room? Possibly not, and yet I *see* it as being there to *sit* in: its perceptual presence consists precisely in its practical significance.

Suppose on the contrary, Merleau-Ponty writes, that perception were merely the effect of discrete and determinate stimuli.

> We ought, then, to perceive a segment of the world precisely delimited, surrounded by a zone of blackness, packed full of qualities with no interval between them, held together by definite relationships of size similar to those lying on the retina. The fact is that experience offers nothing like this, and we shall never, using the world as our starting point, understand what a *field of vision* is.
>
> (*PP* 11/5/6)

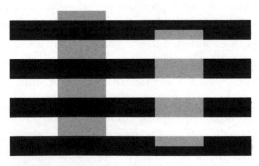

Figure 2: White's illusion

The edges of my visual field are nothing like the edges of a canvas or a movie screen, since they are in principle not objects I can look at, but the horizons of my looking: "The region surrounding the visual field is not easy to describe, but what is certain is that it is neither black nor gray." Moreover, it is not as if things that fall just outside my visual field simply lapse into perceptual oblivion. Instead, "what is behind my back is not without some element of visual presence," for it still has a kind of perceptual availability as something there to be seen when I turn to look at it (PP 12/6/6). The perceptual field thus cannot be equated with that range of objects directly affecting my sense organs at a given time.

"There is no physiological definition of sensation" (PP 16/9/11), yet it is tempting to try to define sensations in terms of the stimuli that cause them. Indeed, philosophical intuitions about the real character of our sensations, abstracted from the distorting effects of judgment, are regularly driven by assumptions concerning the external causes of our experience. If the Müller–Lyer illusion (Figure 1) involves a mistaken judgment about the relative lengths of the two lines, it is tempting to suppose that the underlying sensations must be sensations of lines of equal length. The lines themselves are the same length, after all, and surely our sensations do no more than register the effects of those causal sources of our experience.

However, this "constancy hypothesis,"[13] which stipulates a strict correlation between stimulus and sensation, immediately confronts a plethora of counterexamples. Small patches of yellow and black side by side together look green, while red and green patches together look gray. Motion pictures create an effect of movement by presenting the eye with a series of discrete still pictures in rapid succession. The gray segments in White's illusion (Figure 2) look strikingly different, though they are all the same shade.

So, while it is tempting to define sensations in terms of stimuli, there is no isomorphism between the contents and the causes of perception. And even if there were, the concept of sensation would be no better off. For the ordinary notion of sensation is meant to capture *how things look*. Since stimuli do not line up in any neat way with how things look, the concept of sensation they motivate could only stand in a dubious relation at best to the phenomenology it was meant to describe.

The constancy hypothesis thus stands in need of auxiliary hypotheses to save it from total implausibility, and Merleau-Ponty first considers the classic empiricist response, namely, that sensations, having been fixed by stimuli, subsequently undergo modification by the effects of association and memory. But *ad hoc* appeals to such cognitive operations are doomed to obscurity and circularity: obscurity because those notions tell us only *that* some sensations elicit others, not *how* they do so, that is, in virtue of what features or powers; circularity because the concepts of association and memory themselves presuppose the perceptual significance they were meant to explain.

The sensation of one segment or path in the figure of a circle, for example, may trigger an association by resembling another, "but this resemblance means no more than that one path makes one think of the other," so that our knowledge of objects "appears as a system of substitutions in which one impression announces others without ever justifying the announcement." The introduction of association and memory in the analysis sheds no light on the putative transition from discrete atoms of sensation to a perceptually coherent gestalt. Instead, for empiricism, "The significance of the perceived is nothing but a cluster of images that begin to reappear without reason" (PP 22/15/17).

Worse yet, the empiricist principle of the "association of ideas" takes for granted precisely the kind of perceptual coherence it is intended to explain. For what we in fact associate or group together, when we do, are things and the meaningful features of things, not sensations or atomic qualities. And what is a *thing*? A coherent whole, an ensemble, not a collection of discrete parts: "The parts of a thing are not bound together by a merely external association"

(PP 23/15/18); rather, the inner coherence of the things we perceive is what enables us to abstract aspects or features we can then associate with one another:

> It is not indifferent data that set about combining into a thing because *de facto* contiguities or resemblances cause them to associate; it is, on the contrary, because we perceive a grouping as a thing that the analytical attitude can then discern resemblances and contiguities.
>
> (*PP* 23/16/18–19)

As an attempt to save the concept of sensation, the empiricist principle of association reverses the true order of explanation, mistaking an effect of perceptual significance for its cause. The principle of association thus begs the question of perceptual meaning, for "the unity of the thing in perception is not constructed by association, but is a condition of association" (PP 24/ 17/19–20).

In addition to this negative point, Merleau-Ponty adds a positive phenomenological account of the emergence of perceptual coherence as an alternative to the crudely mechanistic theory of the association of ideas. Perception, he suggests, involves the organism in a constant fluctuation between states of tension and equilibrium, and the very unity of a perceived object amounts to a kind of solution, or anticipated solution, to a problem we register not intellectually, but "in the form of a vague uneasiness" (PP 25/17/ 20). I adjust my body, for example by turning my head and moving my eyes, squinting or cupping a hand around my ear, leaning forward, standing up, reaching, trying all the while to achieve a "best grip" (*meilleure prise*) on the world (PP 309/267/311). Eventually, things come into focus, and my environment strikes me as organized and coherent; my surroundings make sense to me, and I can find my way about. Only then do I recognize things and establish "associations" among them. An impression can arouse another impression, Merleau-Ponty remarks, "only provided that it is already understood in the light of the past experience in which it coexisted with those we are concerned to arouse" (PP 25/17/20).

Appealing to memory as a way of salvaging the constancy hypothesis is subject to the same objections. For memory, like association, is possible only against a background of perceptual coherence and cannot, on pain of circularity, be invoked to explain it. Memory cannot "fill in" the gaps in the sensations that must, on the constancy hypothesis, result from the poverty of our retinal images, for "in order to fill out perception, memories need to have been made possible by the character [physionomie] of what is given." What is capable of evoking a memory is not a decontextualized sense datum, but something one perceives and recognizes as familiar and meaningful under an aspect. Like association,

> the appeal to memory presupposes what it is supposed to explain: the patterning of data, the imposition of meaning on a chaos of sensation. At the moment the evocation of memories is made possible, it becomes superfluous, since the work we put it to is already done.
>
> (PP 27/19/23)

My present experience must already have some definite character or aspect, after all, in order to evoke this particular memory and not some other. In the end, Merleau-Ponty concludes, reference to the mind's unconscious "projection of memories" as a constitutive principle at work in all perceptual experience is a "bad metaphor" that obscures the structure of perception and memory alike (PP 28/20/23).

The distinctions between figure and ground, things and the empty spaces between them, past and present are not rooted in sensation, but are "structures of consciousness irreducible to the qualities that appear in them" (PP 30/22/26). Merleau-Ponty knows that he has no knock-down *a priori* argument against the atomism of empiricist epistemology, but it is enough to show that the concept of sensation lacks the phenomenological support and the explanatory force that would have to speak in its favor to vindicate it. The atomistic level of description will seem to be providing a more accurate picture of reality, he says, "as long as we keep trying to construct the shape of the world, life, perception, the mind, instead of recognizing as the immanent source and as the final authority of our knowledge of such things, the *experience* we have of them" (PP 31/23/27).

The concept of sensation is incoherent, since it is meant to serve two incompatible functions: first, to capture the actual content of perceptual experience; second, to explain how that experience is brought about by causal impingements on our sensory surfaces. The concept fails in the first effort precisely because of its service to the second, and vice versa. For when it describes the phenomena adequately, it explains nothing, and when it is subsequently invoked, along with auxiliary hypotheses concerning association and memory, to explain away the manifest phenomena, it no longer describes them as they are.

2. Judgment

Since perceptual phenomena so clearly depart from what the concepts of sensation, association, and memory seem to demand, it is natural to suppose that the actual order of appearance must lie buried beneath a layer of cognition that actively restructures it, either wholly or in part. This is what Merleau-Ponty calls the "intellectualist antithesis" of empiricism, which lay at the heart of Cartesian and Kantian epistemology, and which continues to inform cognitivist theories of perception today. Descartes was perhaps an extreme case, insisting as he did that perception is not strictly speaking a bodily process at all, but the activity of an incorporeal mind. And yet contemporary physicalists like Daniel Dennett are no less adamant than their rationalist predecessors that perception must be organized by, indeed that it just *is*, thought or judgment. For Descartes and Kant, the very fact that it is *things* that we see, as opposed to mere clusters of qualities, is due to our application of the concept of substance to the manifold of intuition provided passively by the senses.[14]

As we have seen, the constancy hypothesis assumes an isomorphism between stimulus and perception. One might suppose that this assumption is peculiar to empiricism, but as Merleau-Ponty points out, intellectualist theories rely on it as much or more, precisely in order to demonstrate that perceptual awareness is a product of active cognition, not of passive receptivity. Sensations, if they exist at all, are perfectly determinate, but lie buried beneath the threshold of conscious awareness, then the spotlight of attention shines on them and brings them to consciousness. Thus in the Second Meditation Descartes insists that objects are strictly speaking "perceived by the mind alone," not by the senses. Perception of a piece of wax melting, changing its qualities, and yet remaining one and the same piece of wax is a "purely mental scrutiny; and this can be imperfect and confused, as it was before, or clear and distinct as it is now, depending on how carefully I concentrate on what the wax consists in."[15] For Descartes, imperfect or confused perception is not a matter of having defective or obscure material available for mental scrutiny, but of scrutinizing it imperfectly or confusedly. What is given is given by God and cannot be imperfect; error and illusion flow from our own willful misconstructions. So, for the intellectualist, as Merleau-Ponty says, "The moon on the horizon is not, and is not seen to be, bigger than at its zenith: if we look at it attentively, for example through a cardboard tube or a telescope, we see that its apparent diameter remains constant" (PP 35/27/32). What is literally given in perception, the intellectualist and the empiricist agree, is fixed by the stimulus.

But this means that attention and judgment can effect no change from perceptual obscurity to clarity after all, since there was no confusion in the sensations themselves to begin with, only in the vagaries of thought or will. Consequently, "attention remains an

abstract and ineffective power, because it has no work to perform."
It is not as if our experience is a muddle and then the mind oper-
ates on it and sorts it out; rather, perceptual indistinctness is always
only a matter of failing to attend carefully and judge correctly.
"What intellectualism lacks," Merleau-Ponty observes, "is contingency in the occasions of thought" (PP 36/28/32). In this way,
empiricism and intellectualism are two sides of a coin, the former
rendering the transition from experience to judgment inexplicable,
the latter taking it for granted by building thought into the very
definition of perceptual objectivity: "Empiricism cannot see that
we need to know what we are looking for, otherwise we would not
be looking for it, and intellectualism fails to see that we need to be
ignorant of what we are looking for, or equally again we should not
be searching." In both, "the indeterminate does not enter into the
definition of the mind" (PP 36/28/33).

More recent cognitivist theories of perception have tried to dispense with this problem about the relation between experience and
judgment by dispensing with the very idea that anything is really
given in experience at all, prior to or independent of our judgment
about it. Daniel Dennett, for example, radicalizing Wilfrid Sellars's
attack on the Myth of the Given, insists that there can be no difference between the way things seem to us and the way we think they
seem. For Dennett, there is no difference in principle between a
perceptual experience and a judgment about a perceptual experience. For him, quite literally, seeing is believing: to lack a belief
about a perceptual experience is to lack the experience.[16]

To be sure, there are borderline cases between perception and
judgment. It is not always easy, or even possible, to say whether
an experience is simply one or the other. We hear words in our
native language as discrete units, whereas foreign speech sounds
like an undifferentiated stream of babble. We hear words, but do
we literally hear gaps between them or do we, as it were, insert
them in thought? You hate anchovies, but is it literally just the
taste on your tongue or also partly the idea of them that gives

you the creeps? Intellectualism often thrives on ambiguous cases like these, which tempt us to construe all kinds of intentionality as either explicitly or implicitly judgmental.

But why should we suppose that borderline cases threaten the very distinction between experience and judgment? To say that there is only a gradual difference between the two, rather than a sharp boundary, is in no way to deny that there are unambiguous instances of each. I perceive the clouds in the sky without any deliberation or commitment of judgment at all, just as I judge that $2 + 2 = 4$ without the faintest glimmer of qualitative feeling. As Merleau-Ponty says,

> Ordinary experience draws a very clear distinction between sensing [*le sentir*] and judgment. For it, judgment is the taking [*prise*] of a position, it aims at knowing something valid for me at every moment of my life, and for other minds, actual or possible; sensing, by contrast, is giving oneself over to appearance without trying to possess it and know its truth. This distinction disappears in intellectualism, because judgment is everywhere pure sensation is not, which is to say everywhere. The testimony of phenomena will therefore everywhere be impugned.
>
> (*PP* 43/34/39)

One could almost believe Merleau-Ponty had more recent cognitivists like Dennett in mind when he wrote those words.

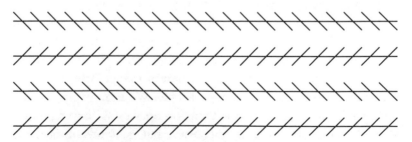

Figure 3: Zöllner's illusion

Indeed, one of the ironic effects of intellectualism is a reinstatement of one of the prejudices of the Cartesian conception of the mind of which materialists like Dennett are otherwise so suspicious, namely the idea that we are incorrigible about our own mental states. For if my consciousness and my beliefs about my consciousness collapse into a single effect, it will be impossible for my beliefs to be wrong *about* my experience. Intellectualism thus entails a doctrine of incorrigibility:

> if we see what we judge, how can we distinguish between true and false perception? How will we then be able to say that the halluciné or the madman "think they see what they do not see"? What will be the difference between "seeing" and "thinking one sees"?
>
> (*PP* 44/34–5/40)

There is a difference between seeing and merely thinking one sees, not just because "see" is a success verb, but because things do not always *actually* appear to me the way I *think* they appear, and intellectualism can make no sense of that distinction.

Intellectualism thus begs the questions, At *what* are the operations of the intellect directed? and, How do minds *orient* themselves at the outset vis-à-vis their objects? Consider a concrete example. In Zöllner's illusion (Figure 3), the horizontal lines are parallel, but they seem to converge.

"Intellectualism," Merleau-Ponty observes, "reduces the phenomenon to a simple mistake." But the mistake remains inexplicable. "The question ought to arise: how does it come about that it is so difficult in Zöllner's illusion to compare in isolation the very lines that have to be compared in the given task? Why do they refuse in this way to be separated from the auxiliary lines?" (PP 44/35/40–41). The erroneous judgment that is supposed to explain the perceptual appearance in this case begs a question that can only be answered by further phenomenological description of the recalcitrant appearance itself. If I judge falsely, it is because my judgment is motivated by an appearance that is not itself a judgment, but rather "the spontaneous organization and the particular configuration of the phenomena." The auxiliary lines break up the parallelism, "But why do they break it up?" (PP 45/36/41–42). Is that, too, the effect of a mistaken judgment? But why do I continue to make the mistake? Our ordinary concept of intellectual error presumes at least the possibility of some account of the perceptual source of the mistake, but intellectualism cannot in principle acknowledge that presumption, since it denies the availability, or indeed the very existence, of phenomenal appearances underlying the judgments we make about them.

What intellectualist theories of perception fail to acknowledge, according to Merleau-Ponty, is the embodiment and situatedness of experience, for they reduce perceptual content to the free-floating cognition of a disembodied subject:

> Perception is thus thought about perceiving. Its incarnation furnishes no positive characteristic that has to be accounted for, and its hæcceity is simply its own ignorance of itself. Reflective analysis becomes a purely regressive doctrine, according to which every perception is just confused intellection, every determination a negation. It thus does away with all problems except one: that of its own beginning. The finitude of a perception, which give me, as Spinoza put it, "conclusions without premises," the inherence of consciousness in a point of view, all this reduces to my ignorance of myself, to my negative power of not reflecting. But that ignorance, how is it itself possible?
>
> (PP 47–48/38/44)

Intellectualism is not just a phenomenological distortion, but an incoherent doctrine pretending to explain appearances the very existence of which the doctrine cannot consistently admit. And yet descriptions of supposedly constitutive perceptual judgments always turn out to be descriptions of perceptual receptivity. For intellectualism, "Perception is a judgment, but one that is unaware of its own foundations,[17] which amounts to saying that the perceived object is given as a totality and a unity before we have apprehended the intelligible law governing it" (PP 52/42/48). What Descartes describes as the innate inclinations of the mind, and what Malebranche calls "natural judgment," is just perception itself in its receptive aspect, in contrast to the spontaneity of the intellect. "The result," Merleau-Ponty concludes, "is that the intellectualist analysis ends by rendering incomprehensible the perceptual phenomena it is supposed to explain" (PP 43/34/39).

The perceptual foundations of judgment become clearer when we consider aspects or gestalts that shift even while the discrete parts of objects remain constant. As Merleau-Ponty says, "perception is not an act of understanding. I have only to look at a landscape upside down to recognize nothing in it" (PP 57/46/54). Faces and handwriting undergo similar jarring transformations of character when viewed upside down or backwards, yet their objective structures remain the same from a purely intellectual point of view. Thus Merleau-Ponty concludes that intellectualism, like empiricism, tacitly thrives on the constancy hypothesis: the sensory stimuli are in a certain sense objectively the same forward as backward, right side up as upside down, therefore the qualitative difference in perceptual aspect can only be an artifact of a change of intellectual attitude. You cannot see what is not there, so when a perceptual effect fails to correspond to the supplied stimulus, you are not literally *seeing* what you seem to see, but merely *thinking* you see it. Arguments purporting to uncover massive illusions in normal visual experience take the constancy hypothesis for granted in just this way. You seem to see a regular pattern across a large expanse of wallpaper, more or less instantaneously, but your eyes cannot be saccading to all the discrete spots on the wall in order to piece together the pattern bit by bit, therefore you must be *judging* rather than literally *seeing* its regularity. The illusion is not that you are seeing something that is not there, but that you think you are *seeing* what you are in fact merely *surmising*.[18]

But why should we accept the constancy hypothesis? Why not suppose instead that we often see things precisely by having them in our peripheral vision, especially in cases where we are sensitized to notice just those salient features that make them relevant to what we are looking at, or looking for? Parafoveal vision is not just an impoverished but otherwise phenomenologically equivalent form of foveal vision. Peripheral vision has abilities and liabilities all its own, quite unlike those of direct visual scrutiny. By arbitrarily applying a single preconceived criterion of perceptual success across the board, namely accurate registration of discrete stimuli, intellectualism systematically ignores the qualitative phenomenological differences that distinguish our diverse sensory capacities and therefore underestimates the complexity and sophistication of the perceptual mechanisms involved in bringing the world before our eyes.

For Merleau-Ponty, although perception is not grounded in sensations, the gestalts in which things are perceptually given constitute a primitive aspect of experience, irreducible to cognition: "there is a significance of the percept that has no equivalent in the universe of the understanding, a perceptual milieu that is not yet the objective world, a perceptual being that is not yet determinate being" (PP 58/46–7/54). Intellectualism ignores the indeterminacy of perception and helps itself uncritically to a view of the world as described by the physical sciences: "the real flaw of intellectualism lies precisely in its taking as given the determinate universe of science" (PP 58/47/54). Only by bracketing that fully objective description of the world, the description that aspires to a view from nowhere, as it were, and stepping back from the theoretical achievements of scientific theory to our ordinary situated perspective on our familiar environment, can we recover the abiding naïveté that constitutes the positive organizing principle of our conscious lives. For the world as given in perception is not the world as described by science, nor even the world as described in prescientific cognition: "Perception is not a science of the world, it is not even an act, a deliberate taking up of a position; it is the background from which all acts stand out, and is presupposed by them" (PP v/x–xi/xi).

Perception understood as a background condition of intelligibility, the intelligibility both of judgments and of the misbegotten concept of sensation, is an inheritance we are already intimately familiar with as children, long before we are in a position to comprehend the world or ourselves from the depersonalized standpoint of science:

> The child lives in a world he unhesitatingly believes to be accessible to all around him; he has no consciousness of himself or of others as private subjectivities, nor does he suspect that we are all, himself included, limited to a certain point of view on the world. ... Men are, for him, empty heads turned toward a single self-evident world.
>
> (PP 407/355/413)

That naïve mentality of the child, Merleau-Ponty believes, harbors a wisdom of its own precisely in virtue of its prereflective, pretheoretical phenomenal integrity, which survives vestigially but unmistakably beneath the cognitive accretions of self-conscious maturity. Indeed, "it must be that children are right in some sense, as opposed to adults ... and that the primitive thinking of our early years abides as an indispensable acquisition underlying those of adulthood, if there is to be for the adult a single intersubjective world" (PP 408/355/414). It is that underlying phenomenal inheritance or acquisition that an adequate phenomenology of perception must aspire to describe.

4. THE PHENOMENAL FIELD

But if perception is neither sensation nor judgment, why have philosophers and psychologists so regularly and so persistently misunderstood it by pressing it into such evidently inadequate conceptual categories? As we have seen, Merleau-Ponty does not rest content with criticizing the errors that have plagued traditional theories of perception; he also tries to diagnose those errors by describing the tendencies inherent in ordinary perceptual life that motivate and sustain them. He then offers what he thinks is a more faithful description of the things themselves prior to their distortion in theoretical (and pretheoretical) reflection.

So, although the concepts of sensation and judgment are useless as fundamental explanatory notions, perception itself clearly has two broadly discernible aspects, which Merleau-Ponty calls, respectively, "sensing" (*sentir*) or "sensoriality" (*sensorialité*) and "knowing" (alternately *connaître* or *savoir*). These are not the abstract notions of pure impression and pure concept, as one finds in Humean and Kantian epistemology, but are at home in common sense, ordinary language, and culture. Romantic discourse in literature and the arts, for example, relies heavily on a robust notion of sense and sensibility, just as vague but indispensable notions of judgment are vital to legal and scientific practice.

So, for example, when we "sense" something in the familiar and perfectly legitimate sense of the word, we *grasp* it: an unburdened wheel *looks* different from a wheel bearing a heavy load; a flame *looks* different to a child (namely hot, dangerous, threatening) after a burn. "Vision," Merleau-Ponty says, playing on the multiple senses of the word *sens*, "is already inhabited by a meaning [*sens*]" (PP 64/52/60). To sense something in this sense is not merely to register or feel it, but to comprehend it, to make sense of it. And yet, what the ordinary notion has in common with its bastardized theoretical counterpart, indeed what breathes life into that concept construed abstractly, is the suggestion of passivity, receptivity, being given over to the world as it is given to us. This phenomenon, as we have seen, is precisely what rationalism forgets, or suppresses: "A critical philosophy, in the last analysis, accords no importance to the resistance of passivity ... It thus tacitly assumes that the philosopher's thinking is not subject to any situation" (PP 75/61/71).

What makes sense experience a kind of *experience*, rather than an unconstrained form of awareness, Merleau-Ponty maintains, is its subjection to the world. Experience, in this sense, is "the communication of a finite subject with an opaque being from which it emerges, but to which it remains bound [*engagé*]" (PP 253/219/254).

What, then, in our ordinary experience gave rise to the abstract notion of sensation as pure quality? A very familiar, hence inconspicuous, experience, namely looking intently at an object and momentarily ignoring the background context that presented it to us as something to look more closely at in the first place. The perceptual world could be conceived as consisting of nothing but such qualities only if perception itself were nothing but the relentless, focused inspection of discrete features: "The pure *quale* would be given to us only if the world were a spectacle and one's own body a mechanism that some impartial mind acquainted itself with" (PP 64/52/61).

When I stare directly at a white piece of paper, for example, trying to determine the exact apparent shade of the part of it falling in shadow, Merleau-Ponty says, "I have made the quality appear by fixing my eyes on one portion of the visual field: then and only then have I found myself in the presence of a certain quale that absorbs my gaze." Pure sensible qualities are not original ingredients of perception, but artifacts of concentrated attention and reflection:

> The sensible quality, far from being coextensive with perception,
> is the peculiar product of an attitude of curiosity or observation. It
> appears when, instead of abandoning my entire gaze to the world,
> I turn toward the gaze itself, and when I ask myself *exactly what it
> is I see.*
>
> (*PP* 261/226/263)

Something similar is true of judgment. Explicitly articulated judgments with propositional contents are not conditions of perception, but conditioned achievements built on a more fundamental form of bodily intelligence guiding our behavior, including even our most basic ways of seeing and hearing things. Judgment presupposes a more primordial form of sensory understanding, one that does not involve the application of concepts. Consequently, "Understanding also needs to be redefined, since the general connective function ultimately attributed to it by Kantianism is now spread over the whole of intentional life and no longer suffices to distinguish it" (PP 65/53/61). In the acquisition of a motor skill, for example, "it is the body"—not the mind—"that 'understands'" (PP 168/144/167).

Merleau-Ponty thus wants to draw our attention back to the sensory background underlying our perception of isolated qualities and our formulation of explicit judgments. He calls this background the *phenomenal field*, which suggests that it is neither an object in our experience nor merely a subjective effect cut off from the world: "This phenomenal field is not an 'inner world,' the 'phenomenon' is not a 'state of consciousness' or a 'psychic fact'" (PP 69–70/57/66). It is, as it were, that aspect of the world always already carved out and made available and familiar to us by our involuntary bodily perceptual capacities and unthinking behaviors. The phenomenal field presents things to us as "infused [*imprégné*] with an immanent meaning [*signification*]" (PP 70/58/67). How? By having an *intentional* structure in the primitive sense discussed earlier in this chapter, that is to say, a directional orientation in an environment, in a materially inhabited space. So, for example, others are immediately present to us; we see them *as* others, not as objects, certainly not as mere sensory data. But what notion of immediacy is this? For Merleau-Ponty, "the immediate is no longer the impression, the object that is one with the subject, but the sense [*sens*], the structure, the spontaneous arrangement of parts" (PP 70/58/67). Again, what makes this kind of sense *sensible* rather than intellectual, what makes it receptive, is that it constrains us by giving us over to the world. So, although seeing is a kind of understanding, it is bound by what is given to it: "Vision is *a thought subject to a certain field*, and this is what is called a *sense*" (PP 251/217/251–52).

What then, more specifically, is this direction or sense (*sens*) belonging to the phenomenal field? Again, in the next chapter we will see how the field is itself constituted by our active bodily skills. For now we want to concentrate on its specifically sensory aspect, which Merleau-Ponty in no way wants to downplay, much less deny: the directional structure of the field is irreducibly bodily, but it is also irreducibly sensory. That is, we sense things in the world as tending toward ends that we at the same time sense ourselves tending toward, both perceptually and behaviorally.

The phenomenal field is consequently elusive, precisely because its function is to draw us out into the world. This is why reflection is so difficult, for in resisting the temptation to reify sensory experience in pure discrete qualities, the psychologist "goes against the natural movement of knowledge, which blindly traverses the operations of perception and goes straight on to their teleological result," namely some always more finely determinable object. The phenomenal field constantly pushes us away from itself, and this is why "Nothing is more difficult than knowing precisely *what we see*," for "perception hides itself from itself ... it is the essence of awareness to forget its own phenomena" (PP 71/58/67).

Merleau-Ponty's insistence that sensory experience always has the form of a *field*, rather than a mere sum or accumulation of data, is thus a refinement of the seemingly obvious claim I mentioned at the beginning of Chapter 1, namely, that perception is always essentially *perspectival*. For to construe a perspective as a field is to appreciate that it is neither a mere collection of objects, a homogeneous segment of space, nor finally somehow just another bundle of sensations or judgments. A field is, irreducibly, a kind of space or place (*lieu*); it is *where* objects and their qualities appear to us, relative to us. It therefore cannot be understood as a conditioned product of sensations or judgments. Just as space and time were for Kant, so the phenomenal field is for Merleau-Ponty a *transcendental* condition of the possibility of our being perceptually open to the world at all. Thus,

> phenomenology, alone among philosophies, speaks of a
> transcendental *field*. This word indicates that reflection never has
> the whole world and the plurality of monads arrayed and
> objectified before its gaze and that its view is never other than
> partial and of limited power.
>
> (*PP* 74/61/71)

Perceptual perspective is not a geometrical fact about the objective position of my sense organs in relation to objects; it is the immanent orientation of my experience toward things as ends available to me in virtue of my bodily attitudes and behaviors. It is what makes the perceived world meaningful to me *as* a world:

> the thinking Ego can never abolish its inherence in an individual
> subject that knows all things in a particular perspective.
> Reflection can never bring it about that I cease to perceive the
> sun as two hundred yards away on a misty day, or see it "rise"
> and "set," or think with the cultural apparatus provided me by my
> education, my past efforts, my history.
>
> (*PP* 74–75/61/71)

For Merleau-Ponty, the meaningfulness of sense experience is an effect of its cohering around a concrete perspective naturally oriented outward, away from itself, toward the world. There is thus a deep and necessary connection between the unity of the perceived object and the unity of the sensory perspective to which alone it can appear. Philosophers have tended to prise those two poles of experience apart, treating the unity of the object as a metaphysical problem in contrast to the unity and diversity of the senses, which then became an epistemological issue in its own right.

5. MOLYNEUX'S PROBLEM

The *locus classicus* of the epistemological issue is known as Molyneux's Problem, so called because John Locke inserted it from his correspondence with William Molyneux of Dublin into the second edition (1694) of *An Essay Concerning Human Understanding*. The question Molyneux asked is this: suppose someone born blind, who could distinguish a cube from a sphere by touch, suddenly regained vision; could the person then distinguish the cube from the sphere by sight, before touching them?[19] Molyneux and Locke said no, as did Berkeley. Leibniz said yes. The question became a *cause célèbre*; indeed, Ernst Cassirer has called it "the common center" of all "the special problems of eighteenth century epistemology and psychology."[20]

Unfortunately, the question, as stated, is a bit of a muddle. Is it an empirical question? So, apparently, it seemed in the eighteenth century, for when the English surgeon and anatomist William Cheselden successfully restored the vision of a fourteen-year-old boy, blind almost from birth, by means of a cataract operation in 1728, observations of the boy's slowness in gaining what Merleau-Ponty would call a visual *grip* on the world seemed to many to confirm the negative *a priori* predictions of empiricists like Locke and Berkeley. And yet that matter of empirical fact, whatever it amounts to, obscures what is philosophically interesting about the question, namely the conceptual and phenomenological issues it raises concerning the organization and intelligibility of sense experience in normal cases.[21]

Merleau-Ponty, for his part, regards the unity of the object and the unity of the senses as bound up together, not simply and directly, but by the intentional structure of the body and the underlying coherence of the phenomenal field: "I could not grasp the unity of the object without the mediation of bodily experience" (PP 235/203/235). He therefore devotes much of chapter 1, Part 2 of *Phenomenology of Perception*, entitled "Sensing" (*Le Sentir*), to the problem (or puzzle) of the unity and plurality of the senses, precisely because he thinks the problem can appear to be a problem only if we forget that the senses *are* senses only by working together in a unified phenomenal and bodily field, opening onto a single world. Philosophers had things backwards when they took the five senses as separately given and unproblematic, each on its own, and then concluded that it is our unified access to the world that somehow stands in need of explanation. On the contrary, it is the disclosed world itself that allows us to reflect on our unified phenomenal field, to the extent that we can, which in turn allows us to distinguish (roughly) among the sense modalities and finally, at an extreme, regard our sense organs themselves as mere objects.

In truth, talk of the "five" senses is a convenient but misleading simplification. Is proprioception a sixth sense? Is our sense of being warm or cold a function of the same sense as our sense of balance or movement? Taste and smell are two parts of a single system, but then so are all the senses. The commonsense prejudice that the senses come neatly packaged in five discrete bundles is precisely the mistake that prompts Molyneux's question: "It is a commonplace to say that we have five senses, and it would seem at first glance that each of them is like a world out of touch with the others" (SNS 63/49). But if this were so, how could we find it so natural to speak "of hot, cold, shrill, or hard colors, of sounds that are clear, sharp, brilliant, rough, or mellow, of soft noises and of penetrating fragrances" (SNS 63/50)? Is it arbitrary that we associate the sound of a cello with dark shades, with warmth, with heaviness, and the high pitch of a flute with lightness, sharpness, spaciousness? Or is it not rather more plausible to say that such associations are already prefigured in the holistic organization of embodied sensory life?

Nor is it even obvious where (and how) one sense modality ends and another begins. What part of the experience of eating or drinking is *purely* gustatory, and what part *purely* olfactory? In fact, the two systems work together, and a disruption in the sense of smell interferes with one's ability to taste things. Even the effort to enumerate the senses is a bit arbitrary, rather like counting up the corners or edges of a piece of furniture: the criteria are not only vague, but variable relative to different aspects of the organization of the system as a whole and the context in which it functions. The seat of a chair shows up as significant for sitting, while the protruding end of the arm may become salient only when you try to maneuver it into the next room. Similarly, the sense of smell seems most like a separate sense, distinct from taste, when eating is out of the question, for example when we smell flowers or perfume rather than soup. We are closer to hearing something like pure sounds when we deliberately suspend our other senses, for example by standing still and closing our eyes; otherwise, what we hear is the wind in the trees, the traffic, the conversation.

Properly understood, Merleau-Ponty insists, "sensation is literally a communion" (PP 246/212/246). It is our most concrete contact with the world. To say, however, that "any sensation belongs to a certain field" (PP 250/216/251) is to say that sensing cannot be understood in abstraction from the sensible world itself. That world, the world of things and the world we inhabit, is extended in space, and we perceive it as spatial. How? Presumably not by taste and smell. Then how? By touching things, by moving our bodies, by seeing, by hearing? Which of the five senses is primarily and intrinsically spatial?

Merleau-Ponty thinks the question takes for granted an abstraction of the senses both from each other and from the world we sense, which in effect renders them unintelligible as senses, as openings onto the world. Once we forget their world-disclosing function and regard them as mere sensitive surfaces or data input points, it begins to seem as if there could be no empirical evidence for their inherent spatial orientation. The spatiality of the senses cannot be inferred from their nonintentional causal functions, but must be presupposed in regarding them as senses at all: "There is reason, then, to say *a priori* that all the senses are spatial, and the problem of knowing which one presents us with space must be considered unintelligible if we reflect on what a sense is" (PP 252/

218/253). For Merleau-Ponty, since the senses *are* senses only by being embedded in and revealing the world, and since that world is a spatial world, "Every sensation is spatial" (PP 255/221/256). This is not because each sense modality contains its own discrete representation of space, but "because our experience is the experience of a world" (PP 256/221/257).

The unity of sense experience therefore cannot be derived from some function of their putative underlying intrinsic heterogeneity: "the unity and the diversity of the senses are truths of the same order" (PP 256/221/257). The senses are not completely separate and independent, but neither are they simply homogeneous and coextensive. A blind patient who regains his sight after cataract surgery is surprised and fascinated by the space now open to him visually; it is somehow not what he expected based on his prior motor and tactile experience. As a result, "he is quite prepared to admit that he never had the experience of space before the operation" (PP 257/222/258).

But of course we cannot take that admission at face value, for as Merleau-Ponty asks, if his prior tactile experience "was not spatial at all, would the subject stretch out his hand toward the object shown to him? This gesture presupposes that touch opens onto a setting at least analogous to that of what is given visually" (PP 258/223/259). Like many pathological phenomena seemingly foreign to normal life, the astonishment of the newly sighted patient has analogues in ordinary experience. "After the operation he marvels that there should be 'such a difference' between a tree and a human body" (PP 259/224/261). What did he expect? Plainly, his sense of touch had failed profoundly to anticipate the peculiar texture of visual experience and the visible differences it presents. This is striking, but then we often have exactly the same sense of irreducible novelty when we first see someone we have previously only heard on the telephone or the radio, or when we first hear the voice of someone we previously knew only from portraits or photographs. Even in normal experience, "we always find a man different from what we have heard about him" (PP 259/224/261).

What is crucial to Merleau-Ponty's account of the unity and plurality of the senses is his insistence that the "analogy" between touch and vision is not merely intellectual, but *sensory*: "the constitution of an intersensory world must be effected in the domain of sense itself" (PP 260/225/261). The interweaving and overlapping of the senses is a feature of the phenomenal field itself and, as we shall see in the next chapter, a reflection of the concrete coherence of the organism:

> The senses are distinct from one another and distinct from intellection inasmuch as each of them brings with it a structure of being that is never exactly transposable. We can recognize this because we have rejected any formalism of consciousness and made the body the subject of perception.
>
> (*PP* 260/225/261)

Trying to absorb our attention wholly in a single sense at the expense of the others—in the pure blue of the sky, for example—is precisely to lose "the unique grip our body has on the world" (PP 318/275/321), including those features of the world we might have thought lay in their pristine state as discrete qualities in a single sense modality.[22]

Like discrete sensory qualities, "the experience of separate 'senses' finds a place only in a very particular attitude and cannot serve in the analysis of direct awareness" (PP 261/225/262). Rather, experience is irreducibly multisensory, and the senses are what they are only in relation to one another:

> The senses intercommunicate by opening onto the structure of the thing. One sees the hardness and the brittleness of the glass, and when it shatters with a crystalline sound, the sound is borne by the visible glass. One sees the springiness of the steel, the malleability of the red-hot steel, the rigidity of the plane blade, the softness of the wood shavings.
>
> (*PP* 265/229/266–67)

Similarly, we see the flexibility of the branch, the heaviness of the stone, the fluidity of water, the viscosity of syrup, and we speak literally, not metaphorically, of "soft," "dull," and "sharp" sounds (PP 265/230/267). Consequently, in my normal perception of a table, "It is the same table that I touch and that I see" (PP 266/230/267).

Merleau-Ponty suggests two analogies, which, though they cannot solve the problem Molyneux's question seems to pose, may nonetheless dampen the mystery it threatens to inflame. The first analogy is between the diversity of the five senses and the cooperation of the two eyes in binocular vision. Merleau-Ponty writes, "perception reunites our sensory experiences in a single world ... in the way binocular vision grasps a single object" (PP 266/230/268). Do we originally see double and then blend the two retinal images into a single visual representation? Does one eye then cease to contribute directly to our visual awareness, or do we forget that we are really seeing two images rather than one? These are misguided questions for the same reason that anxiety about the heterogeneity of the five senses is misguided, for the supposedly discrete and independent factors are familiar and intelligible to us in the first place thanks only to their integration in a coherent phenomenal field grounded in the body and open onto the world.

That the integration of the senses is itself a sensory phenomenon becomes clear when we feel their divergence and disharmony as a perceptual disturbance in need of correction and adjustment. Seeing double, for example, is not the true original condition of sight, but a breakdown of visual orientation:

> For my gaze to be directed to nearby objects and my eyes to fix on them, it must feel the diplopia as a disequilibrium or as imperfect vision and orient itself toward the single object as toward the resolution of that tension and the achievement of vision. "One must 'look' in order to see." (PP 268/232/270)[23]

Similarly, our perceptual behavior as a whole guides and organizes our multisensory experience, so that "the senses communicate in perception as the two eyes collaborate in vision" (PP 270/234/271–72). That we perceive things by seeing, hearing, touching, tasting, and smelling—not to mention moving around—is therefore no more mysterious or problematic than that we see with two eyes and hear with two ears. And that in turn ought to be no more worrisome than that we walk with two legs and grab with five fingers. All such forms of bodily differentiation are dimensions of the body's underlying coherence and organization.

To say that the integration of the senses is itself a sensory phenomenon is also to caution against positing a transcendental subject to combine the sensory manifold in an act of judgment. The two eyes, Merleau-Ponty writes,

> are used as a single organ by a single gaze. It is not the
> epistemological subject that effects the synthesis, it is the body
> when it pulls itself out of its dispersion, gathers itself up, carries
> itself by all its means toward the sole aim of its movement.
>
> (PP 269/232/270)

Consequently, "the unity of the senses ... is not to be understood in terms of their subsumption under one originary consciousness, but rather their never completed integration in a single knowing organism" (PP 270/233/271). The senses are not sensorially disjoint and in need of intellectual synchronization, as it were; instead, they are always already intermeshed and interdependent, so that their individual ways of comprehending the world outwardly are at once ways of comprehending one another laterally: "The senses translate one another without any need of an interpreter, they understand one another without having to pass through an idea" (PP 271/235/273).

The second demystifying analogy Merleau-Ponty draws is between the plurality of the senses and plurality of persons. The otherness of others is not just a theoretical problem, but an abiding mystery of the human condition. It is also a profound reminder that irreducible difference is and must in principle be compatible with openness and transparency. The plurality of the senses must be understood in the same way as the plurality of points of view on the world, namely as open onto each other only by being irreducibly distinct and finite: "Like the perspective of others on the world for me, the spatial realm of each sense is an unknowable absolute for the others, and to that extent limits their spatiality" (PP 257/222/258). The analogy might seem to make matters worse, for surely the problem of others' minds is an even deeper and murkier conundrum that Molyneux's question. Does it not compound rather than divide the present difficulty? But Merleau-Ponty's purpose is to treat both problems by seeing them as instances of a general pattern of unity and diversity in all aspects of our experience. Problems often seem intractable when viewed in isolation, after all, and coming to see resemblances and patterns underlying them recurring in different contexts often serves to reconfigure and assuage them individually. We will return to the problem and the puzzle and the mystery of others in Chapter 4 when we examine Merleau-Ponty's reflections on society, history, and politics.

SUMMARY

Merleau-Ponty's most important contribution to philosophy is his account of perception as neither a subjective experience nor an objective property of the mind, but an aspect of our *being in the world*. Merleau-Ponty's philosophy is thus neither psychology nor epistemology, but *ontology*. Like Heidegger, he believes that an ontology of human existence must proceed from a phenomenological description of human experience.

What does phenomenology purport to describe? In a word, *intentionality*—the *of*-ness or "aboutness" of experience. Since the late Middle Ages, intentionality has been understood in two ways: as

the sheer *directedness* of the mind toward the world, and as the discursive or *semantic content* of thought and language. The theory of
ideas in Descartes and Locke effectively obscured both of those
notions, and by the late nineteenth century, for example in Brentano and Husserl, the *semantic paradigm* had begun to eclipse not only
the early modern "way of ideas," but also the more primitive
notion of intentional directedness itself.

Merleau-Ponty phenomenology is in large part a critical reaction
to that rationalistic semantic paradigm, an attempt to free the
phenomenon of perceptual awareness from the dominant conception
of intentional content as abstract, discursive, and generally *thought*-like.
Since the semantic conception of intentionality encourages an image
of consciousness as a closed and contained domain of meaning,
sharply delineated from the world to which it purports to refer,
Merleau-Ponty's alternative phenomenology emphasizes the essential bodily intertwining of perception and the perceived world.
Whereas Husserl was an internalist, Merleau-Ponty is an *externalist*.

Husserl's internalism manifests most explicitly in his methodological device known as the *transcendental reduction*, that is, the bracketing or exclusion of the external world itself from all immanent
descriptions of the contents of consciousness. Although Merleau-
Ponty writes with great sympathy and admiration for Husserl's
work, like Heidegger, he rejects the transcendental reduction as
impossible, indeed incoherent.

In *Phenomenology of Perception* Merleau-Ponty launches a two-pronged
attack on *empiricism* and *intellectualism*. Empiricism regards perception
as grounded in *sensation*; intellectualism sees it as a function of
judgment. Merleau-Ponty argues that neither theory can be correct.
Perception cannot be grounded in sensation because the very concept of sensation is confused. We see *things*, not sensations. Indeed,
words supposedly descriptive of mere sensations ("burning,"
"ringing," "spot," "patch") are in fact abstract, fragmentary bits of
language originally referring to full-fledged things (fires, bells,
swatches of cloth). The very concept of sensation is parasitic on our

concept of objects. Worse, the concept of sensation is caught between two often incompatible tasks: to describe the immediate *stimulus* to our senses, and to describe how things *seem*. The perceptual appearance of things differs widely from the array of sensory stimuli, though, so the very concept of sensation has no consistent role to play in a theory of perception. Perception cannot be grounded in judgment because judgments presuppose something given, *about which* a judgment may then be made. If intellectualism insists that perception is really judgment "all the way down," then it robs itself of any appeal to the ordinary phenomenon that seemed to give it content, namely judgment understood as an attitude taken up with respect to a world *given* in perception. What both empiricism and intellectualism lose sight of is the *phenomenal field* itself, the givenness of the world to a situated bodily perspective that is neither merely sensory nor intellectual. The unity of perceptual objects as such, problematized in the seventeenth century by Molyneux's famous question concerning the relation between visual and tactile sensory content, is grounded in the unity of the human body, "the material subject of the world," as Samuel Todes puts it.[24]

FURTHER READING

Carman, T. "Sensation, Judgment, and the Phenomenal Field." An account of Merleau-Ponty's critiques of *empiricist* and *intellectualist* attempts to reduce perceptual content to meaningless sense data or discursive thought, respectively.

Dreyfus, H. "Merleau-Ponty's Critique of Husserl's (and Searle's) Concept of Intentionality." An explanation and defense of Merleau-Ponty's account of action and perception, in contrast to the internal representationalist theories of Husserl and, more recently, John Searle.

Evans, G. "Molyneux's Question." Critical discussion of the formulation and reception of Molyneux's Problem and an original argument for the *identity* of the spatiality of the visual field and the "behavioral space" of motor action.

Kelly, S. D. "Seeing Things in Merleau-Ponty." A critical analysis and constructive interpretation of Merleau-Ponty's view that vision of full-fledged objects in an environment is bound up with solicitations and inhibitions of intelligent motor action.

———. "What Do We See (When We Do)?" Defense of a Merleau-Pontyan account of perceptual constancy in terms of the *normativity* of perceptual experience, that is, that we adjust our bodily position and perspective to see things *properly*, as they *should* appear.

Seebohm, T. M. "The Phenomenological Movement: A Tradition Without Method? Merleau-Ponty and Husserl." Argues that Merleau-Ponty's ambivalence about Husserl, including the implausibility of his "existential" reading of Husserl's later writings, conceal a deconstructive critique of Husserl's phenomenological method.

Taylor, C. "Merleau-Ponty and the Epistemological Picture." A general discussion of Merleau-Ponty's phenomenology as a rejection of all "mediational" accounts of experience as an inner representation of an outer reality, in particular the antirealism of recent analytic philosophers such as Donald Davidson and Richard Rorty.

Three

Body and World

Merleau-Ponty's central original idea about perception is that it is not just contingently but essentially a *bodily* phenomenon. Perception is not a private mental event, nor is the body just one more material object set alongside others. We lose sight of perception itself when we place it on either side of a sharp distinction between inner subjective experiences and external objective facts. In its most concrete form, perception manifests itself instead as an aspect of our *bodily* being in the world. Interior and exterior, mental and physical, subjective and objective—such notions are simply too crude and misleading to capture it. For perception is both intentional and bodily, both sensory and motor, and so neither merely subjective nor objective, inner nor outer, spiritual nor mechanical.

Moreover, the middle ground between such traditional categories is not just their middle but indeed their *ground*, for it is what they depend on and presuppose. There are such things as subjective sensations and sensory qualities, of course, but only because we can sometimes generate them by abstracting away from our original openness onto the world and zeroing in on isolated features of things, and on bits of experience, which we suppose (rightly or wrongly) must correspond to those features, just as we can abstract in the other direction away from ourselves toward a world independent of perspective on it.

It is possible in that primitive middle ground to draw a distinction for analytical purposes between two aspects of perception that arguably underlie and motivate subsequent distinctions between subjective and objective, inner and outer, and mental and physical. The two underlying or primal aspects of perception are (1) the (relative) *passivity* of sense experience and (2) the (relative) *activity* of bodily skills. The Kantian contrast between receptivity and spontaneity, though crude and abstract in its own way, comes closer than other competing theoretical distinctions to capturing the two essential aspects of perception, namely its *sensory* and its *motor* dimensions. As Merleau-Ponty puts it, "The structure of the world, with its double moment of sedimentation and spontaneity, is at the center of consciousness" (PP 152/130/150). Of course, he regards those two moments not as sharply distinct, self-sufficient states, but as interwoven and inseparable aspects of a unified phenomenon. They are not, like Kantian intuitions and concepts, discrete parts or ingredients of a composite product, but more like two sides of a coin, or two dimensions of a figure. Perception is always both passive and active, situational and practical, conditioned and free.

Whereas the previous chapter focused on the receptive sensory aspect of perception, abstracting provisionally (and admittedly somewhat artificially) from the bodily infrastructure on which it rests, the present chapter makes more explicit perception's bodily dimension, which is at the heart of Merleau-Ponty's phenomenology. The individual sections of this chapter are again divided roughly into the critical and the constructive, beginning with Merleau-Ponty's rejection of traditional theories of the body's role in perception and then proceeding to his own account of sensorimotor phenomena in terms of what he calls the *body schema* and *motor intentionality.*

The chapter concludes with a brief discussion of later developments in Merleau-Ponty's view of our place in nature and the ontology of body and world. For by the late 1950s he was apparently dissatisfied with what he had come to regard as the still too dualistic framework of *Phenomenology of Perception.* In its place he now insisted more emphatically that body and world must be seen as overlapping sinews in a common "flesh" (*chair*), related not as situation and reaction (let alone stimulus and response), but as a kind of "chiasm," an "interweaving" or "interlacing" (*entrelacs*) of threads in a single fabric. Merleau-Ponty scholars often write as if these new metaphors amount to a radical break with his earlier work, but I think this is only half right. For although Merleau-Ponty's concept of flesh does mark an abandonment of the primacy of *consciousness* in his account of being in the world, the images of chiasm and interlacing are elaborations on an idea he had already been expounding in his early work, decades before.

It is worth getting clear first about the kind of philosophical claim Merleau-Ponty is making, both early and late, about the role of the body in perception. Perception, I said, is the *ground* of both the subjectivity and the objectivity of experience, of its inner feel and its intentional grip on the world. Furthermore, perception is not a *mental* phenomenon, if by "mental" we mean something in contrast to material or physical. Rather, perception is a *bodily* phenomenon, which is to say that we experience our own sensory states not as mere states of *mind*, but as states of our bodies. Even Descartes had to concede this to phenomenology, precisely in his attempt to argue us out of it by means of abstract, often strikingly counterintuitive considerations to the contrary. We feel pains in our bodies, he admitted, but only because we are confused, for a pain can exist only in a mind. Similarly, we imagine that we see with our eyes, but this is impossible, for seeing is not a physical but a mental event.[1]

Like many philosophers today, Descartes regarded phenomena as mere appearances, eminently revisable, indeed supplantable, by the discoveries of rational inquiry. Our naïve experience of ourselves as bodies, he thought, could be accommodated simply by acknowledging a close causal relation between physical and mental states. Of course we do not *feel* like minds housed or lodged in our bodies, "as a sailor is present in a ship."[2] And yet, for Descartes, the metaphysical fact of the matter is that the relation between experience and the body is a *causal* relation, not an identity.

But suppose body and experience are not just causally connected, but identical. Is that identity conceptually necessary, deducible *a priori*? Do our concepts or judgments about perception *entail* concepts or judgments about the body? How so? What purely rational inferences to bodily phenomena can be drawn from the *concepts* of perception, sensation, recognition, judgment?

For Merleau-Ponty, the relation between perception and the body is neither causal nor conceptual, for those two categories are not the only two ways in which the coincidences and dependencies between the body and perceptual experience are intelligible to us. Instead, traditional concepts pertaining to perception are parasitic on a more basic understanding we have of ourselves in virtue of *being* embodied perceivers. We have a prereflective understanding of our own experiences, not as causally or conceptually linked to our bodies, but as coinciding with them in relations of mutual motivation. To say that perception is essentially bodily is to say that we do not and cannot understand it in abstraction from its concrete corporeal conditions. The phenomenal field is neither caused nor defined, but *constituted* by the sensorimotor structures and capacities of the body. The structure of perception, we might say, just is the structure of the body. As Merleau-Ponty says, my body "is my point of view on the world" (PP 85/70/81).

Of course, from a third-person point of view, the structures and capacities of the body are mere contingent, arbitrary facts about the kinds of creatures we happen to be. And yet those facts can never manifest themselves *as* contingent and arbitrary for us, from our point of view, for they *are* our perspective on the world. The body is not just one more object in the environment, for we do not —indeed *cannot*—understand our own bodies as accidentally occurring things. The point is not just that the boundary between my body and the environment cannot be drawn sharply from a third-person point of view, for what matters here is not *where* the boundary lies, but rather *that* there is a deep difference in principle between myself and my world. My body cannot be understood simply as that chunk of the material world that sits in closest contact with my mind:

> if I am a prisoner, the church will be reduced for me to a truncated steeple. If I did not take off my clothes, I could never see their insides, and we will indeed see that my clothes may become extensions of my body. But this fact does not prove that the presence of my body is comparable to the *de facto* permanence of certain objects, or the organ to a tool that is always available.
>
> (*PP* 107/91/104)

However shifting or indeterminate the boundary between body and environment may be, it cannot collapse entirely, for an environment is an environment only for a body that cannot perceive itself as just one more object among others: "I observe external objects with my body, I handle them, examine them, walk around them, but as for my body, I do not observe it itself: to be able to do so, I would need to use a second body that would itself not be observable" (PP 107/91/104).

My body is my perspective on the world and so cannot be for me just one more contingent object or fact about the world. Instead, it constitutes a kind of background field of perceptual *necessity* against which genuine sensorimotor contingencies show up *as* contingent. Manifestly contingent facts about perception presuppose (more or less) invariant structures of the phenomenal field, for example perspectival orientation in space and time and figure/ground contrast. Although it can change somewhat while our basic relation to the world remains fixed and intact, the phenomenal field is always for Merleau-Ponty a "transcendental field" (PP 74/61/71), that is, a space of possibilities, impossibilities, and necessities *constitutive* of our perceptual world. The body is not just a causal but a transcendental condition of perception, which is itself not just an inner subjective state, but a mode of being in the world. In short, we have no understanding of perception in abstraction from the body and the world.

1. WHAT THE BODY IS *NOT*

To say that the structure of perception just *is* the structure of the body might sound odd. For whereas we often think of perception from a first-person perspective, since Descartes we have grown accustomed to thinking of the body from a detached third-person point of view, as a mere object. We regard perception as subjective, the body as objective. How then could the structure of the one be *identical* with the structure of the other, over and beyond their being somehow causally connected? As Merleau-Ponty says, thanks to the Cartesian legacy, "it is difficult to see what ground could be common to 'physiological facts' that are in space and 'psychic facts' that are nowhere," or in Sartrean terms, "objective processes like nervous influxes that belong to the realm of the in-itself [*en soi*], and *cogitationes* ... that are of the order of the for-itself [*pour soi*]" (PP 91–92/77/89).

What led Descartes and others to draw such a sharp conceptual distinction between the mental and the physical, rendering the two incommensurable? Arguably, the initial motivation was not an intuition about the mind at all, but an assumption about the body, namely, that it must be a *machine*. What is a machine? A free-standing physical system whose behavior as a whole is a function of the workings of its individual parts, which interact rigidly by direct causal contact. Machines are strictly speaking the sums of their parts, hence analyzable into mechanical subsystems:

> The definition of the object is ... that it exists *partes extra partes*, and that consequently it acknowledges between its parts, or between itself and other objects, only external and mechanical relationships, whether in the narrow sense of motion received and transmitted, or in the broad sense of the relation of function to variable.
>
> (*PP* 87/73/84)

Machines are extended objects—"parts outside of parts," in scholastic lingo—hence explicable from the bottom up, as macroscopic systems supervening deterministically on their underlying microstructures. As we shall see later in this chapter, it is unclear whether such a conception of bodies can in principle adequately describe the vital processes of living organisms, though the assumption that it can and must is what underwrites the reductive program of contemporary molecular biology.

For Descartes and the tradition that followed him, the body is just that chunk of the physical world that happens to be causally contiguous with the soul, the last link in a chain of causes and effects that ends with the perceptual experience. Of course, Descartes was not the first dualist in the history of philosophy; Plato was a dualist, too. The difference, though, is that Descartes distinguishes the soul from the body only by first drawing a sharp distinction between *having a soul* and *being alive*. For Plato and the Aristotelian-scholastic tradition, the soul is the principle of life: a thing lives and initiates its own movements by having a soul, and when the soul leaves the body, the thing dies. For Descartes, by contrast, life is a mechanical phenomenon and has nothing in principle to do with having a soul or mind (which are for him the same thing). It is not the soul that constitutes life, but life that allows the immaterial soul to be united with the material body. Likewise, death is a mechanical failure of the body and "never occurs through the absence of the soul, but only because one of the principal parts of the body decays."[3]

It is easy, from a safe historical distance, to scoff at Descartes's crudely mechanical understanding of the body, with all its quaint pulleys and levers,[4] and yet the ontology underlying it has filtered so far into scientific common sense that in many ways we now simply take it for granted. Consider, for example, the ambiguity infecting our concept of *behavior*. We might think the English word refers to a single thing, and yet human *conduct*, what the *Oxford English Dictionary* calls "demeanor, deportment, bearing, manners," is something profoundly different from, as another definition of "behavior" has it, "the manner in which a thing acts under specified conditions or circumstances, or in relation to other things." Indeed, whereas references to human behavior date back in English to the fifteenth century, the OED cites only one source under the latter generic and depersonalized definition from 1674; the rest are from the nineteenth century. It is only the more recent conception, applying indifferently to personal actions and impersonal events, that seems to vindicate intuitively what must have struck many in the seventeenth century—and arguably still ought to strike us—as a bizarre conflation of flesh and engine: "The body becomes the highly polished machine that the ambiguous concept of behavior [comportement] nearly made us forget" (PP 90/76/87).

Of course, as Merleau-Ponty insists, Descartes's mechanistic theory of the body, which in effect pushes all intentional phenomena back into a worldless, incorporeal mind, has no echo in ordinary experience. We feel pains, for example, not as *caused by* our bodies, but as *inhabiting* them. Better yet, what I experience is not *pains* as distinct from my body, but my body (myself) *in pain*:

> if I say my foot hurts, I do not simply mean that it is a cause of pain in the same way as the nail that is cutting into it, differing only in being nearer to me; I do not mean that it is the last of the objects in the external world, after which a more intimate kind of pain should begin, an unlocalized awareness of pain in itself, related to the foot only by some causal connection and within the closed system of experience. I mean that the pain reveals itself as localized, that it is constitutive of a "pain-infested space." "I have a pain in my foot" does not mean *I think my foot is the cause of this pain*, but rather, *the pain is coming from my foot*, or again, *my foot is in pain*.
> (PP 109–10/93/107)

In spite of its official demise in the nineteenth century, the spirit of dualism lived on, for example in the psychological theory of the *reflex arc*—the supposedly isolated neural pathway linking particulate sensory inputs with particulate behavioral outputs—and more recently in functionalist theories of mental content. On these views, psychological phenomena can be understood as representations or functions linking incoming sensory stimuli to outgoing behavioral responses.

As early as 1896, John Dewey criticized the concept of the reflex arc by pointing out that what is in fact empirically given is neither isolated sensations nor discrete physical movements, but the more basic phenomenon of sensorimotor "coordination."[5] Bodily behaviors are already at work actively selecting and differentiating sensory stimuli, just as the phenomenal field as a whole already elicits and constrains voluntary and involuntary actions. Consequently,

> the reflex arc idea ... is defective in that it assumes sensory stimulus and motor response as distinct psychical existences, while in reality they are always inside a coordination and have their significance purely from the part played in maintaining or reconstituting the coordination.[6]

Moreover, the senses are integrated with one another, so that "What happens is a certain relative prominence and subsidence as between the various organs which maintain the organic equilibrium."[7] In the end,

> What we have is a circuit, not an arc or broken segment of a circle. This circuit is more truly termed organic than reflex, because the motor response determines the stimulus, just as truly as sensory stimulus determines movement.[8]

Only against such a background of meaningfully integrated sensorimotor coordination is it possible to pick out particular experiences and bodily movements *as* stimuli and responses. They are not conditions, but products of the interpretation of experience and behavior. Construing them as givens, Dewey argues, is virtually the psychological or historical fallacy. A set of considerations which hold good only because of a completed process, is read into the content of the process which conditions this completed result. A state of things characterizing an outcome is regarded as a true description of the events which led up to this outcome.[9]

Others, including the neurologist Kurt Goldstein, later dealt the reflex-arc theory a further empirical blow by showing in detail that it contributes virtually nothing to the actual explanation of behavior. In fact, as Goldstein observed, it is not obvious that there is any such thing as a pure reflex. Even the patellar reflex (the kick in your leg when the doctor taps on the ligament just below your knee) turns out to be highly variable, increasing for example as a result of lesions in the pyramidal tract lying outside the putative reflex arc, which in this case reaches only partway up the spinal cord. "To explain all these variations," Goldstein reports, "it was necessary to go beyond the processes in the so-called reflex arc and to assume that the course of a reflex is influenced by other factors."[10] Like the concept of sensation, the idea of an isolated reflex arc enjoys an entirely specious obviousness and simplicity. It appeals to theorists a priori, but turns out to be empirically useless. Just as it is unclear what role (if any) pure sensations play in ordinary perception, so too it is unclear what role (if any) pure reflexes play in normal behavior.

Following Goldstein, Merleau-Ponty observes that perception and movement are not related to one another as causes and effects, but coexist in a complex interconnected whole, against which the stimuli and responses of the psychology laboratory are mere abstractions, artifacts of analysis:

When the eye and the ear follow an animal in flight, it is impossible to say "which came first" in the exchange of stimuli and responses. Since all the movements of the organism are always conditioned

by external influences, one can, if one wishes, readily treat
behavior as an effect of the environment. But in the same way,
since all the stimulations that the organism receives were in turn
possible only through its prior movements, which culminated in
exposing the receptor organ to the external influences, one could
also say the behavior is the first cause of all the stimulations.

(*SC* 11/13)

Actual empirical evidence of perception and behavior reveals the
abstractness and explanatory impotence of the reflex-arc model:

Before any systematic interpretation, the description of the *known*
facts shows that the fate of an excitation is determined by its
relation to the whole of the organic state and to the simultaneous
or preceding excitations, and that the relations between the
organism and its environment are not relations of linear
causality, but of circular causality.

(*SC* 13/15)

In short,

there is never any pure exteroceptive reflex—that is, one that
needs only the intervention of an external stimulus in order to
exist. All reflexes demand the concurrence of a multitude of
conditions in the organism external to the reflex arc, which have
as much right as the "stimulus" to be called the causes of the
reaction.

(*SC* 15/17)

Moreover, stimulus and reflex do not occur in nature at all as they
do in the laboratory:

The reflex as it is defined in the classical conception does not
represent the normal activity of the animal, but the reaction

obtained from the organism when it is made to work, so to speak, with detached parts, to respond not to complex *situations* but to isolated *stimuli*. Which is to say, it corresponds to the behavior of a sick organism ...

(SC 45/43–44)

Normal healthy animals do not produce discrete responses to isolated stimuli; they react in coordinated ways to whole (more or less) coherent situations. Unlike stimulus and response, "situation and reaction ... cannot be set one after the other as cause and effect: they are two moments of a circular process" (SC 140/130).

Stimuli and responses are abstract, artificially elicited moments in complex dynamic interactions between organisms and their environments. There is no simple correlation between discrete neurological parts, either central or peripheral, and pure sensory phenomena. For example, "injuries to centers and even to conductors are not translated into the loss of certain qualities of sensation or of certain sensory data, but into loss of differentiation in the function. ... for example, a decay of sensitivity to color" (PP 88/73–74/85). So too, loss of a precise sense of the localization of tactile stimuli in some brain-damaged patients "is not explained by the destruction of a localizing center, but by the reduction to a uniform level of sensations, which are no longer capable of organizing themselves into a stable grouping in which each of them receives a univocal value" (PP 88–89/74/86). More generally, as we have seen, the givenness of something in perception is never just the effect of an external cause; rather, perception is the perspective of the organism as a whole on its world, which it confronts not as a meaningless collection of objects, but as a significant situation:

the "sensible quality," the spatial limits set to the percept, and even the presence or absence of a perception, are not *de facto* effects of the situation outside the organism, but represent the way in which it meets stimulation and is related to it. An excitation is not perceived when it strikes a sensory organ that is not "attuned" to it. The function of the organism in receiving stimuli is, so to speak, to "conceive" a certain form of excitation. ... exteroceptivity demands that stimuli be given a shape.

(*PP* 89–90/75/86–87)

In reality the reflexes themselves are never blind processes: they adjust themselves to a "sense" [*sens*] of the situation, they express our orientation toward a "behavioral milieu," just as the "geographical milieu" acts on us. ... It is this global presence of the situation that gives a sense to the partial stimuli and makes them matter, have value, and exist for the organism. The reflex does not arise from objective stimuli, but moves back toward them and invests them with a sense that they do not possess taken singly as psychological agents, but only when taken as a situation. It makes them be, qua situation ... The reflex, insofar as it opens itself to the sense of a situation, and perception, insofar as it does not first of all posit an object of knowledge and is an intention of our whole being, are modalities of a *preobjective view*, which is what we call being in the world.

(*PP* 94/79/91–92)

The Aristotelian-scholastic image of the soul diffused throughout the body, an image Descartes seemed to render obsolete by conceiving of the body as a machine tethered to an incorporeal mind through the metaphysical bottleneck of the pineal gland,[11] turns out to capture something right about the generality and nonspecificity of many neurological functions. As Merleau-Ponty says, "awareness of the body invades the body, the soul spreads over all its parts, and behavior overspills its central sector" (PP 90/75/87).

But although he relies heavily on Goldstein's findings, Merleau-Ponty's real objection to the reflex-arc theory is a not an empirical but a philosophical objection, and is thus closer in spirit to Dewey's. The point is not that perception and behavior are too complex and the reflex-arc theory too crude to capture them, but that the very notions of stimulus and response are abstractions that can apply to perception and behavior only by presupposing what they purport to explain. Only by already having a robust understanding of perception can you even try to identify something like a sensation, for example by staring at a bright light and then closing your eyes and concentrating on the afterimage, or by trying to think about a pain without thinking about the part of your body that hurts. So too, only by already having a robust understanding of intelligent, coordinated behavior can you even try to identify something like an isolated reflex, for example by dangling your leg and tapping the ligament just below your knee. In both cases, the effect depends crucially on setting up artificial conditions precisely in order to generate phenomena answering to a theoretical preconception. It is the pre-existing perceptions and behaviors themselves that make intelligible such things as sensations and reflexes, not vice versa.

Of course, perceptual awareness is not an inner sanctum distinct from the peripheral nervous system, much less the body as a whole: "The phenomenal field is not an 'inner world,' the 'phenomenon' is not a 'state of consciousness' or a 'psychic fact,' and the experience of phenomena is not an act of introspection or an intuition" (PP 69–70/57/66). More precisely, experience is simply not the sort of thing that has sharp metaphysical boundaries, either inside or outside the material world.

But why did anyone ever think it was? The reason, Merleau-Ponty argues, lies in the attenuated concept of the body as a mere object or machine, which in turn yielded the image of the mind as a kind of additional inner realm lying outside the physical world altogether, or perhaps in contact with it at some vanishingly small point in the brain. That exclusion then produced, or perhaps merely reinforced, a notion of the mind as a distinct thing alongside the body, a kind of mental mechanism parallel to that of the physical world. As Gilbert Ryle observed, the "ghost in the machine," precisely because Descartes construed it as a thinking *substance* alongside and so in the same conceptual category as extended substance, took on a kind of "paramechanical" character of its own, curiously mirroring the mechanism of physical nature.[12]

Later, even as substance dualism came to seem increasingly absurd, psychologists persisted in trying to carve out a special place for the mind in some kind of gap or vacuum in nature, however narrowly straitened by the presumably rigid mechanical parts of the physical organism. Although the aim was in one sense to define an interior realm, the effort was guided by what Merleau-Ponty calls "the prejudice of the exterior" (PP 70/57/66):

> Introspective psychology detected, on the margins of the physical world, a zone of consciousness in which physical concepts no longer apply, but the psychologist still believed consciousness to be no more than a sector of being, and he decided to explore this sector as the physicist explores his. He tried to describe the givens of consciousness, but without putting into question the absolute existence of the world surrounding it. Together with the scientist and common sense, he presupposed the objective world as the logical framework of all his descriptions, and as the setting of his thought.
>
> (*PP* 72/59/68)

While not banishing the mind from nature altogether, the effect was nonetheless a peculiar reification of mental phenomena as inner duplicates or representations of things in the external world, including the body itself. Intentionality, our intelligent situatedness in the world, now appeared as a mere " 'psychic fact' ... a world of inner events" (PP 72/59/68).

To relieve this conceptual cramp, which afflicts not just dualism, but introspective psychology and recent versions of functionalism

and eliminativism as well, we must rethink the mechanistic conception of the body that brought it on. Our reluctance to abandon
that conception rests on the entrenched but wrongheaded notion
that doing so would amount to abandoning science itself, and that
only a resolutely third-person, mechanical conception of the world
is compatible with genuine scientific inquiry.[13] And yet the first-
person, phenomenological dimension of experience is part of the
world, too, however we choose to describe it. Our intentional
directedness toward the world is itself a fact about the world, after
all, which somehow manages to include us and our experience. We
must avoid hypostatizing that experience as a mere bundle of isolated psychic facts residing in the mind or brain, outside or alongside the world, but we cannot simply think it out of existence.

What we need is a richer phenomenological description not just
of the mind, but of the body too—not in its objective aspect, as
something distinct from mental phenomena, but as it figures in
our ordinary experience of ourselves, from the first-person point of
view. More precisely, we need an account of the body as it informs
our intuitive sense of perceptual sensitivity and agency, oriented in
and open on the world. As Merleau-Ponty says, "I can understand
the function of the living body only by enacting it myself, and
insofar as I am a body that rises toward the world" (PP 90/75/87).
We must return to our pretheoretical understanding of the body
not as an object or a machine, but as our embeddedness in and
direction toward the world. Cutting through the dualism that persists in philosophy and psychology, we need to make room for an
understanding of the body itself as the locus of intentionality.

2. THE BODILY POINT OF VIEW

Merleau-Ponty's account of the bodily nature of perception thus
steers between two competing but equally inadequate alternatives.
The first is the perspective of an as it were disembodied thinking
subject, a pure intellect, the supposedly spontaneous source and
autonomous agent of its own cognition. Merleau-Ponty dismisses

that rationalistic self-image as incoherent and delusional: incoherent because reflection is not self-sufficient, but grows essentially
out of intuition; delusional because, in rationalizing itself, it also
rationalizes phenomena it ought merely to be describing: "philosophy, as soon as it declares itself to be reflection or coincidence,
prejudges what it will find" (VI 172/130). The other phenomenologically inadequate perspective is the objective, impersonal stance
of the physical sciences, which renounces the myth of the
sovereignty of the subject, but in so doing abstracts from the first-
person dimension of experience altogether, which is however
precisely what a theory of perception is obliged to acknowledge
and describe.

Merleau-Ponty's *via media* between the two is what I shall call *the
bodily point of view*, which is to say the ordinary intuitive understanding we have of ourselves as embodied perceivers. The bodily
point of view is the first-person point of view, but it is not the
subjective or personal point of view traditionally theorized, for
again only some of our experience centers around a self-conscious
subject, a locus of personal identity and responsibility—in short, an
I. Underlying that (more or less) transparent personal subject is a
more primitive, one might say merely *translucent* layer of bodily
experience that has a more impersonal character better captured by
the French pronoun *on* ("one" or "we"), as in *one blinks every few
seconds*, or *we breathe through our noses*. The prepersonal bodily subject of
perception is thus not my conscious, reflective self, but simply "the
one" (*le "on"*) (PP 400/348/405):

> All perception takes place in an atmosphere of generality and is
> given to us as anonymous. I cannot say *I* see the blue of the sky in
> the sense in which I say I understand a book, or again in which I
> say I decide to devote my life to mathematics ... if I wanted to
> render precisely the perceptual experience, I ought to say that
> *one* perceives in me, not that I perceive.
>
> (*PP* 249/215/250)[14]

The bodily point of view is our ordinary point of view on the world. It is not just one more arbitrary perspective among others, nor is it a mere methodological contrivance, for we inhabit it every day of our lives. Taking it seriously in philosophy is not just a neat way of solving a theoretical problem, but a necessary presupposition for speaking intelligibly about the bodily nature of perception at all, for it is simply the acknowledgment that we ourselves *are* the phenomenon that a phenomenology of perception must try to describe. Perception is not some exotic object or process somewhere out there in the world, it is us.

One might object at this point that appealing to the bodily point of view is just another way of substituting subjectivity for objectivity, flimsy testimony for hard evidence, rhetoric for science. Doesn't the third-person point of view necessarily trump the first, rendering it irrelevant for theoretical purposes? Isn't the attempt to describe the bodily point of view *from within* just another hopeless attempt on the part of the subject to catch itself out as subject rather than as object? And isn't that like trying to jump over one's own shadow? Surely the only sensible approach is to reflect from a detached, objective point of view, which, though it always fails to grasp itself in its own act of reflection, nevertheless at the end of the day eventually gets around to everything in principle susceptible to description. We cannot see backwards or sideways, but that doesn't mean we don't have objective backs and sides. A subject trying to grasp itself as subject, Ryle says, "is always a day late for the fair, but every day he reaches the place of yesterday's fair. He never succeeds in jumping on to the shadow of his own head, yet he is never more than one jump behind."[15]

Put another way, it may seem as if phenomenology faces a dilemma, for either its putative data, which it regards as occupying a privileged intermediary position between subjective appearance and objective fact, are themselves just more objective facts—viewed obscurely, from an oblique angle, as it were—or else they constitute a distinct subjective realm after all, a separate interior slice of reality, which would in effect expose phenomenology as the sort of closet dualism its physicalist critics have always suspected it of being. Surely either the phenomena of phenomenology are real facts, in principle describable from a third-person point of view, however far removed that may be from our ordinary intuitions, or else they fall altogether outside the physical world, the world described by the natural sciences. Even if there is something worth calling "the bodily point of view," why should we give it any credence when we theorize about perception?[16]

The objection is an attempt to explain away what Merleau-Ponty calls the phenomenal field by reducing it to something merely subjective, something notional but unreal in itself, in deference to a wholly external point of view. Merleau-Ponty insists, on the contrary, that the first-person dimension of experience is *constitutive* of perception. The body has a distinctive experience of itself, an experience that is not just a contingent subjective obstacle to some ideally detached, sidelong view of it. The fact that we can never peer around our own corner is not an accidental epistemic limitation, but an essential structure of perception itself, one that stands in need of description and interpretation. The bodily point of view thus cannot simply be dismissed a kind of error or illusion. Indeed, any adequate account of the body qua *perceiving subject* must include an account of its own experience of itself *prior to* its self-objectification in reflection, which is in any case always incomplete and imperfect.

Merleau-Ponty is not a dualist, however. He knows that experience is an objective physical phenomenon inasmuch as it is realized in the brain and nervous system, or rather the organism as a whole, and not in some distinct metaphysical realm:

> Our aim is not to oppose to the facts objective science coordinates a
> group of facts that "escape" it—whether one calls them "psychism"
> or "subjective facts" or "internal facts"—but to demonstrate that
> the object-being, and so too the subject-being conceived in

opposition to it and relative to it, are not alternative, that the
perceived world is beneath or beyond that antinomy.

(VI 41/22)

The mind is not a thing distinct or separate from the body. Nevertheless, experience has an irreducible first-person character, for
even as realized in the body it remains uniquely, though not
exclusively, accessible to the subject whose body it is:

The function of the organism in the reception of stimuli is, so to
speak, to "conceive" a certain form of excitation ... [But] I cannot
represent this form to myself as a series of processes in the third
person ... I cannot gain a detached knowledge of it.

(PP 89–90/75/86–87)

Experience is nothing metaphysically distinct from the coherent
configuration of the body, but neither is it a mere representation of
the body that could in principle be grasped from a third-person
point of view. Is this intelligible? Can we have a nonrepresenta-
tional experience of our own bodies? Merleau-Ponty writes,

one might reply that this "bodily experience" is itself a
"representation," a "psychic fact," and that as such it is at the end
of a chain of physical and physiological events that alone can be
ascribed to the "real body." Is not my body, exactly like external
bodies, an object that acts on receptors and finally gives rise to
the awareness of the body? Is there not a "interoceptivity," just as
there is an "exteroceptivity"? Can't I find in the body message wires
sent by the internal organs to the brain, which are installed by
nature to provide the soul with the opportunity of feeling its body?

(PP 90/75–76/87)

Ordinary experience provides a striking counterexample to the
putative dilemma between subjective appearance and objective reality,

namely *proprioception*, or immediate perceptual self-awareness. Proprioception is our direct sensorimotor awareness of our own bodies, and it differs in both form and content from *exteroception*, our perception of external things. We are proprioceptively aware of being warm or cold, of the positions and movements of our limbs, of whether and which parts of our bodies are being touched—all without observing ourselves or forming judgments on the basis of observation. Yet proprioception is not a sixth sense distinct from and additional to the five (so-called) "external" senses. Rather, "External perception and the perception of one's own body vary together because they are two sides of one and the same act" (PP 237/205/237). "Every external perception is immediately synonymous with a certain perception of my body, just as every perception of my body makes itself explicit in the language of external perception" (PP 239/206/239).[17]

Consider the famous *phantom limb* syndrome, in which people continue to feel the presence of an amputated or missing limb, sense its movements, and (often agonizingly) feel pains where the limb once was.[18] The illusion is not just a false judgment, for the subject knows perfectly well that the limb is not there: "the experience of the amputated arm as present, or of the disabled arm as absent, is not on the order of 'I think that … '" (PP 96/81/94). But neither is it a brute sensation, for it has intentional content informing the subject's intuitive sense of his own body, its positions and possibilities, what is happening to it and what it can do. Moreover, such conditions often dissipate or correct themselves with the passage of time, which suggests a kind of recalibration of a long-term with a short-term sense of one's body, what Merleau-Ponty calls "the habitual body" and "the present body," respectively (PP 97/82/95). A similar disturbance in your sense of bodily position and capacity occurs when you stand up and try to walk on a leg that has "fallen asleep" for lack of circulation. Like *anosognosia*, in which patients fail to recognize or admit their own seemingly obvious physical impairments, phantom limb syndrome is neither a judgment nor a sensation, but a modification of the intuitive bodily understanding essential to perception.

For the tradition, of course, the phrase "bodily understanding" is an oxymoron, for it cuts across entrenched distinctions between sensation and judgment, mechanism and mind, extension and thought:

> The phantom limb is no mere effect of objective causality, nor is it a *cogitatio*. It could be a mixture of the two only if we could find a way of linking the one to the other, the "psychical" and the "physiological," the "for itself" and the "in itself," and to bring about a connection between them, if the processes in the third person and the personal acts could be integrated in a middle common to them.
>
> (*PP* 92/77/89)

Those conceptual distinctions are drawn precisely to resist any such synthesis, so we can hardly hope to reconstruct the kind of primitive bodily understanding at work in the experience of the phantom limb simply by, so to speak, pasting such categories back together again piecemeal. Rather, Merleau-Ponty observes, the emphatically "un-Cartesian terms" required to describe the phenomena, which are themselves neither cognitive nor mechanical, "force us to form the idea of an organic thought through which the relation of the 'psychic' to the 'physiological' becomes conceivable" (PP 92/77/89).

In insisting that the bodily point of view occupies a middle ground between beliefs and desires on the one hand and physiological mechanisms on the other, Merleau-Ponty is not denying that perceptual understanding has psychological and causal features. Indeed, by moving outward from the primitive middle ground, rather than inward from the abstract and reified extremes, he hopes to show how such a seemingly paradoxical blend of reasons and causes is possible. What he does deny, perhaps somewhat implausibly, is

that there are purely physiological behaviors devoid of any psychological significance or pure rational states devoid of any bodily character: "there is not a single movement in a living body that is
entirely fortuitous with respect to psychic intentions, not a single
psychic act that has not found at least its germ or its general outline
in physiological tendencies" (PP 104/88/101).

It is important to keep in mind that the kind of bodily self-
understanding Merleau-Ponty is describing is not unique to human
beings, or even higher organisms. When an insect loses a leg and
uses another to compensate the loss, the substitution does not
simply enlist a mechanism designed and ready for that purpose in
advance, but neither is it the result of an idea representing an end
to be achieved. It is instead part of the organism's global reor-
ientation to its tasks in its environment taken as a whole:

> The insect simply continues to be in the same world and moves in
> it with all its powers. ... There is no more choice here than in a
> drop of oil that uses all its internal forces to solve practically the
> maximum-minimum problem confronting it.
>
> (*PP* 92–93/78/90)

Like the insect's adjustment to the loss of its leg, our normal (and
abnormal) sense of our own bodies is neither merely mechanical
nor cognitive, but "has to do with an a priori of the species and not
a personal choice" (PP 93/78/90).

> It is because it is a preobjective view that being in the world can
> be distinguished from every third-person process, from every
> modality of the *res extensa*, as from every *cogitatio*, from every
> first-person form of knowledge—and that it can effect the union
> of the "psychic" and the "physiological." ... Anosognosia and the
> phantom limb lend themselves neither to a physiological nor to a
> psychological explanation, nor yet to a mixture of the two.
>
> (*PP* 95/80/92)

Anosognosia is a bizarre condition; phantom limbs, however, should not really strike us as so strange. After all, people frequently feel "referred pains" in parts of their bodies other than those directly stimulated, for example when a heart attack is felt in the left arm, or when lower back trouble sends pain shooting down the legs. The proverbial "ice cream headache" is a similarly misplaced pain. If it seems incredible that a person can feel pain in a missing limb, ask yourself how we manage to feel pains in the limbs we actually have, rather than in our brains, where the final neural processing actually occurs. Is that mundane fact really any less astonishing? On the other hand, come to think of it, why should we expect to feel pains in our brains? From this Cartesian angle, it is tempting to say that all pains are phantom pains, all bodily feelings merely virtual, wherever we happen to locate them. Yet if all proprioceptive awareness is anomalous in this way, then none of it is, including referred and phantom pains, and the mystery dissolves.

Why then are we so surprised and intrigued when we first hear about the abnormal cases? For one thing, such anomalies force us to recognize our own tacitly abiding bodily understanding, which is so basic and so familiar that we are normally unaware of it. It is so inconspicuous and so transparent to our ordinary perceptual sense of ourselves as to be invisible. This is also why abnormal syndromes are so valuable to phenomenology: they are vital to the effort of description not just because they supply us with new weird data, but because our initial intuitive response to them casts light on the prior background understanding we bring with us from prereflective experience. Phantom limb syndrome is fascinating in part precisely because it reminds us that we always already have an intuitive understanding of our own bodies as, for example, *where* we feel pain and *where* our actions are initiated and performed. *That* we have such an immediate and intuitive bodily sense of ourselves is what Merleau-Ponty wants to recover and explore in his phenomenology.

In addition to that concrete bodily sense of self, moreover, we have an intuitive sense of personal and emotional space, which also

often adjusts itself to new worldly conditions only gradually, involuntarily, and sometimes only with the painful effort of rehabilita-
tion. As Merleau-Ponty remarks, "We do not understand the
absence or death of a friend until the moment we expect a reply
from him and realize there will never be one" (PP 96/80–81/93).
The phantom limb is literally like a lost companion: our bodies
originally attune us to their presence, just as they then absorb and
become habituated to their absence. "To be moved is to find oneself caught up [engagé] in a situation one is failing to face up to, and
yet which one does not want to flee" (PP 101–2/86/99). Emotional intelligence, like the phantom limb, constitutes a kind of
"preconscious knowledge" (PP 96/81/93), not because it falls
below the threshold of explicit awareness, but because it is different
in kind from the rationally articulated contents of self-conscious
beliefs and desires. This is why Merleau-Ponty can maintain that
"memory, emotion, and phantom limb are equivalents with regard
to being in the world" (PP 102/86/99). Moreover, such prearticulate intelligence straddles nature and culture, for it shapes not
only our sense of bodily and emotional space, but also our perception
and understanding of the cultural worlds we inhabit and negotiate
in virtue of our socially conditioned skills and sensibilities.[19]

3. THE BODY SCHEMA

As we saw at the beginning of this chapter, the philosophical significance of the bodily nature of perception is neither that the body
is the cause of sensory awareness nor that our concepts about perception
entail concepts about the body; it is rather that my body constitutes
my perspective on the world, and a perspective on the world cannot
be understood as an object merely occurring in the world.

Put another way, it is obvious and yet important that my relation
to my body is structurally unlike my relation to anything else to
which it affords me perceptual access. For example, since my body
is my means of observation, I cannot simply observe it by means of
itself, or rather I can do so only partially, imperfectly, only up to a

point, for example with the help of mirrors or cameras. Of course, I can observe some parts of my body by means of others: I can look at my foot or touch the back of my head. But I cannot make my body as a whole an object of contemplation, for as Merleau-Ponty says, "to do so, I would have to use a second body, which would itself be unobservable" (PP 107/91/104).

This peculiar unobservability of one's own body is not just a material or geometrical problem, an artifact of, say, the position of our eyes in our heads. Instead, it has to do with the impossibility of shedding our own perceptual agency and simply observing ourselves. This is why hearing your own voice as you talk is so unlike hearing a recording of it, and why looking in the mirror is so unlike seeing a photograph or yourself:

> I can just barely catch my living glance when a mirror in the
> street unexpectedly reflects my image back at me. My body in the
> mirror never stops following my intentions like their shadow, and
> if observation consists in varying the point of view while keeping
> the object fixed, it escapes observation and is given to me as a
> simulacrum of my tactile body since it imitates its initiatives
> instead of responding to them by a free unfolding of perspectives.
> (PP 107/91/105)

This asymmetry of bodily perspective and objective observation points up the way in which the structure of perception is not just caused or conditioned but *constituted* by the structure of the body. Perception is not just the presence of objects to a subject, but has, as Husserl observed, a *horizonal* structure. No matter how accurately a photograph may represent an object, seeing the photograph is never quite like seeing the object itself, for whereas the visual field has *horizons* peculiar to the body, photographs merely have *edges*:

> When, in a film, the camera focuses on an object and zooms in on
> it for a closeup, we can of course *remember* that this is the

ashtray or an actor's hand; we do not actually identify it. For the screen has no horizons. In normal vision, by contrast, I direct my gaze on a fragment of the landscape, which comes to life and is disclosed while the other objects recede into the periphery and become dormant, though they do not cease to be there. For with them, I have at my disposal their horizons, in which there is implied, in peripheral vision, the object on which my eyes are now fixed. The horizon is thus what guarantees the identify of the object in the course of the exploration.

(*PP* 82/68/78)

The horizons of perceptual experience are thus functions of the body in which it is realized. For example, all perception has a figure/ground structure. Why? It is not as if figure/ground contrast is deducible a priori from the concept of perception, hence applicable to all possible perceivers, including angels and insects. But neither is it a merely contingent feature that we can imagine our own experience lacking:

To see an object is either to have it on the margin of the visual field and be able to fix on it, or to respond to the solicitation by fixing on it. When I do fix on it, I become anchored in it ... I continue inside one object the exploration that just now hovered over them all, and in one movement I close up the landscape and open up the object. The two operations do not just coincide by accident: it is not the contingencies of my bodily organization, for example the structure of my retina, that oblige me to see my surroundings vaguely if I want to see the object clearly. Even if I knew nothing of rods and cones, I would know [*je concevrais*] that it is necessary to put the surroundings in abeyance to see the object better, and lose in ground what one gains in figure, because to look at the object is to sink into it, and because objects form a system in which one cannot show itself without concealing others.

(*PP* 81–82/67–68/78)

The phenomenological figure/ground contrast is not identical with the physiological structure of the eye, nor is it equivalent to measurable differences between foveal and parafoveal vision. Parafoveal vision, for example, is supposedly insensitive to color and about ten times less discriminating than foveal vision, and indeed we all know that we have to move our eyes, not just our heads, to get a good look at things. But does our peripheral vision *seem* ten times less discerning that our focal point? Do the outer horizons of our visual field *seem* colorless?[20]

The figure/ground contrast is not a physiological fact, but part of what we might call the *contingent a priori* structure of perception. It is contingent because it is, after all, a phenomenological function of the structures and capacities of the body, yet it is *a priori* inasmuch as it provides a stable ground or framework within which we are able to recognize some aspects of our experience *as* genuinely contingent and changeable. The phenomenal field is not just a bundle of sensory facts, but instead constitutes a "transcendental field" (PP 74/61/71), a space of abiding perceptual possibilities, impossibilities, and necessities. That space of possibilities is articulated by what Merleau-Ponty calls the *body schema* (*schéma corporel*). This notion plays a crucial role in his phenomenology, indeed it could be said to anchor his account of the bodily nature of perception as a whole, for as he says, "The theory of the body schema is implicitly a theory of perception" (PP 239/206/239).

What is the body schema? Crucially, it is *not* what psychologists call the body *image*.[21] The distinction between schema and image has an important philosophical pedigree that can be traced at least as far back as Kant's *Critique of Pure Reason*. The idea of schematism provides the solution to a problem posed by Kant's sharp distinction between understanding and sensibility, pure concepts and raw intuitions. The problem is, as Kant asks, "how is the *subsumption* of the latter under the former, hence the *application* of the category to appearances, possible?" (A137/B176).[22] We cannot literally see (or feel or hear) such things as number, possibility, causality, or substance, and yet we perceive things as *exhibiting* those concepts. How?

Kant concludes that "there must be a third thing" mediating between concepts and intuitions, namely by having something in common with both, and this third thing he calls "the *transcendental schema*" (A138/B177). The schema of a concept is a procedure by which the imagination provides the concept with an image. Consequently, "the schema is to be distinguished from an image" (A140/B179), for whereas images are always concrete particulars, schemata must anticipate in advance an indefinitely wide range of possible applications of the concept. It is thus the imagination, not the intellect, that carves out the space of possibilities within which we can then subsequently apprehend objects as falling under concepts. The body schema is thus precisely *not* an image of the body, for images are *objects of awareness*, whereas schemata sketch out in advance and hence structure our *awareness of objects*.

The body schema is not a representation of the body, then, but our ability to anticipate and (literally) incorporate the world prior to applying concepts to objects. This ability, which Merleau-Ponty also calls "habit," is not objective knowledge, nor is it internal to the mind, for "it is the body that 'understands' in the acquisition of habit" (PP 168/144/167).

Aristotle observed, for example, that if you forcibly cross your fingers around a small object, you will seem to feel two objects instead of one.[23] "Aristotle's illusion," Merleau-Ponty remarks, "is primarily a disturbance of the body schema." For it is not just that your fingers are rarely in such an awkward position, but that they cannot get themselves there by their own effort: "The synthesis of the object here is thus effected through the synthesis of one's own body" (PP 237/205/238). Your perception of objects is already structured by your body and its sense of its own possibilities.

The body schema thus constitutes our precognitive familiarity with ourselves and the world we inhabit: "I am aware of my body *via* the world," Merleau-Ponty says, just as "I am aware of the world through the medium of my body" (PP 97/82/94–95). My body is not an extraneous container or instrument of my agency, but comprises "stable organs and preestablished circuits" (PP 103/87/ 100) that operate according to their own logic, as it were, below the threshold of self-conscious intention. Moreover, like Kantian schemata, "our reflexes translate a specific *a priori*," and we respond to and anticipate familiar situations as typical instances or "stereotypes" (PP 104/87/101).

Moreover, the body schema is not a static representation, but a "*dynamic*" capacity, inasmuch as

> my body appears to me as a posture with a view to a certain actual or possible task. ... If I stand in front of my desk and lean on it with both hands, only my hands are accentuated and the whole of my body trails behind them like the tail of a comet.
>
> (*PP* 116/100/114–15)

Conversely, it is our direct contact with the world that in turn gives us a reflexive sense of our own bodies: "I know where my pipe is with absolute certainty, and thereby I know where my hand is and where my body is" (PP 116–17/100/115). The body is not an object of which I have an internal image or internal representation, rather "it is polarized by its tasks, it *exists toward* them, it gathers itself up to reach its goal, and 'body schema' is in the end a way of expressing that my body is in the world" (PP 117/101/115).

To explain more precisely how the body schema orients us in the world, Merleau-Ponty drew inspiration—but then characteristically departed—from Husserl's account of embodiment in the manuscripts of the second book of *Ideas*. Merleau-Ponty relies especially on Husserl's claim that movement and perception are interrelated neither as reasons nor as causes, but rather as "motives":

> the phenomenological notion of *motivation* is one of those "fluid" concepts that must be formed if we want to get back to the

phenomena. One phenomenon releases another, not by some
objective efficacy, like that which links events in nature, but by the
sense [*sens*] it offers—there is a *raison d'être* that orients the flux
of phenomena without being explicitly posited in any one of them,
a sort of operant reason.

(*PP* 61/49–50/57)[24]

What is this "operant reason" at work in perception?

We normally perceive a landscape as solid and immobile, but
someone whose ocularmotor muscles have been temporarily para-
lyzed sees the entire landscape shift to the left when he thinks he is
turning his eyes in that direction (PP 58–59/47–48/55). Why?
Merleau-Ponty rejects intellectualist and empiricist accounts of the
illusion: the subject does not infer the movement of the landscape
from beliefs he has about the position of his eyes and the location
of the landscape before him, nor is the stationary retinal image a
mere cause of the ensuing sensory effect. The effect is not just a false
judgment, for the logic of perception is not the logic of deliberation, but "a lived logic that cannot account for itself," and its meaning is
not abstract, but "an immanent meaning that is not clear to itself and
becomes fully aware of itself only through the experience of certain
natural signs" (PP 61/49/57). The turning of my gaze is thus neither a reason nor a cause, but a kind of sign that motivates my
apprehension of my own orientation:

For the illusion to be produced, the subject must have intended
to look to the left and must have thought he moved his eye.
The illusion concerning one's own body leads to [*entraîne*] the
appearance of movement in the object. The movements of one's
own body are naturally invested with a certain perceptual
significance and form, with the external phenomena, such a
tightly woven [*bien lié*] system that external perception "takes
account" of the displacement of the perceptual organs, finding in
them, if not the *explicit explanation*, then at least the *motive* of

the intervening changes in the spectacle, and can thus
understand them straight away.

(*PP* 59/47–48/55)

Motivational connections forge bonds of meaning in experience, allowing us to preserve and maintain a "best grip" (*meilleure prise*) on the world (PP 309/267/311):

> my body at grips with [*en prise sur*] the world when my perception offers me a spectacle as varied and as clearly articulated as possible, and when my motor intentions, as they unfold, receive from the world the responses they anticipate. This maximum distinctness in perception and action defines a perceptual *ground*, a basis of my life, a general milieu for the coexistence of my body and the world.
>
> (*PP* 289–90/250/292).

The body is in the first instance not an object of knowledge, but part of the normative structure of intentionality: "our body is not the object of an 'I think': it is an ensemble of lived meanings that finds its equilibrium" (PP 179/153/177).

This insistence on a dovetailing of perception and movement constitutes a radical challenge to the mind–body dichotomy still taken for granted even by materialists, whose aversion to the mental merely reinforces the conceptual distinction they have taken over from the dualist tradition. Again, Merleau-Ponty's point is not that movement and perception are very closely linked causally, but that they are two sides of the same coin. So too, my body and the world itself are essentially intermingled: this body is my body only because I find myself oriented in an environment, just as the world confronts me only relative to the hinge or "pivot" that is my body (PP 97/82/94; cf. VI 243/189).

This interdependence of self and world manifests itself in the body schema, which gives us a normatively rich but precognitive grip on our environment. What allows our attitudes to be right or wrong about the world in the most basic way is the sense of bodily equilibrium that determines which postures and positions allow us to perceive things *properly*, and which constitute liabilities, incapacities, discomforts, and distortions. Again, as Merleau-Ponty says, we have—and *know* and *feel* ourselves to have—*optimal* bodily attitudes that afford us a "*best* grip" on things, for example the right distance and angle from which to see something, a preferred posture in which to listen or concentrate, or to achieve poise and balance. Our bodies are constantly, though unconsciously and involuntarily, adjusting themselves to secure and integrate our experience and maintain our grip on the environment. This ongoing self-correcting bodily orientation constitutes the perceptual background against which discrete sensory particulars and explicit judgments can occur.

Again, it is obvious that bodily capacities and dispositions of various sorts *causally* underlie our perceptual orientation in the world; what is not obvious is that those capacities and dispositions establish a *normative* dimension without which perception could not be intentional at all. What makes motor "intentionality" worthy of the name is precisely its normativity, the felt rightness and wrongness of the various bodily attitudes we unthinkingly assume and maintain throughout our waking (and sleeping) lives. Felt differences between manifestly better and worse attitudes mark differences between right and wrong, or true and false, perceptual appearances: the words on the chalkboard are indistinct, so I squint and crane my neck to see them better; the voice at the back of the room is muffled, so I lean forward and put my hand to my ear; the sweater looks brown until I hold it directly under the light and see that it is green.[25]

The intentionality of perception thus depends crucially on the normativity of the body schema. The rightness and wrongness of perceptual appearances are interwoven with the felt rightness and wrongness of our bodily attitudes. We have a *feel* for the kinds of balance and posture that afford us a correct and proper view of the world, and that feel is neither the buzz and hum of sensation nor the rationality of deliberate thought.

4. MOTOR INTENTIONALITY

To shed light on the noncognitive intelligence of bodily awareness, Merleau-Ponty relies heavily on Adhémar Gelb and Kurt Goldstein's study of a case of visual form agnosia, or what used to be called "mind blindness" (*Seelenblindheit*). The patient, whom they call Schneider, suffered brain damage in World War I that left him "unable to perform 'abstract' movements with his eyes closed, that is, movements that are not relevant to any actual situation" (PP 119/103/118). He could still perform "concrete" movements, that is, "movements necessary for life, provided they have become habitual for him: he takes his handkerchief from his pocket and blows his nose, takes a match out of a box and lights a lamp" (PP 120/103/118). Schneider could not simply point to his eyebrow, out of the blue, as it were, yet he could go through the repertoire of movements constituting a military salute. When he did so, however, he would not just move his hand to his brow, but throw his whole body into the performance of a meaningful action, which he managed to pull off only by putting himself into the situation entirely.

What Schneider's condition reveals, Goldstein argues, is that two distinct neurological functions are involved in normal bodily behavior: one for "pointing" (*Zeigen*), the other for "grasping" (*Greifen*). Although Schneider has lost the ability to point to things out of context, his grasping skills remain remarkably intact. This difference has been confirmed more recently by Melvyn Goodale and David Milner, who have shown that two distinct neural pathways in the brain, the ventral and the dorsal streams, are responsible for, in their words, "vision for perception" and "vision for action."[26] Patients suffering from various forms brain damage may lose the one ability while retaining the other: either they can no longer identify *what* something is by pointing at it or drawing a picture of it, though they can still see *how* to grasp and manipulate it skillfully, or vice versa.[27]

What should we make of these discoveries? Two questions immediately arise. First, what, if anything, do the pathological cases tell us about normal perception? And second, what, if anything, do such findings have to do with phenomenology? After all, pointing and grasping are normally so integrated that it never previously occurred to anyone to suppose they might rest on distinct under-lying neurological mechanisms. And why should we suppose that such facts makes any difference to the felt character of normal experience, any more than any of the other subterranean processes going on undetected in our internal organs? If the distinction between pointing and grasping did not just happen to go unnoticed for centuries due to some kind of collective inattention or care-lessness, but was strictly unobservable in the absence of carefully controlled studies of impaired subjects like Schneider, can it be relevant to a phenomenology of perception?

To answer these questions, it is worth reminding ourselves of the distinction Heidegger draws in *Being and Time* between our pri-mary understanding of things "available" (*zuhanden*) for use—not only literally manipulable equipment like hammers and nails, but more generally things we rely on, for example the wind and the stars for sailing and navigation—and a secondary, parasitic way in which we encounter things as objects of contemplation or judgment, as merely present or "occurrent" (*vorhanden*). Heidegger's aim is to show that *availing* oneself of things skillfully neither involves nor presupposes observing or thinking about them; rather, observation and thought consist in a kind of detachment or abstraction from our initial absorption in the world through the exercise of practical skills.[28] Both forms of understanding must be susceptible to phenomenological description; after all, Hei-degger is inviting us to notice in our own experience a difference he has noticed in his.

Merleau-Ponty's point is very similar, indeed he alludes to Heidegger's notion of availability when he refers to the perceptual environment as "a set of *manipulanda*," as opposed to "objects in the Kantian sense" (PP 122/105/120). What Schneider's condition shows, Merleau-Ponty suggests, is that intelligent motor skills are not extensions or applications of a theoretical representation of objective space. "When I signal to my friend to come near, my intention is not a thought I prepare in myself, and I do not perceive the signal in my body" (PP 128–29/111/127). If my friend resists, and I insist, "my gesture of impatience emerges from the situation without any intervening thought" (PP 129/111/127). Intelligent bodily behavior is not based on the contemplative and reflective attitudes on which philosophers have traditionally modeled their theories of experience and understanding. Indeed, dealing skillfully with things in a spatial environment requires no conscious or reflective grasp of objects standing in determinate spatial configurations at all.

This much, however, might suggest that Merleau-Ponty, like Goldstein, simply regards normal behavior as a composite of two distinct functions, only one of which Schneider has lost. Schneider's condition, on this view, has robbed him of the ability to point, leaving his ability to grasp intact, so that we can now see that latter capacity more clearly and appreciate its specific contribution to normal sensorimotor competence. After all, much of what Merleau-Ponty says about Schneider is true of normal perceivers, too, for example: "The patient, stung by a mosquito, does not have to look for the place he was stung, but finds it straight away" (PP 122/105/121). Similarly, in performing his job, making wallets, "the subject, when placed in front of his scissors, his needle, and his familiar tasks, does not have to look for his hands or his fingers, for they are not objects to find in objective space" (PP 123/106/121). When he sets to work,

the task elicits the necessary movements from him by a kind of attraction at a distance, just as the phenomenal forces at work in

> my visual field elicit from me, without calculation, the motor
> reactions that establish the best equilibrium between them, or as
> the conventions of our milieu, or our group of listeners,
> immediately elicit from us the words, the attitudes, the tone
> suited to them.
>
> (PP 123–24/106/122)

At some level, unreflective motor skills are what we have in common with agnosics like Schneider. For in spite of his deficit in conscious objective intuition, he is not blind; his concrete movement is guided by a kind of visual grip on the world.[29]

But this is not Merleau-Ponty's point. To see why, it is worth quoting the following passage at length. After observing that Schneider lacks immediate intuitive knowledge of whether he is, for example, lying down or standing up, but must infer such things from, say, the pressure he feels on his back or his feet, Merleau-Ponty writes,

> How are we to coordinate these facts, and how are we to grasp,
> by means of them, the function that is present in the normal
> person and absent in the patient? It cannot be a question of
> simply transferring to the normal person what the patient lacks
> and is trying to recover. Illness, like childhood and the state of the
> "primitive," is a complete form of existence, and the procedures it
> employs to replace normal functions that have been destroyed
> are themselves pathological phenomena. One cannot deduce the
> normal from the pathological, deficiencies from the surrogate
> functions, by a mere change of sign. We must take surrogates as
> surrogates, as allusions to some fundamental function they are
> trying to replace ... Nothing would be more misleading than to
> take for granted the same procedures with the normal person,
> shortened merely by habituation. The patient looks for these
> explicit perceptions only to stand in for a certain presence of body
> and object that is given in the case of normal subjects.
>
> (PP 125/107–8/123–24)

The point here is twofold. First, when we recognize things passively or point them out abstractly, we do not simply do what
Schneider does, only more quickly and discreetly, namely enlist a
whole ensemble of exploratory movements and hopefully stumble
upon the forms that then merely *seem* to be given. Rather, we have a
capacity that Schneider lacks, in virtue of which our bodies and
worlds *really are* given to us in sensory intuition. Schneider's way of
identifying and describing things in his environment is profoundly
unlike ours.[30]

Second, motor action itself is not for Schneider the same as it is
for those of us who do not need to rely on it exclusively, as he
does, in order to recognize objects around us and know our own
position and orientation in space. What is lacking in Schneider's
sensorimotor experience? Not just spatial intuition as an isolated
function, but a kind of bodily awareness that allows us to encounter
the environment *as* an environment, as opposed to being submerged in it skillfully but unconsciously. Schneider can perform
concrete movements on order, but

> if the order has for him an *intellectual significance* and no *motor
> significance*, it conveys nothing to him as a mobile subject ... he
> can never convert the thought of a movement into actual movement.
> What he lacks is neither motility nor thought, and we are led to
> recognize between movement as a third-person process and
> thought as the representation of movement an anticipation or
> arrival at a result, ensured by the body itself as a motor power, a
> "motor projection" (*Bewegungsentwurf*) or "motor intentionality"
> in the absence of which the order remains a dead letter.
>
> (*PP* 128/110/126–27)

Lacking any direct intuition of objective spatial relations, Schneider
also lacks the ability to project himself into imaginary actions and
imaginary worlds. Asked to salute, he takes up the role of the
soldier with a kind of earnestness, a wholehearted engagement

unnecessary for normal actors, who can simply "detach their real body from the living situation to make it breathe, speak, and if need be weep in the imaginary. This is what our patient can no longer do" (PP 122/105/120). Instead, he "throws his body into blind trials," whereas normals can literally *see* what they're doing, "which can be expressed by saying that for the normal person every movement has a *background* and that movement and its background are [as Goldstein says] 'moments of a unified whole'" (PP 128/110/127). Schneider can perform concrete movements, but he lacks the perceptual background that ordinarily imbues such movements with their worldly significance. His concrete movements are thus in a sense blind:

> Abstract movement carves out from the interior of that thick world [*monde plein*] in which concrete movement took place a zone of reflection and subjectivity; it superimposes on physical space a virtual or human space. Concrete movement is thus centripetal while abstract movement is centrifugal; the former occurs in being or in the actual, the latter in the possible or in nonbeing; the former adheres to a given background, the latter projects [*déploie*] its own background.
>
> (*PP* 129/111/128)

Schneider's movements do not open up their own background, but are embedded in a kind of plenum. Consequently, "in a word, the world no longer has any *physiognomy* for him" (PP 153/132/152).[31]

Merleau-Ponty's purpose here is not simply to report or reiterate Goldstein's experimental results, nor does he claim to have made his own original contribution to empirical psychology. Instead, he goes behind the empirical issues to make a philosophical point, namely, that the neurological distinction between grasping (dorsal stream) and pointing (ventral stream) *misses* the crucial intermediary phenomenon of *motor intentionality*, which involves the projection of a world *given* in intuition, as opposed to constructed in thought.[32]

Motor intentionality is not a neurological datum, nor is it simply Merleau-Ponty's name for concrete movement, grasping, or dorsal stream processing. It is instead the normal unity and integration of our bodily movement and our intuitive awareness of a given, stable environment.[33]

Merleau-Ponty is making a philosophical point, then, but one enriched by Goldstein's description of Schneider, whose behavior reveals—albeit in distorted, pathological form—an aspect of normal perception ordinarily so inconspicuous as to have gone virtually unnoticed for centuries. In this way Merleau-Ponty, more than any of the other major figures in the phenomenological movement, draws on psychological evidence, demonstrating that phenomenology is not a purely conceptual exercise, yet without entirely collapsing the distinction between phenomenological description and empirical inquiry, as if there were nothing distinctive about the bodily point of view from which we experience ourselves and the world.

How then ought we to coordinate empirical findings like Goldstein's, or more recently those of Goodale and Milner, with a phenomenology of perception like Merleau-Ponty's?[34] Does the discovery of the dorsal and ventral streams in the visual system threaten our commonsense understanding of vision? Goodale and Milner write, "It seems intuitively obvious that the visual image that allows us to recognize a coffee cup is the same one that guides our hand when we pick it up. But this belief is an illusion."[35] Vision, they think they have shown, is not one thing, but two: one genuinely phenomenal, the other merely action-guiding. What about the phenomenology? Does vision present itself to ordinary experience and understanding as one thing or two? The question, as it stands, is meaningless. Is a pair of scissors one thing or two? Neurologically speaking, apparently, sensorimotor capacities are segregated in distinct but normally interacting systems in the brain. Should we then say, as Goodale and Milner suggest, that they are intuitively or phenomenologically *one*? Not quite, it seems, since it is not clear that the individuation of systems and subsystems arises at the level of ordinary perceptual awareness at all. But then what should we say?

The fact is that psychological findings like these impinge on phenomenology in much the same way novel scientific discoveries impinge on our intuitions generally. For centuries people took it for granted that the earth is motionless. When Copernicus and Galileo established that it is not, educated people gave up that belief and yet continued to have pretty much the same perceptual experience they had before. Beliefs, even theories, often trickle down and shape our perceptions, but the heliocentric model of the solar system can hardly be said to have caused us to see the earth *as* moving under our feet, or the sun as fixed and motionless: terra firma is still firm, and we still see the sun rise and set. An (apocryphal) story has it that Wittgenstein once asked, "Why did people centuries ago believe that the sun goes around the earth?" When a student suggested it was because that's how it *looks*, Wittgenstein replied, "And how would it look if it *looked like* the earth was going around the sun?"

Similarly, we might ask ourselves why people believe (if they do) that visuomotor action is a function of one system and not two. Is that how it seems? How would it seem if it *seemed* like two? It might be tempting to reply that it would seem like two systems if, say, we could *feel* the difference between them, or perhaps feel ourselves *shifting* from one to the other. But this is a mistake. After all, when you see, does it seem as if you're seeing with two eyes? One could reasonably answer either yes or no. No, since it doesn't usually seem one way or the other, any more than it seems as if you have two lungs or one stomach. But yes, since it doesn't usually seem as if one eye is closed or blind. If we answer yes, that is, it is not because we continually feel the distinctness of our two eyes, or feel ourselves shifting visually from one to the other; it's just that there doesn't seem to be anything wrong with either of them.

Or consider an analogy with memory. There is empirical evidence for the existence of two distinct memory systems. On one model, a *temporal* boundary of a few seconds separates *long-term* from *short-term* memory. On another model, the companion to long-term memory is not short-term but *working* memory, that is, the two systems work together according to the amount of information at play, just as the hard drive differs from the random access memory in a computer. Phenomenology has nothing to say between those hypothesized systems, and for all we know it might turn out that we have some combination of the two pairs. That is, there does not seem to be a joint or seam in our retention of the past lagging a few seconds or minutes behind us, dividing long-term from short-term memory, nor is it intuitively evident how much information we can hold in our attention before having to offload it somewhere for future retrieval. Does it therefore seem as if our memories form a continuous stream trailing behind us, gradually tapering off into the remote past? Well, no. The phenomenology of memory is a subtle and delicate undertaking, but it swings wide of the empirical research that relies crucially on experimental data unavailable to consciousness.

It is no more true to say that visuomotor action *seems* like a single neurological function than to say it seems like two, or dozens for that matter.[36] The *seeming*—the phenomenology—is silent about what neurological structures (if any) underlie our sensorimotor capacities; it is, after all, possible that some features of experience have no specific physiological correlates at all. Dualists have sometimes argued that the mind *cannot* be anything physical since mental states do not *seem* like physical states. But again, how would they seem if they *did* seem like physical states? Experience itself does not favor dualism over physicalism. Unfortunately, the argument cuts both ways, for neither does it assure us that perception *must* be a physical process. We (most of us) take for granted that it is, but arguably for a different reason, namely that the ever widening scope of the concept of the physical over the past few centuries has made it increasingly obscure what it would even *mean* to call something real like perception *non*physical.[37]

5. FLESH AND CHIASM

Although Merleau-Ponty never abandoned phenomenology, by the late 1950s his understanding of it, and with it his understanding of perception and embodiment, had taken a new direction. Some argue that the change was radical, constituting a kind of paradigm shift of the sort one finds in Heidegger and Wittgenstein, whose later thinking took a sharp turn from the early works that made them famous. Although Merleau-Ponty wrote essays in the years leading up to his death in 1961 that give no hint of the new project, he also left behind a highly original but unfinished work, *The Visible and the Invisible*, which was posthumously published in 1964 along with working notes from his manuscripts. The fourth chapter of the published text, entitled "The Intertwining—The Chiasm" (*L'entrelacs—le chiasme*), spells out the substance of the new line of thought, with further, often cryptic elaboration in the notes. In the notes there are also occasional critical references to his own earlier work, in particular *Phenomenology of Perception*, from which some have inferred a profound transformation in his entire approach to philosophy.

That something had changed is clear, but was the change radical? The best way to proceed is to consider the new ideas first, and then try to assess how far they depart from what Merleau-Ponty had already been saying 15 and 20 years earlier. My own view is that although scholars, understandably eager for news of a dramatic philosophical breakthrough at the eleventh hour, have tended to overestimate the novelty of Merleau-Ponty's late work, there are indeed some genuinely interesting and original ideas in *The Visible and the Invisible*, ideas that at times extend and amplify themes in his earlier work, but also occasionally cast doubt on some of its basic assumptions.[38]

What did Merleau-Ponty take for granted in the 1930s and 1940s, and then abandon by the late 1950s? In a word, the primacy of *consciousness*. In a working note of May 2, 1959, he considers the phenomenon of insight, the involuntary crystallization or formation (*Gestaltung*) of meaningful wholes, what the Gestalt psychologists called the "Aha experience," for example when you suddenly see the figure of a dog in a picture that a moment ago looked like nothing but a chaotic pattern of black and white splotches. Seeing such figures is not a product of reflection, but a flash of perceptual recognition; moreover, once you see them, it's virtually impossible *not* to see them: "one can no longer free oneself from what has once been thought," for "one finds it again in the materials themselves." Thought and insight do not come first, but follow as effects or achievements from a prior unreflective perceptual groping and exploration: "there is a *germination* of what *will have been* understood" (VI 243/189).

So far, nothing in these remarks goes beyond the standard Gestalt theory Merleau-Ponty had been invoking and elaborating for years. But then he draws a startling conclusion: "And that means: perception is unconscious. What is the unconscious? That which functions as a pivot, an existential, and in that sense is and is not perceived." This "pivot," he goes on to say, is the body schema, "the *hinge* of the for itself and the for others—To have a body is to be looked at (it is not only that), it is to be *visible*" (VI 243/189).

This might sound like a minor terminological variation on the account of perception and the body schema that we have already seen elaborated in *Phenomenology of Perception*, but Merleau-Ponty evidently considered it a major departure with profound implications. What is at issue, it seems, is the *ontological* ground of phenomenology, which is confined to what is available to experience, however dimly or marginally. Thus, in a working note from February 1959, Merleau-Ponty writes, "Results of Ph.P.—Necessity of bringing them to ontological explicitation. ... The problems that remain ... are due to the fact that in part I retained the philosophy of 'consciousness'" (VI 237/183). And in July of that year, more critically: "The problems posed in Ph.P. are insoluble because I start there from the 'consciousness'–'object' distinction"—

One will never understand, starting from that distinction, how a particular fact of the "objective" order (a particular cerebral lesion) could entail a particular disturbance of the relation with the world—a massive disturbance that seems to demonstrate that "consciousness" as a whole is a function of the objective body—It is these problems themselves that must be dismissed by asking: *what is* the supposed *objective* conditioning? Answer: it is a way of expressing and noting an event of the order of brute or savage being that is ontologically primary.

(VI 253/200)

"Brute or savage being" is now prior to consciousness, and the task of philosophy is no longer to describe even the bodily and existential dimensions of *conscious* experience, but to say how experience itself is possible as a mode of our *unconscious* bodily immersion in the world.[39]

Why does Merleau-Ponty renounce the primacy of consciousness? The answer, I think, appears in the second paragraph of the passage above, in which Merleau-Ponty, some fifteen years after his reflections on Schneider in the *Phenomenology*, considers once again the potentially catastrophic effects of brain damage. As we have seen, he rejects any sharp distinction between the mental and the physical, in light of which purely mechanical events in the brain could be straightforwardly correlated with discrete psychological effects described in abstraction from the subject's bodily being in the world. Goldstein was wrong to think that Schneider's condition simply removed all visual contribution to his motor action, leaving pure tactile perception in its pristine state. On the contrary, Merleau-Ponty insists, Schneider suffered a profound loss of motor intentionality, which is to say visuomotor *awareness* of the world, the abiding background of perception and action grasped as a coherent whole. Schneider no longer has a world *given* in conscious intuition.

What then *does* he have? He certainly has visuomotor skills. That is, his bodily movements are still guided by vision of some sort—not *conscious* visual experience by way of the ventral stream, but *unconscious* dorsal-stream vision for action. This peculiar form of blind vision, so to speak, remained a mystery in Merleau-Ponty's earlier account, the point of which was to emphasize Schneider's *loss* of motor intentionality, or normally integrated visuomotor *experience*. But now that Merleau-Ponty no longer regards conscious experience as fundamental to our being in the world, Schneider's strange unconscious immersion in the world appears more peculiar and more significant than ever. What is original in *The Visible and the Invisible*, then, is Merleau-Ponty's new way of describing that unconscious ground of conscious experience, the ontological bed-rock on which sense experience and bodily comportment rest.

The underlying ontological foundation of sensory receptivity and motor spontaneity is what Merleau-Ponty now calls *flesh* (*chair*). Flesh is the stuff common to ourselves and the world, what we and it are both made of, as it were. And yet the term is not just another name for physical or material stuff: "flesh is not matter, it is not spirit, it is not substance" (*VI* 184/139; cf. *VI* 191/146). What is it? The *sensibility* of things, the perceptibility both of the perceptual environment and of ourselves as perceivers—the *visibility* of vision, the *tangibility* of touch, the *exposure* of anything to which the world itself can be exposed in experience, including the bodily sense or experience of motor intentionality.

Merleau-Ponty had always insisted that to stand *before* the world, one must be *in* the world; he now goes further by insisting that to be in the world, one must be *of* the world. One must, so to speak, be of the same flesh as the world one inhabits and perceives. What is new in this is that it gives pride of place to what he had previously tended to brush off as merely "objective," namely the blind, unconscious bedrock of being that underlies perceptual experience. Now that blind, unconscious world turns out to have profound significance precisely because *we are it*. For in sensing, we ourselves must be thoroughly and inescapably sensible: "the body as sensible and the body as sentient," he explains, is "what we previously called objective body and phenomenal body" (*VI* 180/136). Whereas earlier he posited the objective body as secondary and relative to the phenomenal body of sensorimotor awareness—"the genesis of the objective body is only a moment in the constitution of the object" (PP 86/72/83)—he now reverses course and construes conscious experience as a whole, even its proprioceptive and motor elements, as grounded in a new kind of prephenomenal being, namely the flesh of visibility.

How are we to understand this new idea? It is not, after all, as if Merleau-Ponty (or anyone) ever doubted that the body is *de facto* empirically visible. The point is rather that its unconscious visibility, far from being a merely dependent moment of its motor-intentional awareness, is in fact the *ontological ground* of the phenomenal manifestation of being in the world as a whole. That my body can be seen and touched is not just the empirical fact that I (or anyone) can be aware of it as an object; it is rather the underlying condition of my encountering and inhabiting a world at all in the first place. It is our "brute or savage being," which makes possible everything explicitly realizable in phenomenological reflection itself. To see the world, we must already be in a kind of bodily communion with it. We will return to this idea in Chapter 6 in connection with Merleau-Ponty's essays on painting, especially "Cézanne's Doubt" and "Eye and Mind."

Although chapter 4 of *The Visible and the Invisible* is called "The Intertwining—The Chiasm," it is in the working notes at the end of the volume that we find Merleau-Ponty taking full advantage of those terms as he presumably would have had he lived to finish the book. The metaphor is clear enough: a *chiasm* or *chiasma* is an x-shape or crisscross pattern; in grammar, a *chiasmus* is an inversion of parallel phrases, such as *When the going gets tough, the tough get going*, or *Working hard or hardly working?* And so it is, Merleau-Ponty believes, with body and world: they are not two distinct things, but sinews of a common flesh, threads in the same fabric, related to one another not as situation and reaction (not to mention stimulus and response), but as a single woven texture, like the overlapping and interlocking lizards and birds in an Escher drawing.

Unlike his concept of the flesh, however, which it is precisely meant to incorporate and contain, the notion of intertwining or chiasm is nothing new in Merleau-Ponty's later thought, but an elaboration of an idea that already figured prominently in *Phenomenology of Perception*. For example, he refers to

> peculiar relations woven [*se tissent*] between the parts of the landscape, or between it and me as incarnate subject ... Sense experience is that vital communication with the world that renders it present to us as the familiar setting of our life. It is to it that the perceived object and the perceiving subject owe their thickness. It is the intentional fabric [*tissu*] that the exercise of knowledge will try to pull apart.
>
> (*PP* 64–65/52–53/61)

And further on:

> since the genesis of the objective body is only a moment in the constitution of the object, the body, by withdrawing from the objective world, will carry with it the intentional threads linking it to its surrounding and finally reveal to us the perceiving subject as the perceived world.
>
> (*PP* 86/72/83)

Finally, he writes of our primitive experience of others, "Inasmuch as I have been born and have a body and a natural world, I can find in that world other comportments with which my own are interwoven [*s'entrelace*]" (PP 410/357/416), just as "nature penetrates to the center of my life and is interwoven [*s'entrelace*] with it" (PP 399/347/405).

Merleau-Ponty's fascination with the image of chiasmic intertwining was inspired, or perhaps merely confirmed and reinforced, by contemporary work in the sciences. Like Kurt Goldstein and the Gestalt psychologists, for example, biologists such as G. E. Coghill and Jakob von Uexküll defended holistic conceptions of organic form against reductive mechanistic models of biological function. The parallel is instructive, for just as contemporary cognitive science might seem to have rendered obsolete the psychology that inspired Merleau-Ponty's phenomenology, so too, after his death, the reductive agenda of molecular biology gradually seems to have eclipsed the holistic literature he was drawing on in his lectures on nature in the late 1950s.

In Merleau-Ponty's 1957–58 course on "The Concept of Nature," subtitled "Animality, the Human Body, and the Passage to Culture," he discusses the work of the psychologist and physician Arnold Gesell. Gesell insists on the unity of body and behavior; the two cannot be disentangled, since behavior is part and parcel of the body's organization, while the body is the concrete manifestation of its behaviors. The body is not a passive medium that also happens to move, as for example a machine can either function or not function and still remain the thing it is. For human beings, moving and being at rest, like waking and sleeping, are equally dynamic states that preserve the body's very morphological structure. Even embryological development is not an entirely "blind" process, but is constantly conditioned by optimizing tendencies and states of relative equilibrium, which imbue all future growth with a distinctive "style" or "bearing" of life (allure de la vie) (N 199/149).[40] For Gesell, "the enigma of form is omnipresent," indeed it constitutes "the fundamental enigma of science" (N 200/150). The organism is a kind of balance of spontaneity and constraint. So too, strictly conditioned impulses and spontaneous improvisations are always intertwined, so that the distinction between nature and nurture proves to be a false dichotomy. Gesell's "principle of reciprocal intertwining," "weaving," and "meeting of threads" (N 198/149) clearly inspired Merleau-Ponty's elaboration of the concept of chiasm.

It was always Merleau-Ponty's view that we are, as it were, woven corporeally both into the material world we perceive and into the social world we inhabit; that we do not stand outside the world, peering in at it, but already inhabit and incorporate it from within: "Our own body is in the world as the heart is in the organism" (PP 235/203/235); "The sentient and the sensible do not stand over against each other as two mutually external terms, nor is sensation an invasion of the sensible into the sentient" (PP 247–48/214/ 248). The metaphor of an intertwined fabric or tissue was always part of his conceptual vocabulary: "My body is the texture common to all objects" (PP 272/235/273).

The point of the metaphor is that there is no sharp line between what is internal and what is external to us, for self and world are interdependent aspects of a unified whole. As J. J. Gibson puts it, "The supposedly separate realms of the subjective and the objective are actually only poles of attention."[41] Nor are our perceptions sharply divided between inner and outer, for all sense experience is simultaneously open onto the world and reflexively self-sensitive; the senses are both proprioceptive and exteroceptive: "Consciousness of the world is not *based* on self-consciousness; rather, they are strictly contemporary: there is a world for me because I am not ignorant of myself; I am not concealed from myself because I have a world" (PP 344/298/347).

Merleau-Ponty insists on this duality of sense experience, in particular against Husserl, who maintained in the second book of *Ideas* that only the sense of touch has this double aspect. When we see, Husserl notes, we do not see our own eyes: "The eye does not appear visually" (Id II 147). Of course, I can see my eyes in a mirror, but that kind of seeing is a form of third-person observation, not first-person proprioception: "For I do not perceive ... the seeing *qua* seeing. I see something, of which I judge indirectly, through 'empathy,' that it is identical with my eye (constituted, say, by touch), just as I see the eye of another" (Id II 148n). To say that I cannot see my eye *seeing* is to say that I do not locate visual sensations in my eyes. So too with hearing: "The ear is 'there,' but the sensed tone is not localized in the ear" (Id II 149).

The situation is importantly different, Husserl thinks, to the sense of touch. When I touch something with my hand, not only do I feel the qualities of the object, I also feel, and can turn my attention to, tactile sensations localized in the hand itself; hence the difference between the transitive sense of "feel" (feeling a cool breeze) and the intransitive (feeling exhausted). The body can feel itself feeling in a way that the eye cannot, even with the aid of a mirror, see itself seeing. I do not locate visual sensations in my eye or auditory sensations in my ear, but I do locate tactile sensations in the part of my body with which I touch something.[42]

Husserl's theory of bodily intentionality is thus predicated on what he deems "the privilege of the localization of touch sensations" (Id II 150), that is, the double aspect of tactile sensation that he thinks grounds our sense of our bodily self-awareness. Free bodily movement also plays a role, for among the "material bodies [Körper] of this nature I ... find uniquely singled out my body [Leib] ... the only one in which I immediately have free rein and ... govern in each of its organs." For Husserl, however, such acts do not make this body my body, for the sense of body ownership requires the reflexive perception of one of its parts by means of another:

> As perceptually active, I experience ... my own bodiliness [Leiblichkeit], which is thereby related back to itself. This becomes possible inasmuch as I can in each case perceive the one hand by means of the other, an eye by means of a hand, etc., so that the functioning organ must become an object, the object a functioning organ.[43]

For Husserl, the intentional reflexivity of the body is not a primitive or ubiquitous feature of perception, but depends crucially on the double aspect peculiar to the sense of touch:

> A subject with eyes only could not have an appearing body at all. ... The body as such can be constituted originally only in

tactuality and in everything localized within the sensations of
touch, such as warmth, cold, pain, and the like. ... the body ...
becomes a body only through the introduction of sensations in
touch, the introduction of pain sensations, etc., in short, through
the localization of sensations qua sensations.

(*Id II* 150–51)

In its most primitive manifestation, the body does not strictly
speaking coincide with the subject of experience, but is instead a
sensitive "field of localization" belonging to the subject: "The subject,
constituted as the counterpart of material nature, is ... an I, to
which a body belongs as the field of localization of its sensations"
(Id II 152); "the entire consciousness of a human being is in a
certain sense bound to its body by its hyletic substrate" (Id II 153).
For Husserl, the body is "a bearer of sensations ... a thing 'inserted'
between the rest of the material world and the 'subjective' sphere"
(Id II 161).

But Husserl's insistence on the primacy of touch is problematic
on two counts. First, it is unclear why the body's transparent role
in action should count any less toward its intentional constitution
than its passive role as the bearer of tactile sensations. Why must
my body appear to me as the site of localized sensations in order
for me to experience my actions and perceptions as embodied at
all? Suppose I lack a sense of this body being my body. Now suppose
I locate my sensations in this same body. It remains an open question in principle whose body this is in which I locate my sensations.
For there is nothing conceptually incoherent about locating one's
sensations in the body of another, or in a prosthesis, or in a table
and a chair for that matter.[44] If I do not already have a sense of
body ownership, or rather bodily self-identification, it is unclear
what difference the localization of my sensations in this body could
make. Locating my sensations in parts of my own body means that
I already understand the body in which I locate them as my own. But
if I already identify this body as my own body, then the localization

of sensation itself arrives on the scene too late to play the founding role Husserl wants it to play.

Second, if it is just in virtue of the sense of touch and free bodily movement that I understand myself as having a body at all, this can only be because I enjoy some prior consciousness of my self, some distinct means of self-identification, apart from my epistemic relation to the body housing the sensations I feel subjectively. Not surprisingly, Husserl argues that I do indeed have such an abiding sense of self, logically prior to and independent of anything outside my consciousness, including my body, namely my awareness of myself as the "pure" or "transcendental ego" standing at the center of all my intentional acts.[45] For Husserl, as for Descartes, "all sensings belong to my soul [*Seele*], everything extended [belongs] to the material thing" (*Id* II 150).

But this seems to imply that my ordinary identification with my body is not only a kind of mistake, but an utterly unaccountable and unintelligible mistake. If our bodies are not ourselves, how could we ever have thought they were?

> if one's own body and the empirical self are nothing but elements of the system of experience, objects among other objects in the eyes of the true I, how can we ever confuse ourselves with our body, how could we believe that we saw with our eyes what we in truth grasp with an inspection of the mind?
>
> (*PP* 241/208/241)

I see not with my eyes, Descartes said, but "by the faculty of judgment which is in my mind."[46] Husserl is not a substance dualist, but like Descartes he ascribes visual experience to the transcendental subject, not the perceiving body. For I experience my eyes as *mine*, he argues, not just by seeing, but by touching them or by their hurting. But then why do we say, why are we even tempted to say, that we see with our eyes? "If it is true that I do not see with my eyes, how can I ever have been ignorant of this truth?" (PP 246–47/213/247).

For Merleau-Ponty, by contrast, the body is not just somehow attached to the self, or merely "inserted," as Husserl puts it, between subject and object. The body just *is* the self. Our experience of ourselves and the world "does not require and even excludes a constituting subject" (PP 465/406/472). Nor does my immediate identification with my body depend on the localization of sensations within it. It is nothing unique to the sense of touch that renders our bodies our own. Instead, the duality of exteroception and proprioception, of receptivity and spontaneity, is ubiquitous. My hand can touch only because it can be touched:

> Through this crisscrossing within it of the touching and the tangible, its own movements are incorporated into the universe they interrogate, are recorded on the same map ... It is no different for vision, except, it is said, that here the exploration and the information it gathers do not belong "to the same sense." But this delimitation of the senses is crude.
>
> (*VI* 176/133)

This is clearly an allusion to Husserl, and the point becomes explicit in a note from November 1960:

> In *Ideas II*, Husserl, "disentangle" "unravel" what is entangled [...]
>   The idea of chiasm and *Ineinander* is on the contrary the idea that every analysis that *disentangles* renders unintelligible [...]
>   It is a question of creating a new kind of intelligibility
>
> (*VI* 321–22/268)

Merleau-Ponty had always been dissatisfied with the hyper-reflective, analytical tendencies that threatened to pull Husserlian phenomenology into a kind of intellectualism.[47] By the end of his life that sense of dissatisfaction had compounded, for he had come to believe that the true task of philosophy is not just to describe experience, but to extend a kind of ontological insight into something ultimately opaque to reflection. The "new kind of intelligibility" he opposes to the "disentangling" strategy of Husserlian eidetic analysis is therefore not just "a *lived logic* that cannot account for itself," or "an *immanent meaning* that is not clear to itself," as he put it in *Phenomenology of Perception* (PP 61/49/57). Instead, it is the flesh that is already present, and somehow already even present to itself in the most primitive manifestations of life.

What is new in Merleau-Ponty's late work is not the image of chiasm as such, then, but the terms onto which that image is projected. The point is no longer simply that the body, in being aware of the world, is also always reflexively aware of itself, or that its conscious sensory and motor capacities are dependent moments of a unified whole. Instead, he now wants to make the more radical ontological claim that organisms, conscious or not, just by being alive, are already woven into their environments, not as minds, or even preminds or protominds, but as flesh, as both sense and sensibility.

SUMMARY

Perception is not a mental but a *bodily* phenomenon. In making this *ontological* claim about perceptual awareness and the body, Merleau-Ponty is neither reporting a subjective appearance nor advancing an empirical or metaphysical theory about the underlying nature of reality. He is instead describing, articulating, and clarifying the ordinary intuitive point of view from which we understand ourselves as neither disembodied intellects nor physical mechanisms, but living bodily subjects. I have called this phenomenological perspective, from which Merleau-Ponty advances his claims, the *bodily point of view*. It is this point of view as such that both traditional and contemporary theories of perception fail to recognize as a proper subject of inquiry, let alone a legitimate framework within which to understand intentional phenomena.

How, more specifically, does the body function as the subject of perceptual experience? By means of the *body schema*, the set of abiding noncognitive dispositions and capacities that orient, guide, and inform our bodily sensitivities and motor actions. To say that perception is grounded in the body is to say that the *phenomenal field* is constituted by the *body schema*. Our bodily skills and dispositions carve out a perceptual world with perspectival horizons and a contrast between figure and ground.

The kind of intentionality made possible by the body schema is not mental but *motor intentionality*. Brain-damaged patients, such as Goldstein's "Schneider" who suffer from visual form agnosia retain many motor skills and are able to think abstractly about spatial relations, but have lost an intermediate intuitive *motor intentional* sense of spatial position and orientation. Space is no longer *given* in their intuitive awareness, but now resides in pathologically segregated domains of "blind" motor action on the one hand and decontextualized judgment on the other.

Merleau-Ponty's posthumously published manuscript, The *Visible and the Invisible*, elaborates two metaphors, *flesh* and *chiasm*. Some believe these themes constitute a significant shift in his philosophical views, an idea encouraged by Merleau-Ponty's occasional critical references to his own former adherence to a philosophy of consciousness and its attendant subject–object distinction. On closer inspection, it appears that the image of chiasm—crisscrossing, overlapping, interlacing (*entrelacs*)—already informed his account of perception as an aspect of our bodily embeddedness in an environment. The notion of flesh, however, arguably marks a genuine departure from *Phenomenology of Perception*, for whereas that book was essentially a description of perceptual *experience*, the word "flesh" is meant to refer to our more basic *unconscious* bodily continuity with the world we perceive. Flesh is the *identity* of perception and perceptibility, even below the threshold of conscious awareness. As bodily perceivers, we are necessarily part of the perceptible world we perceive; we are not just *in* the world, but *of* it.

FURTHER READING

Barbaras, R. *The Being of the Phenomenon: Merleau-Ponty's Ontology.* Advances an ontological reading of Merleau-Ponty's philosophy, both early and late. Barbaras argues that only in his later, posthumously published works, especially *The Visible and the Invisible*, did Merleau-Ponty begin to free himself from the crippling dualist and idealistic presuppositions that doomed *Phenomenology of Perception* to failure.

Dreyfus, H. "Merleau-Ponty and Recent Cognitive Science." Argues for the relevance of Merleau-Ponty's account of action to contemporary cognitive science, particularly simulated neural networks and reinforcement learning.

———. "Reply to Romdenh-Romluc." In reply to Romdenh-Romluc's essay (see below), Dreyfus argues that Merleau-Ponty's phenomenology has the resources to describe intelligent lateral shifts of attention *within* a situation, but concedes that Merleau-Ponty says nothing about what makes possible *detached* reflection and deliberate, thought-driven action.

Kelly, S. D. "Grasping at Straws." Argues for the relevance of Merleau-Ponty's account of "motor intentionality" to contemporary cognitive science, especially recent neurological studies of "grasping" and "pointing," or *how* and *what* visual content.

Romdenh-Romluc, K. "Merleau-Ponty and the Power to Reckon with the Possible." Argues that Hubert Dreyfus's reading of Merleau-Ponty's phenomenology of action, which emphasizes our ordinary unreflective "absorbed coping," fails to account for the possibility of deliberate intention-driven behavior.

Smith, A. D. "The Flesh of Perception." A discussion of Merleau-Ponty's account of perception and embodiment vis-à-vis Husserl's. Smith argues that Husserl's theory is not intellectualist, nor did Merleau-Ponty consider it so, and that Merleau-Ponty introduces "nothing *radically* new" beyond Husserl's theory of perception.

Todes, S. *Body and World.* Todes's 1963 Harvard Ph.D. dissertation, "The Human Body as Material Subject of the World," plus three short texts written later, in 1969, 1990, and 1993. A highly original critical history of theories of perception in Descartes, Leibniz, Hume, and Kant, culminating in the claim that Kant fundamentally misconstrued perception as a kind of imagination. Todes weaves his own phenomenological insights into his critical history, and then explains his own project in more general terms in the conclusion and appendices (262–92).

Wrathall, M. "Motives, Reasons, and Causes." An account of Merleau-Ponty's view of perceptual meaning as grounded in bodily *motivation*, which is neither rational nor causal. Wrathall presents Merleau-Ponty's position as an attractive alternative to Donald Davidson's and John McDowell's accounts of the relation between perception and belief.

Four

Self and Others

One of the most original and important products of Merleau-Ponty's description of our bodily being in the world is his account in *Phenomenology of Perception* of our experience of others. The account belongs to what is traditionally considered an epistemological problem, the problem of other minds. Do minds other than my own exist? Am I the only one? How can I know?

But is this a problem? Can it be? What, after all, is a mind? Perhaps something like a bundle or system of perceptions, beliefs, desires, and judgments ascribable to a *person*. But what is a person? Not just owners or subjects of experience, but bodily beings. We originally encounter others, that is, not just as minds, but as fellow flesh-and-blood creatures with whom we share a common material world. If our conception of others as minds seems to pose a problem, Merleau Ponty suggests, then "What we have said about the body provides the beginning of a solution to this problem" (PP 401/349/406). The (alleged) problem stands in need of phenomenological clarification of our experience of others before we come to regard them as minds lurking *behind*, rather than incarnate in and as it were visibly animating, their bodies.

Strictly speaking, then, Merleau-Ponty sets out not to solve the problem of other minds, but to dissolve it by reminding us of our nonepistemic, precognitive experience of others, an experience he believes lies at the source of various alienated social attitudes that can then, if only at a perverse extreme, generate skeptical doubts concerning the very existence of other minds. Precisely because of their recognizable *social* origins, however, such doubts are necessarily senseless. Like Heidegger and Wittgenstein, Merleau-Ponty rejects skepticism about other minds as utterly as he rejects skepticism about the external world. According to Heidegger, though the skeptic may not be refutable *a priori*, the fact that human being is essentially being-in-the-world inevitably drains skeptical doubt of all content: "The question whether there is a world at all, and whether its being can be proved, makes no sense as a question raised by *Dasein* as being-in-the-world—and who else would raise it?"[1] Likewise, for Merleau-Ponty, "To ask whether the world is real is not to know what one is saying" (PP 396/344/401).

So too, he argues, I and others *inhere* in bodies and in the world, and "If I feel this inherence of my consciousness in its body and its world, the perception of others and the plurality of consciousnesses no longer present any difficulty" (PP 403/351/408–9). An adequate phenomenological account of ourselves and our experience of others ought to *silence* rather than answer the epistemological question, just as our concrete experience of the world and others always inevitably smothers such doubts in real life. It is worth pondering that irresistible resurgence of credulity—or rather that inescapable erosion of doubt—in real life. Is it irrational, the blind force of unthinking habit, as Hume argued? Evidently not, for in that case its denial would be equally a matter of indifference to reason and common sense. And yet solipsism seems not just mistaken, but quite literally insane. We must therefore describe our experience of others and its role in what we (somehow) know is the only rational view available, namely immediate total acknowledgment of the plurality of persons.

The problem (so called) of other minds, however, conceals and obscures a mystery, the mystery of other selves, and we can see this by recalling that others are present to us, just as we are present to ourselves, in a bodily way *before* we are able to conceive of either them or ourselves as minds standing in relations of mutual distrust, suspicion, or uncertainty. This reminder of our bodily coexistence in the world constitutes Merleau-Ponty's most original and important contribution to philosophical reflections on sociality. It is unparalleled in any other treatment of the subject, including those of Heidegger and Wittgenstein, and only the recent discovery of "mirror neurons" in the brain suggests a similar way of dispelling this peculiar conundrum.

1. HUSSERL AND SARTRE ON OTHER MINDS

Merleau-Ponty's approach to the problem of others contrasts sharply with two of his predecessors in the phenomenological tradition, Husserl and Sartre. Husserl argues in *Cartesian Meditations* that although I do not literally perceive other minds—in which case, he supposes, they would no longer be *other* minds at all, but facets of my own consciousness—neither do I infer their existence from a prior perception of their bodies as mere objects. Rather, others are given in what he calls an "appresentation" or "analogical apperception," in which "the material body [*Körper*] over there, which is apprehended as a living body [*Leib*], must acquire this sense *from an apperceptive transfer from my body*, and then in a manner that excludes any actual direct ... genuine perception."[2] I neither literally see nor merely judge that others are present: "Apperception is not inference, not an act of thinking."[3] Rather, I see others *as* present in the same way in which I see objects *as* having hidden interiors that I do not directly see.

But whereas my awareness of the insides of objects may be informed by prior experiences of opening things up and looking into them, others minds are never directly perceptible, and my awareness of them must instead be founded on an analogical transfer from my perception of myself as an embodied consciousness. Thus, "ego and alter ego are always and necessarily given in an original *pairing*."[4] I come to see the body of the other as linked or bound to his consciousness, just as I experience my own body as linked or bound (by the sense of touch) to experiences I must somehow independently recognize as my own, as belonging to myself not as a *bodily* but as a *transcendental* ego. Only because I originally perceive myself as what Husserl calls a "psycho-physical unity," a blend of consciousness and body, am I able to *apperceive* others as minds perceptually hidden from me by the visible exterior of their bodies.

Merleau-Ponty rejects this distinction between the bodily and the transcendental ego, and the wrongness of that distinction as a description of my experience of myself can be seen as the source of its wrongness as a description of my experience of others. I do not originally perceive myself as a psychophysical unity, for ordinary experience draws no distinction between psychical and physical phenomena. My identity with my body is at once more basic and more thoroughgoing than Husserl supposes. There is indeed a kind of pairing or mirroring in my perception of others, but it is evidently more primordial than the conceptual distinction between private consciousness and public body, which Husserl takes for granted. Indeed, recent psychological and neurological research suggests that such mirroring is a primitive and innate function of primate brains and is already at work in social perception below the threshold of explicit cognition.[5] There is simply no basis in experience for the kind of analogy Husserl thinks informs our intuitive understanding of others.

For Merleau-Ponty, that is, not only is there no *reasoning* behind our recognition of others, there is no *analogy* either, inferential or noninferential, for such an analogy would require prior acknowledgment of the structure of personhood that is already incomprehensible from a solipsistic perspective. Merleau-Ponty thus concludes, "There is nothing here resembling 'reasoning by analogy.' As Scheler so rightly declares, reasoning by analogy presupposes what it is called on to explain" (PP 404/352/410).[6]

Sartre's account of others in *Being and Nothingness* improves on Husserl's theory of analogical pairing in two ways. First, Sartre recognizes that our primordial experience of others involves affective rather than epistemic attitudes, emotions rather than beliefs:

> Shame, fear, and pride are my original reactions; they are only
> various ways by which I recognize the Other as a subject beyond
> reach, and they include within them a comprehension of my
> selfness which can and must serve as my motivation for
> constituting the Other as an object.[7]

Moreover, according to Sartre, my primitive feeling for others is a
feeling not of seeing (or judging), but of being seen. Whereas
the traditional problem of other minds simply takes for granted that
I am the subject and the other is the object, Sartre ingeniously
turns the tables by insisting that my original confrontation with
others is just the opposite: "the Other is in principle the one who
looks at me."[8]

Unfortunately, Sartre's affective reversal of the epistemological
problem generates problems of its own and arguably misses the
phenomenon in its own way, though from a new and interesting
angle. For what Sartre's theory entails—indeed, what it is designed
to entail—is a theory of interminable metaphysical antagonism
among subjects alternately exposing each other to their gazes,
fixing them as objects, and (seemingly) stripping them of their
agency, until those exposed (temporarily) wiggle free by turning
their own looks back on their tormentors.

The theory—a kind of pessimistic, short-circuited version of the
master-slave dialectic in Hegel's *Phenomenology of Spirit*—highlights the
drama inherent in human relationships, but is it a plausible
description of our actual ordinary dealings with others? Do we
really find ourselves popping in and out of such polarized object
and subject positions, shifting from observed to observer and back
again? That picture looks like a caricature of the actual richness,
complexity, and ambiguity of interpersonal life. More crucially, like
Husserl's theory, though in a different way, it fails to acknowledge
the personally undifferentiated background social space we inhabit
in virtue of our shared bodily being in the world. On that shared
background, we exist with others, alongside them, not over against

them as observers and observed: "positing the other does not reduce me to the status of an object in his field, nor does my perception of the other reduce him to the status of an object in mine" (PP 405/352/411). Indeed, mutually objectifying observation, far from being a primitive phenomenon, must be understood as a modification of social interaction:

> the look of the other transforms me into an object, and my look transforms him into an object, only if ... we each make ourselves into an inhuman look, if each feels his actions are not being taken up and understood, but observed like those of an insect. This is what happens, for example, when I am looked at by a stranger. But even then, the objectification of each by the look of the other feels painful only because it takes the place of possible communication. Being looked at by a dog does not embarrass me. The refusal to communicate is still a form of communication.
>
> (PP 414/361/420)

The dramatic antagonistic experience Sartre regards as metaphysically basic is in fact a kind of interpersonal disturbance or distortion, a felt deviation from a social equilibrium that is ordinarily inconspicuous precisely because it is so pervasive in our experience and our understanding. The pressing phenomenological task, which Sartre neglects, is to describe that background social equilibrium that makes such interpersonal disturbances intelligible as deviations from a preferred state.

Husserl and Sartre disagree about the intentional direction of our experience of others, as well as its cognitive and affective significance, but they both take for granted a theoretical perspective that obscures the phenomenon of shared social space by imagining us in already refined and articulated attitudes of subject and object, knower and known, seer and seen. But how did those social positions and attitudes themselves emerge as possibilities in our interactions with one another?

2. EMPATHY AND SOLIPSISM

Merleau-Ponty's alternative account rests on a recognition of the bodily medium of social perception, a medium common to myself and others, and which always already constitutes us as a community prior to our application of concepts such as mind and consciousness, which abstract from the bodily character of the persons they describe. I perceive others as human bodies, not as material objects. Others are always already persons like myself. My experience of our common character as persons, however, is not based on any analogical or comparative observation of myself and them, for "the perception of others precedes and makes possible such observations" (PP 404/352/410). What, then, does our preobservational perception of others consist in?

Adam Smith already recognized in the 1750s that people naturally respond to the suffering of others with gestures appropriate to the person suffering: "When we see a stroke aimed and just ready to fall upon the leg or arm of another person, we naturally shrink and draw back our own leg or our own arm." Smith attributed such apparently spontaneous intuitive responses to an intervening counterfactual thought, an act of imagination in which we sympathize "by conceiving what we ourselves should feel in the like situation," that is, "by changing places in fancy with the sufferer."[9]

Imagination is surely essential to empathy, as it is to experience in general. But must it be the kind of imagination that has the articulated content of a thought, namely the thought of myself in the position of the other? Or does the projective theory of empathy have things backwards? Do we empathize because we think ourselves into other perspectives, or do we learn to think ourselves into other perspectives only by first being capable of a more primitive form of *unthinking* empathy? Babies spontaneously mimic facial gestures before they are able to observe their own faces, hence before they have any notion of what they look like:

> A baby of fifteen months opens his mouth if I playfully take one of his fingers between my teeth and pretend to bite it. And yet he has hardly looked at his face in a mirror, and his teeth do not resemble mine. The fact is that his own mouth and teeth, as he senses them from the inside, are straightaway for him things for biting, and my jaw, as he sees it from the outside, is straightaway for him capable of the same intentions. "Biting" has immediately for him an intersubjective significance. He perceives his intentions in his body, and my body with his, and thereby my intentions in his body.
>
> (*PP* 404/352/410)

More recent studies have produced even more dramatic results, including facial mimicry in infants as little as 42 minutes old.[10] Clearly, nothing like objective observation or explicit analogical correlation between oneself and others, intuited or inferred, is going on in such cases. Instead, the infant's body is attuned to others in a kind of immediate sympathetic harmony.[11] Consequently, even as an adult, "Inasmuch as I have been born and have a body and a natural world, I can find in that world other comportments with which my own are interwoven [*s'entrelace*]" (PP 410/357/416). There is no room at this level, already manifest in early life, but surely enduring and thriving in adulthood, for observation or judgment to intervene in our bodily interconnectedness: "Between my consciousness and my body, as I intend it, between this phenomenal body and that of another, as I see it from the outside, there exists an internal relation that makes the other appear as the completion of the system" (PP 405/352/410). Quite literally, as Merleau-Ponty says elsewhere, "man is a mirror for man" (Œ 33/168/130).

What this embodied experiential overlapping reveals is the abiding presence of the "prepersonal subject" (PP 405/352/411), or what Merleau-Ponty calls "the one" (*le "on"*) (PP 400–1/348/405–6), a kind of bodily substratum more basic than our experience of ourselves as individuated subjects. Our most basic experience of experience, we might say, is an experience not of distinct, separate, mutually closed, self-contained spheres of private awareness, but of a common openness onto one and the same world. Indeed, this worldly commonality is no different in principle from the way in which we intuitively understand the diverse perspectives and sense modalities in our own experience, not as mutually isolated sensory occurrences, but as converging on—or better, in—the world. Consequently, although experience is variable, and the senses differ among themselves,

> we have learned in individual perception not to regard our perspectival views one apart from another; we know that they slip into one another and converge in the thing. In the same way, we must learn to find the communication of consciousnesses in one and the same world. In reality, the other is not enclosed in my perspective on the world because that perspective itself does not have definite limits, because it slips spontaneously into that of the other, and because they come together in a single world in which we all participate as anonymous subjects of perception.
>
> (PP 405–6/353/411)

This interpersonal, subpersonal convergence of perception on the world is possible only because we experience each other not as isolated minds, but as cohabiting bodies:

> I experience my body as the power of certain behaviors and of a certain world. I am given to myself as a certain grip [*prise*] on the world; it is precisely my body that perceives the body of the other and discovers there a miraculous extension of my own intentions, a familiar way of dealing with the world; henceforth, just as the parts of my body together form a system, the body of the other and my own are a single whole, front and back sides of a single phenomenon, and the anonymous existence, of which my

> body is at each moment the trace, henceforth inhabits both
> bodies at once.
>
> (*PP* 406/353–54/412)

The agent of this primordial social recognition is not the mind, but the body, or more precisely the *body schema*. A child is able to acquire specific bodily and social skills by watching others, not because he can register discrete observations and draw inferences from others to himself, but because his body is both innately attuned and socially habituated, hence prone, to act as others are visibly acting: "the body schema ensures the immediate correspondence of what he sees done and what he himself does" (PP 407/354/412).

This appeal to the shared social space of bodily perception arguably dissolves the problem of other minds, but does it do so at too high a price? After all, unlike babies, adults can and do distinguish their own experience from the experience of others; we do not simply merge into one another in an undifferentiated shared awareness. Merleau-Ponty must therefore do justice not just to our primordial bodily cohabitation in the world, but also to our distinctness as individuated selves or persons.

And so he does. He insists, though, that we must not simply dismiss the infantile experience as error and illusion, as Jean Piaget does.[12] For the primitive experience of the child persists as the vital background and substratum of adult consciousness; indeed, its disappearance would coincide precisely with the absurdity of solipsism:

> The perception of others and the intersubjective world are
> problematic only for adults. The child lives in a world that he
> believes straightaway to be accessible to all those around him; he
> has no awareness either of himself or of others as private
> subjectivities; he does not suspect that we are all, himself included,
> limited to a certain point of view on the world. ... Human beings
> are, for him, empty heads turned toward a single, self-evident
> world where everything happens, even dreams, which are, he

> believes, in his room ... Others are, for him, so many gazes that
> inspect things; they have an almost material existence, so much
> so that a child wonders why the gazes don't break when they
> cross each other.
>
> (PP 407–8/355/413)[13]

Whereas Piaget supposes that children overcome these infantile errors by about the age of 12 and then do without them as rational adults, Merleau-Ponty insists that mature rationality must remain rooted in the child's point of view and can never fully extricate itself from its own naïve history:

> in reality, it must be that children are in some sense right,
> against adults, or against Piaget, and that the primitive thoughts
> of our early years remain as an indispensable acquisition
> underlying those of adulthood, if there is to be for the adult a
> single, intersubjective world.
>
> (PP 408/355/414)

Do we then simply face a dilemma between our infantile sense of shared social space and our mature conception of ourselves as isolated minds closed off to one another? No, for even as adults we continue to experience ourselves as sharing the same world, as immediately visible to one another, not as mental (or physical) objects, but as bodily persons:

> I perceive the other as behavior, for example I perceive the grief
> or the anger of the other in his conduct, in his face and his hands,
> without recourse to any "inner" experience of suffering or anger,
> and because grief and anger are modifications of being in the
> world, undivided between the body and consciousness, alighting
> as much on the other's conduct, visible in his phenomenal body,
> as on my own, as it presents itself to me.
>
> (PP 409/356/414–15)

The perception of others may be problematic only for adults, but this is not to say it is not problematic at all. It is—not as an epistemological problem, but as a kind of mystery, indeed a kind of trouble, haunting the social and political worlds we share. Others come to be mysterious and troubling for adults in a way they cannot be for children, for our mature conception of ourselves as subjects puts us in essential tension, often open conflict, with others, whom we necessarily experience asymmetrically, in the second and third person—not as I myself, but as you and he or she. "Like the gods of polytheism, I have to contend with other gods" (PP 412/359/418).

This perverse polytheism of selves is not just aggravating, but enigmatic. For although we cannot help but recognize the first-person status of other persons, this very recognition yields both food for thought and grist for the political mill, for it seems there are still ways in which "I can ... recognize only one I" (PP 411/358/417). Thus, "Consciousnesses present themselves with the absurdity of a plural solipsism, such is the situation that must be understood" (PP 412/359/418).

This essential asymmetry in our experience of ourselves and others introduces a new level of complexity into Merleau-Ponty's account, one that might appear to raise the specter of skepticism all over again. Others are not a problem, but they are trouble, and the trouble is no accident, but has its roots in the asymmetry without which there could never even seem to be a problem of other minds, nor for that matter mutual recognition of ourselves *as selves*:

> The difficulties in the perception of others do not all stem from objective thought, nor do they all cease with the discovery of behavior, or rather objective thought and the uniqueness of the *cogito*, which is its consequence, are not fictions, but well-founded phenomena, whose foundations we shall have to seek. The conflict of myself and the other does not begin only when we try to *think* the other, nor does it disappear if we reintegrate

thought in nonthetic consciousness and unreflective life: it is
already there if I try to live [the life of] the other, for example in
the blindness of sacrifice.

(*PP* 409/356–57/415)

Just by being myself, I am doomed to regard the other precisely
as *other*, however I might want (impossibly) to appropriate her
experiences or actions as my own. This sounds weird, for surely it
makes no sense to try to be a self other than the self you are. How
could you succeed? And yet the very possibility of solidarity and
conflict seems to allow us to undertake something like this metaphysically incoherent effort, to lose ourselves in a kind of unity
with others or escape and be free of them altogether. And yet we
can only be ourselves, just as we are condemned to be with others.
The self itself thus "seems to preclude any solution to the problem
of others. There is a lived solipsism that is inescapable." My most
basic experience is an experience of myself as among others, and
yet others are *other* precisely because "I am ... the one through
whom they are experienced" (PP 411/358/417).

Merleau-Ponty's acknowledgment of this complexity and asymmetry at the heart of our being with others is in no way a regress
into skepticism, for individuation and interaction are not incompatible ontological conditions, but essentially intertwined and
interdependent aspects of social life:

Solitude and communication cannot be two horns of a dilemma,
but two moments of a single phenomenon, for in fact others
exist for me. We must say of the experience of the other what we
have said elsewhere of reflection: that its object cannot escape
it absolutely, for we have a notion of it only through it. Reflection
must in some way present the unreflected, for otherwise we
would have nothing to contrast it with and it would never
become a problem for us. Similarly, my experience must in
some way present me with others, for if it did not, I would not

speak of solitude at all, and I could not even declare others
inaccessible.

(*PP* 412–13/359/418–19)

Solipsism remains strictly speaking incoherent, for what it envi-
sages is precisely what it itself can make no sense of, namely the
radical absence of the other. For it is precisely the presence of
others that makes the prospect of their absence intelligible as absence.
Without others, I could have no idea what the world would be
lacking were I its only self. The question that exposes solipsism as a
pathology of social life rather than a genuine epistemological problem is the question, *How did I ever acquire the* (seemingly paradoxical)
idea of an "other" self? Where else, indeed, but from my mysterious
and troubled dealings with others?[14]

By the time I am aware of myself as distinct from others, I feel
their presence as something at once primitive and inescapable, as
"the tension of my experience toward another whose existence
on the horizon of my life is beyond doubt, even when my knowledge of him is imperfect" (PP 413/359/419). We experience the
social world

> not as an object or sum of objects, but as a permanent field or
> dimension of existence: I can indeed turn away from it, but not
> without remaining situated in relation to it. Our relation to the
> social is, like our relation to the world, deeper than any explicit
> perception or any judgment. ... The social is already there when
> we know it or judge it.
>
> (*PP* 415/362/421–22)

Thus, as Wittgenstein said of the metaphysical subject, society and
history are not, for Merleau-Ponty, objects but limits of experience:
"my birth and my death cannot be for me objects of thought" (PP
418/364/424).[15] I cannot intuitively grasp or comprehend them,
and yet they remain pervasive and defining aspects of my life:

"although I do not think my death, I live in a general atmosphere of death, there is a kind of essence of death always on the horizon of my thoughts." The same is true of my experience of others: "just as the instant of my death is for me an inaccessible future, so I am certain never to live the presence of the other to himself" (PP 418/364/424). Sociality is an essential structure of my experience inasmuch as it discloses a horizon of others whose point of view on the world cannot in principle be collapsed into my own, nor mine into theirs. Moreover, to see such a structure as essential is precisely to see that it *cannot* constitute an epistemological problem, for there is nothing that could in principle count as occupying the perspective of another, just as there is nothing that could count as escaping one's own body, inhabiting the body of another, stepping outside of space or time, or surviving one's own death.

SUMMARY

Merleau-Ponty's account of our bodily coexistence with others is one of the most original and important elements in his phenomenology. The account is a reply but not an answer to the question of other minds, not a solution but a dissolution of what Merleau-Ponty believes is not a genuine problem. For the problem of other minds, so called, takes for granted a distinction between mind and body that has no echo in our most basic experience of ourselves and others. Merleau-Ponty therefore rejects Husserl's theory of "analogical apperception," according to which I am conscious of others as conscious beings thanks to a pairing association with my awareness of myself as a "psychophysical unity," or mind-body composite. He also rejects Sartre's polarized account of the other as a nonobjectified look that fixes me as an object, for that account arbitrarily dwells on dramatic scenes of conflict and suspicion, my encounter with another as an alien subjectivity standing over against me, in contrast to our more mundane experience of others as simply with us in a shared world.

Merleau-Ponty's own phenomenological description of our experience of others is an extension of his account of the body schema and motor intentionality. Others are for me neither visible objects nor invisible subjects, neither material bodies nor immaterial minds. Indeed, they are not present to me as targets of observation or judgment at all, but as persons, bodily agents I immediately and involuntarily identify with in my own sensitivities and behaviors. Not only do I not infer the existence of other minds from observations of their bodies; there is no "analogy" at all between myself and them, for they are as directly and undeniably present to me as my own body is, though of course in a different way. Only in problematic circumstances must I put myself in their position, think about their perspective on things, their thoughts, their feelings. Even as adults, we are at bottom like children, for whom people are all simply "empty heads" open onto the same world.

But although, barring insanity, others do not—indeed, cannot—constitute a genuine epistemological problem, they are nonetheless always more or less a source of practical, ethical, and political disturbance. Others are not a *problem*, but they are *trouble*. The reason for this is that our perspective on ourselves and on them is essentially asymmetrical: obviously, yet profoundly, I am the only I. Like the gods of polytheism, we find the plurality of sovereign selves perpetually enigmatic and destabilizing.

FURTHER READING

Barbaras, R. *The Being of the Phenomenon: Merleau-Ponty's Ontology.* In chapter 2 Barbaras argues that the account of others in *Phenomenology* remains idealistic and solipsistic, still too Husserlian. See note 12 below.

Eilan, N. "Consciousness, Self-Consciousness, and Communication." A critical discussion of the promise and problems attending Merleau-Ponty's account of shared experience and second-person thought.

Meltzoff, A. N. and M. K. Moore. "Imitation of Facial and Manual Gestures by Human Neonates" and "Newborn Infants Imitate Adult Facial Gestures." These studies provide evidence for the innate mimetic capacities of newborns.

Rizzolatti, G., L. Fogassi, and V. Gallese, "Mirrors of the Mind." An accessible account of research on "mirror neurons" in human and other primate brains, which underlie our immediate intuitive empathic relations to others.

Five

History and Politics

The Cold War, especially during the 1950s, was an age of Manichaean ideological conflict between the communist East and capitalist West. The political landscape was sharply divided, and French intellectual culture absorbed and perpetuated the division with depressing relentlessness. The years immediately following the Liberation saw some effort among noncommunists on the left to articulate and defend a third way, a middle path between the United States and the Soviet Union. In March 1948, opposition within the Socialist Party brought Merleau-Ponty together with Sartre and Simone de Beauvoir, Albert Camus, André Breton, David Rousset, and others in the Rassemblement Démocratique Révolutionnaire (RDR), a short-lived democratic, socialist, antiwar "gathering" led principally by Sartre and Rousset. Unfortunately, within a year the RDR had been infiltrated and corrupted by the CIA, and this experiment in neutralist political activism, like others, came to a sad end.[1]

At around the same time, partly under the influence of Arthur Koestler, Albert Camus—novelist, essayist, journalist, and minor hero of the Resistance—was becoming an ever more passionate anticommunist, though, like Koestler, he still belonged to the political left, broadly speaking. Camus had been, for Sartre and others, a role model of intellectual courage and commitment during the Occupation, but he had no very deep or well worked out political or philosophical ideas; he was a writer and a moral critic, not an original thinker. In the years immediately following the war Sartre's true political "guide," as he later said, was Merleau-Ponty.[2] In 1945, together with Beauvoir, they founded the journal *Les Temps modernes*, and Sartre was deeply impressed, even radicalized, by the political essays Merleau-Ponty published there, and then reprinted in 1947 under the title *Humanism and Terror*.

Sartre's and Merleau-Ponty's ideological paths were crossing, however. In 1952, reacting to the increasingly aggressive and hysterical tone of anticommunism in Europe and the United States, Sartre had a fresh new insight, namely, "Every anticommunist is a dog."[3] From then on, until the Soviet invasion of Hungary in 1956, he was a resolute and deliberately uncritical friend of both the French Communist Party (PCF) and the Soviet Union. He publicly and cruelly ended his friendship with Camus in August 1952 and in December declined to comment on the show trial and execution of Rudolf Slánský and ten other Czech communist leaders, most of them Jewish. Slánský suffered torture in prison, attempted suicide, and was hanged, having been found guilty of "Trotskyite-Titoist-Zionist activities in the service of American imperialism." Sartre refused to protest. Instead, he attended the Stalin-backed World Peace Conference in Vienna, was reconciled with former communist foes, and spoke glowingly of the Congress as one of the high points of his life. In his notebook, still stinging from Sartre's humiliating personal attack a few months before, Camus wrote with characteristic starkness and beauty, "In Vienna, the doves perch on gallows."[4]

Merleau-Ponty, for his part, was moving in the opposite direction ideologically. In the years immediately following the war, he was not just a humanistically inclined Marxist, but a committed, if critical, "fellow traveler" of the PCF and the Soviet Union. By 1950, however, things had changed, and for two reasons. First, reports had begun to emerge from the USSR concerning the scale and brutality of the Soviet concentration camp system. Second, North Korea's invasion of the South in June 1950 showed that the communist regimes of the East could be as aggressive and destabilizing as the United States and other Western colonialist powers. Both developments had a moderating effect on Merleau-Ponty's political thought. As Sartre later wrote, his own (in the end, temporary) conversion to communism was mirrored by Merleau-Ponty's own conversion from it, and indeed from Marxism and revolutionary politics altogether: "Each of us was conditioned, but in opposite directions. Our slowly accumulated disgust made the one discover, in an instant, the horrors of Stalinism, and the other, that of his own class."[5] Merleau-Ponty lost faith in communist practice, Marxian theory, and revolutionary rhetoric as ways of genuinely grasping and dealing with the complexities and ambiguities of modern life.

Merleau-Ponty's thought was always holistic. He regarded the world, ourselves, and our thoughts and experiences as somehow unified and coherent, and his argumentative style invariably involved a kind of reconciling strategy of breaking down and looking behind and beneath familiar conceptual dichotomies—sensation and judgment, inner and outer, mental and physical, mind and world, body and environment. Merleau-Ponty took much the same approach to social and historical phenomena, persistently questioning such seemingly easy and obvious distinctions as those between self and other, individual and society, morality and politics, liberty and equality, principle and practice.

And yet the significance of that approach remained obscure and problematic in his early political writings, emerging more clearly and coherently as he became increasingly disenchanted not just with the direction communism was taking in the East, but with Marx's theory of history itself. Marxism had seemed to promise a nuanced view of social reality, combining an account of the material constraints on life with an acknowledgment of freedom, hence without lapsing into either objectivism or subjectivism, determinism or voluntarism, realism or idealism.

Only when the tyranny of Stalinism and the sterility of official Marxist doctrine became clear to him in 1950, however, did Merleau-Ponty begin to see that Marxism itself, far from escaping or resolving those crippling dichotomies, was fatally impaled upon them. The dialectic was not unfolding, advancing, and transcending itself in historical progress, but collapsing, exposing communism as a fraud, and forcing its intellectual apologists into ever more absurd extremes of either historical determinism, which remained the official party line, or utopian fantasies of revolution, as in Sartre's defense of the PCF and the Soviet Union as legitimate because —but *only* because—they were the only effective vehicles of proletarian action.[6]

That hopeless dilemma between freedom and determinism is not an accident of twentieth-century European politics, Merleau-Ponty now argued, but the inevitable consequence of Marxism itself, which in truth never had at its disposal the theoretical resources for reconciling human beings with history. Trying to be a Marxist in the middle of the twentieth century, Merleau-Ponty concludes, is as much an anachronism as trying to be a Platonist or a Cartesian. "Are you or are you not a Cartesian? The question does not make much sense" (S 17/11). Like Plato's dialogues and Descartes's *Meditations*, Marx's works have become classics in the humanist tradition, they pose essential questions and offer deep insights of enduring philosophical significance, but they are no more keys for understanding contemporary political life than the texts of ancient and medieval metaphysics are tools for the advancement of modern science. Actual political and social history have "so completely shifted the perspectives of proletarian revolution that there is no longer much more reason to preserve these perspectives and to force the facts into them than there is to place them in the context of Plato's *Republic*" (AD 133–34/93).

Merleau-Ponty is not remembered for developing any innovative social or political theory. He was a Marxist in the 1940s, but he made no original contribution to Marxian accounts of the technological causes of historical change, the economic foundations of social practices and political institutions, or the ethics of capitalism. By the early 1950s he had abandoned Marxism and become a kind of liberal leftist, but again he added nothing new to the philosophical or political theory of liberalism. What is new and interesting in his political writings is not their substantive theoretical content, but their attempt to extend phenomenological insights beyond the individual into the public sphere, beyond the personal realm of perceptual experience into the impersonal structures of collective action and social life. The evolution of Merleau-Ponty's political thought, not only his migration from Marxism to liberalism but also his growing disenchantment with the pro-Soviet sympathies of friends and colleagues like Sartre and Beauvoir, are best understood against the background of this troubled effort to generalize and expand phenomenological inquiry into practical and discursive contexts to which it may be fundamentally unsuited.

1. PERCEPTION OF HISTORY

We saw in the last chapter that Merleau-Ponty regards the social world not as an empirical object, but as a transcendental condition or permanent horizon of our recognition of others as others. Several examples he offers in *Phenomenology of Perception* of the special status of social existence move the discussion into the realm of history and politics. He observes, for instance, that in 1917 Russian peasants joined forces with workers in Petrograd and Moscow not because of any explicit judgments about their common political or economic interests, but "because they felt [*sentent*] their lot [*sort*] to be the same" (PP 416/362/422). Quite apart from whatever particular thoughts or experiences they had of one another, their concrete actions were guided, at least momentarily, by an immediate intimation of solidarity, a sense of sharing the same condition, the same fate.

Similarly, an event like the Battle of Waterloo is not an object of observation, either for Napoleon or for the historian—or for Fabrice, the hero of Stendhal's *Charterhouse of Parma*, who is hung over and sleeps through most of the action. Any one person's perspective captures at most only a small slice of what actually happens, either on the battlefield or behind the scenes, and grasping the event in reflection is possible only after it has been experienced concretely, across a tangled web of overlapping points of view. "The true Waterloo resides neither in what Fabrice nor the Emperor nor the historian sees, it is not a determinable object, it is what *comes about* on the fringes of all perspectives" (PP 416/363/422). Collective social entities like classes and nations exist on the horizons of individual awareness and become objects only, if at all, in parasitic acts of abstraction and reflection. Like my own birth, the past is always only an "ambiguous presence" in the present, forever beneath and beyond the limits of my immediate experience (PP 418/364/424). History is not an object, but a structure of inter-subjective experience: "Primordially, the social does not exist as object or in the third person" (PP 416/362/422).

Merleau-Ponty wrote extensively on a wide variety of social and political subjects. Like Sartre, he was a politically "engaged" (*engagé*) intellectual. And yet his interventions in public discourse often remained at a high level of abstraction. The reason for this, I believe, is that his philosophical interest in history, society, and politics flowed from a deeper, more general fascination with perception, embodiment, action, expression, and knowledge. What is interesting and original in his political writings consequently lies less in any particular argument or position he takes than in the style and method of his approach to the subject, rooted as it was in an effort to comprehend social life in its existential dimensions, as exhibiting the same structures, the same unity and coherence he had discerned in his phenomenology of perception and the body.

More specifically, Merleau-Ponty's political texts are interesting for the way in which they reflect his theoretical and practical development, and finally his change of heart and mind on both substantive and methodological matters. By 1950 he had abandoned the antiliberal, utopian Marxism of his early essays, renounced the role of fellow traveler, broken off relations with Sartre, moved closer to the liberalism of Max Weber, and reassessed the relations between East and West, theory and practice, and philosophy and politics. Above all, I want to suggest, he retreated from his initial strategy of treating social, historical, and political questions from the standpoint of phenomenology, that is, on the basis of insights into the structures and contents of individual perceptual experience. For whereas embodied human subjects are coherent organic units, society is irreducibly complex and interpersonal. In short, history does not, perhaps cannot, have the kind of sense or direction (*sens*) manifest in the bodily intentionality of an organism.

Merleau-Ponty's early political essays appeared in 1946 and 1947 in the pages of *Les Temps modernes*, the journal he co-founded with Sartre and Beauvoir after the war, and were then reprinted in 1947 under the title *Humanism and Terror: An Essay on the Communist Problem*. It was and remains Merleau-Ponty's most controversial book and marks the height of his enthusiasm for Marxism and revolutionary politics. Merleau-Ponty was never a doctrinaire Marxist or an uncritical apologist for the Soviet Union or the PCF. On the contrary, *Humanism and Terror* is in part a critique of the crude and regressive tendencies that, as he saw quite clearly, left socialism theoretically and practically vulnerable to charges of dogmatism, authoritarianism, and tyranny, especially from liberal anticommunists.

The central argument of the book, however, is an assault on liberalism, which Merleau-Ponty describes as "a dogma and already an ideology of war" (HT xx/xxiv), fortified by "that shamelessly clear conscience so remarkable at the moment in much Anglo-Saxon writing" (HT 189/175). The book is also therefore a partial defense of terror, the supposedly progressive or emancipatory violence that stands in contrast to both the nihilistic brutality of fascism and the feigned nonviolence of liberal humanism, which merely serves to mask the rapaciousness of capitalism, colonialism, and imperialism. Following the general pattern of Merleau-Ponty's thought, the title *Humanism and Terror* is a reminder that there can be no sharp distinction between morality and violence. Liberal democratic humanism, which claims to deplore and condemn all terror from a standpoint of moral purity, merely perpetuates it by refusing to recognize its own terror as terror. Merleau-Ponty consequently dismisses the liberal critique of communism on the grounds that it rests on a crude dichotomy—naïve at best, cynical at worst—between humanity and violence, justice and expediency, good and evil.

Merleau-Ponty focuses these large and rather abstract questions of morality and politics on a critique of the writings of Arthur Koestler, whose novel *Darkness at Noon* appeared in French in 1945 under the title, *Le Zéro et l'infini*. The novel recounts the fate of Rubashov, a thinly fictionalized portrait of Nicolai Bukharin—Bolshevik old guard revolutionary, head of the Comintern, and one of the dozens of Soviet officials arrested and executed by Stalin in the Moscow Trials in the 1930s. In Koestler's version, Rubashov is a fanatically loyal communist so mindlessly obedient to party discipline that he willingly pleads guilty to trumped-up charges of treason and espionage, blindly sacrificing himself to the cause. Rubashov's nihilistic identification with the regime and his consequent robotic self-liquidation serve as a hard-hitting indictment of what Koestler considered the total moral and ideological bankruptcy of communism. The novel thus takes for granted the crude dichotomies Merleau-Ponty questions, between criticism and obedience, reason and history, ethics and politics, purity and corruption—or, as the title of one of Koestler's essays has it, "The Yogi and the Commissar."

Merleau-Ponty replies that Bukharin's demise, the Moscow Trials, and revolutionary politics are all more complex and ambiguous than Koestler would like to admit. Advancing an idea originating with Machiavelli and later spelled out more explicitly by Hegel,[7] Merleau-Ponty insists that all political action is morally risky, that innocence and guilt are not functions of an individual's intentions, but also depend on accident and circumstance, and that moralistic condemnations of Soviet injustice are therefore too cheap and easy to be taken seriously in actual political debate. He observes furthermore that real-life politicians like Bukharin know all this and that Marxism is the theoretical realization of this insight into both the moral messiness of politics and the political exigencies of morality: "A Marxist knows very well that ... In a world of struggle no one can flatter himself that he has clean hands" (HT 64/60).

On Merleau-Ponty's alternative reading of the reports and transcripts of the 1938 trial, Bukharin did not simply fall on his sword out of slavish obedience to the party. Instead, he sincerely believed in his own (partial) "objective guilt" and in the counter-revolutionary effect—hence the true historical meaning—of his actions, in spite of his good intentions and subjective loyalty to the state (see HT 54ff./50ff.). Evidence of Bukharin's earnestness can be seen, Merleau-Ponty thinks, in the carefulness and precision of his confession. When pressed, Bukharin qualifies, clarifies, distinguishes, tries to identify the degree and nature of his errors, hence his guilt. He pleads guilty to charges of treason, espionage, sabotage, knowing he will be condemned to death. "And yet he refuses to see himself as spy, traitor, saboteur, and terrorist" (HT 49/45). Indeed, "On five occasions Bukharin categorically denies the charge of espionage" (HT 49/46). Such fastidiousness seems at odds with Koestler's image of a man mindlessly sacrificing himself, and any sense of justice he might have had, to the smooth, machine-like functioning of the state. Merleau-Ponty thinks Bukharin was sincerely confessing what he considered his objective guilt: he confesses this, but denies that. Merleau-Ponty asks, "Can one believe in the denials and refuse all credence to the confessions?" (HT 50/46)

Well, yes. As it happens, both Koestler and Merleau-Ponty were seriously mistaken about Bukharin, about his "confession" at his trial in 1938, and about his significance in the rise of Stalinism. To be sure, Bukharin was no Rubashov, but neither did he seriously believe in his own objective guilt as a counter-revolutionary agent. The fact is that his trial was a far more sordid and brutal affair than Merleau-Ponty wanted to believe. True, until his arrest in 1937, he behaved not unlike the subtle, semiprincipled pragmatist Merleau-Ponty envisions. He defied and then broke with Stalin in 1928, thereafter viewing him with "complete hatred," as "a Genghis Khan," a "petty Oriental despot," an "unprincipled intriguer who subordinates everything to the preservation of his power" and "changes theories depending on whom he wants to get rid of at the moment."[8] Nevertheless, in November 1929 he and several other anti-Stalinists signed a statement of political error, conceding that "the party and its Central Committee have turned out to be correct. Our views ... have turned out to be mistaken."[9] In March 1930 he then published an article in Pravda comparing Stalinism to "the 'corpselike' obedience, 'ideological prostitution, and unprincipled toadyism' imposed by Loyola's Jesuit Order."[10] By the following November he had once again signed a statement acknowledging his "mistakes," though he stood by his earlier positions on matters of policy, refusing to admit anything like "guilt" until January 1933, more than four years before his eventual arrest and imprisonment.[11]

Up to this point, Merleau-Ponty's interpretation of Bukharin's conduct is not too implausible. Bukharin was no innocent bystander, but neither was he, like Koestler's Rubashov, an utterly self-abnegating party nihilist. He willingly renewed his alliance with the regime, knowing full well and deploring Stalin's viciousness. Why? Because he was morally committed to communism and saw complicity with the regime as his only way of advancing the cause. When he traveled to Paris in 1936 he knew that Stalin would have him killed upon his return to Moscow. When friends asked why he was going back, he replied with a kind of fatalism. "How could I not return? To become an émigré? ... No, come what may ... ."[12] Merleau-Ponty's view is also partially, but only partially, borne out by Bukharin's candid admission of "a peculiar duality of mind" or "dual psychology" brought on by his devotion to Bolshevik ends and his abhorrence of Stalinist means.[13]

It is worth remembering, however, that by this time as many as 10 million people had already died as a result of forced collectivization in the early 1930s, many of them in the "terror-famine" Stalin deliberately engineered in the Ukraine.[14] The Great Purge of

1936–38 continued on the same order of magnitude. At least 7 million people were arrested, a million of them executed, while another 2 million died in prisons and concentration camps. By the end of 1938 the population of the camps was around 7 million, and by 1952 the number of inmates had risen to about 12 million.[15]

After his arrest, Bukharin held out for three months in prison, relenting "only after the investigators threatened to kill his wife and newborn son"[16]—another sobering reminder of the sheer brutality of the situation, in such stark contrast to the rarified philosophical atmosphere of Merleau-Ponty's reading of the trial transcripts and Bukharin's confessions. Near the end of *Humanism and Terror*, in a moment of grotesque hyperbole, Merleau-Ponty writes, "there is as much 'existentialism'—in the sense of paradox, division, anguish, and resolution—in the *Report of the Court Proceedings* at Moscow as in the works of Heidegger" (HT 205/187). As Raymond Aron would later say, Khrushchev was closer to the truth when he observed in his anti-Stalinist "Secret Speech" to the 20th Party Congress in 1956 that the way despots extract false confessions from prisoners is by humiliation, deprivation, and torture.[17]

Contrary to both Koestler and Merleau-Ponty, Bukharin did not really confess to anything. Instead, by feigning submission and cooperation with the court, he attempted to use his trial as a platform from which to attack the regime. So, for instance, he proclaimed—obviously incoherently—"I plead guilty to ... the sum total of crimes committed by this counter-revolutionary organization, irrespective of whether or not I knew of, whether or not I took a direct part in, any particular act." This is not a philosophically sophisticated meditation on the tragedy of objective guilt, but calculated sophistry. Indeed, as Bukharin himself immediately added, "The confession of the accused is a medieval principle of jurisprudence."[18]

Merleau-Ponty's points about the moral ambiguity of political action and objective guilt may or may not be valid, but they have nothing specifically to do with Bukharin and the Moscow Trials. In spite of its superficial appearance of political engagement, Humanism and Terror remains preoccupied with a cluster of abstract philosophical themes: the nature of political action, the conditions and scope of responsibility, the meaning of guilt, and the substance and application of liberal values, and the legitimacy of representative democratic institutions. It is an interesting and important book, but less for what it has to say about "the communist problem" than for what it signals in the evolution of Merleau-Ponty's thought.

In moving away from and eventually repudiating the Marxism of Humanism and Terror, Merleau-Ponty was arguably coming to have second thoughts about an analogy that informed his political position in the late 1940s. It is an analogy as old as Plato's Republic, namely between the soul and the city, or in Merleau-Ponty's terms the sense and direction (sens) of perceptual experience and the sense and direction of history. For the two are perspectival and indeterminate in essentially the same way:

> There are *perspectives*, but, as the word implies, this involves
> only a horizon of probabilities, comparable to that of our perception,
> which can, as we approach it and it becomes present to us, reveal
> itself to be quite different from what we were expecting.
>
> (*HT* 59/55)

Merleau-Ponty's critique of liberalism thus parallels his critique of intellectualism in Phenomenology of Perception, for just as intellectualism construes our awareness of ourselves and the world in terms of explicit judgment and inference, liberalism attempts to assimilate economic and social life to the rule-governed procedures of legal and political institutions. But just as there is a form of perceptual coherence and significance more primitive than intellect, which makes intellectual attitudes possible, so too there is a coherence and significance in the movement of history more basic than any explicitly codified principles of right and justice; indeed, it is that prior historical significance that makes moral and legal principles intelligible. The determinacy of liberal categories tends to obscure the ambiguity of history, just as the determinacy of cognition obscures the ambiguity of embodied perceptual content.

Yet the analogy is flawed, even relative to Merleau-Ponty's own purposes. For whereas perceiving organisms are unified totalities, the social world is essentially plural, irreducibly complex, perhaps even necessarily fragmented. There is no totalizing perspective for an entire society as there is for a single perceptual subject. The analogy with bodily-perceptual equilibrium breaks down at the level of collective social practices and institutions. Moreover, if there is a kind of self-stabilizing norm or equilibrium inherent in social life, it seems more likely to lie in the arbitrary inertia of custom and established authority than in the spontaneous revolutionary irruption of economic equality and social justice.

Moreover, whereas in *Phenomenology of Perception* Merleau-Ponty was not skeptical about reason itself—in the manner of, say, Hume or Nietzsche—in *Humanism and Terror* he seems to dismiss liberal principles of freedom and justice as such. The point of the book, after all, while neither defending nor justifying the Moscow Trials, is to preempt liberal condemnations of communism by insisting that the trials be understood not simply with reference to abstract principles of justice, but in their concrete social and political setting:

> Any critique of communism or the USSR that makes use of isolated facts without situating them in their context and in relation to the problems of the USSR ... can only serve to mask the problem of capitalism, to threaten the very existence of the USSR and must be considered an act of war.
>
> (*HT* 196–97/179–80)

The concrete context that belies abstract liberal principle is the meaning or direction (*sens*) of history itself. Just as phenomenology must regard experience as it is given in its concrete, lived coherence, so too, Merleau-Ponty insists, philosophy must presuppose that history "is not a simple sum of juxtaposed facts," but "a totality moving toward a privileged state that gives sense and direction [*sens*] to the whole" (HT 165–66/153). Marxism, the philosophy that grasps that historical totality, is thus in effect

> a *perception of history* that brings out at each moment the lines of force and the vectors of the present. Thus it is a theory of violence and a justification of terror, it brings reason out of unreason [*déraison*], and the violence it legitimates must bear a sign that distinguishes it from regressive violence.
>
> (*HT* 105/98)

Merleau-Ponty realistically accepts the ubiquity of violence, but consoles himself with the utopian conviction that history and terror will in the end be somehow self-correcting: "approximation, compromise, terror are inevitable, since history is contingent. But they have their limit inasmuch as within this contingency lines of forces are inscribed, a rational order, the proletarian community" (HT 126/117–18). Rest assured, "Historical terror culminates in revolution" (HT 98/91). Marxism "is not a philosophy of history, it is the philosophy of history, and to renounce it is to dig the grave of historical Reason" (HT 165/153).

But what exactly is that normative "privileged state" lying outside or at the end of history? What does its "privilege" consist in, and how exactly does Marxism manage to "perceive" it? The privileged state is presumably analogous to the bodily equilibrium anchoring our sense of perceptual rightness, which is more basic than, and occasionally in tension with, explicit norms of cognition and reflection. But whereas the coherence and stability of bodily skills and perceptual awareness are manifest phenomena in need of no theoretical justification, Marxian notions of historical totality and teleology are asbstract postulates in the service of a theory. Why should we believe them? Merleau-Ponty has little to say on their behalf, and even less to say about how or why they pose a challenge to principles of individual liberty and the rule of law.

What Merleau-Ponty offers in *Humanism and Terror*, then, is not so much a compelling critique of liberal principle as a forceful reminder of "liberal mystification" and hypocrisy, an insistence that, in current practice, "liberal ideas form a system of violence" (HT ix/xiii). As a criticism of the brutality of Western liberal democratic regimes, the argument is pertinent and compelling—indeed, perhaps even more so today than it was 60 years ago. With extraordinary prescience, for example, Merleau-Ponty describes the way in which "Respect for law and liberty ... serves even to justify military suppression in Indochina or in Palestine and the development of an American empire in the Middle East" (HT ix/xiii).

But does such a critique indicate "the limits of liberalism" itself (HT 37/35)? Does it expose "the dogmatic basis of liberalism" (HT 38/35)? Does it show that the only true humanism is Marxist humanism, which we must accept along with all the violence and lawlessness supposedly necessary to create a decent society for all mankind? One need not concede that the liberal ideal of justice is inherently flawed or illegitimate to agree with Merleau-Ponty that it *de facto* "plays its role in the functioning of conservative societies" (HT 34–5/32). One might instead try to articulate the moral content of liberal humanism and anticommunism as a third alternative to the two moralities Merleau-Ponty tells us they in fact have at their disposal: "the one they profess, celestial and uncompromising, and the one they practice, terrestrial and indeed subterranean" (HT 185–86/172). Again, Merleau-Ponty's point is that there is no sharp line separating humanism and terror, for political violence occurs across the ideological spectrum, and moral decency consists not just in the formal legal protection of freedom and equality, but in concrete mutual recognition and respect: "humanity is humanity in name only as long as most of mankind lives by selling itself, while some are masters and others slaves" (HT 168/155).

Of course, principles are by definition abstract, so, like all principles, liberal principles are vulnerable to hypocrisy. It is possible, however, that the hypocrisy lies not in the principles themselves, but in our failure to live up to them. Indeed, to see the untenability of any stark contrast between principle and expedience is to see that there is an excellent pragmatic reason to maintain ideals of justice in the teeth of cynical tactics. The reason is simply that such ideals function not just as idle wishes and obfuscations of the complexity of events, but as self-fulfilling prophecies, as fostering and promoting what they envision as desirable and worth protecting, as establishing exemplars and precedents. Abstract principles may in a sense be empty taken on their own and out of context, but resigning ourselves to that fact in theory makes it harder to achieve social justice in practice than it would be from a more admittedly naïve liberal standpoint. Paradoxically, there is a purely pragmatic argument for not abandoning abstract principles in light of the ambiguity of practice, namely, that doing so thwarts the progressive efforts one might think such principles merely tend to obscure. (As Sidney Morgenbesser once said, pragmatism is true, it just doesn't work.)

Ironically, then, Merleau-Ponty's approach to "the communist problem" in *Humanism and Terror* turns out to be intellectually disengaged in its own way, for it takes contemporary events as a mere occasion to reflect abstractly on problems about the status of liberal principle and the moral ambiguity of political action. It makes no substantive contribution to our understanding of Leninism, Stalinism, Bukharin, the Moscow Trials, or the meaning or fate of communism. Indeed, if anything, it stands in the way of any genuine critical engagement with those issues by dismissing liberal principles out of hand as a mere disguise and defense of Western imperial aggression.

2. LIQUIDATION OF THE DIALECTIC

Merleau-Ponty's disenchantment with communism grew in part with reports of the vastness and inhumanity of forced collectivization in the USSR: arrests, executions, mass starvation in the Ukraine, 10 million prisoners in labor camps by 1950. Victor Kravchenko, a Soviet official and defector, recounted the horrors in his memoir, I Chose Freedom, published first in 1946 in the United States, and then the following year in France. The French communist weekly Les Lettres françaises promptly denounced Kravchenko as a liar and a spy, he (successfully) sued the paper for libel, and his trial in 1949 became a high-profile occasion for further appalling testimony from camp survivors. A few years later, David Rousset, a survivor of the Nazi camp at Buchenwald, formed the International Commission Against Concentration Camp Practices, brought the Soviet Corrective Labor Code to public attention, and revealed the massive scale of the camps in the USSR. Once again, Les Lettres françaises—sensing their duty—accused him of slander, forgery, and misinformation. Like Kravchenko, Rousset sued and won in 1951.

In January 1950 Merleau-Ponty wrote (and Sartre co-signed) an editorial in Les Temps modernes, later reprinted in Signs, on "The USSR and the Camps" in which he conceded that "there is no socialism when one out of every twenty citizens is in a camp" (S 332/264). "If there are ten million concentration camp inmates ... then quantity changes to quality. The whole system swerves and changes meaning" (S 333/265). He even asks whether the "permanent crisis of the Russian regime" can be dismissed as a purely Stalinist aberration, or was instead "prefigured in the Bolshevist organization of the Party" (S 332/265). On its rhetorical face, the question Merleau-Ponty asks is shockingly naïve:

how has October 1917 been able to end up in the cruelly hierarchical society whose features are gradually becoming clear before our eyes? In Lenin, Trotsky, and a fortiori Marx, there is not a word that is not sane, which does not still speak today to men of all lands, which does not help us understand what is going on in our own. And after so much lucidity, intelligence, and sacrifice—ten million deported Soviet citizens, the stupidity of censorship, the panic of justifications.

(S 333/265)

Merleau-Ponty's view of the growth of the concentration camp system is, it must be said, almost perversely forgiving: "It seems probable that the evolution that leads from October 1917 to millions of slaves ... happened little by little without deliberate intention, from crisis to crisis and expedient to expedient, and that its social significance escapes its own creators" (S 334/266).

Merleau-Ponty tries to walk a fine line of blunt but friendly criticism of the USSR:

we do not draw the conclusion that indulgence must be shown toward communism, but that one can in no case make a pact with one's adversaries ... every political position that is *defined* in opposition to Russia and localizes criticism within it is an absolution given to the capitalist world.

(S 338/269)

Merleau-Ponty accuses Rousset of opportunism and warns that his libel suit against Les Lettres françaises will merely polarize debate and provoke the communists to close ranks. In short, criticism of the USSR merely diverts attention from oppression in other parts of the world, for example Spain and Greece (S 343/273). For loyal fellow travelers, Soviet atrocities are the mirror image of Western imperialism: "the colonies are the democracies' labor camps" (S 340/270).

Either around this time or within a few months, however, Merleau-Ponty's attitude changed. After nearly four decades of tyranny, communism could no longer make excuses for regularly lapsing into authoritarianism and bureaucratic insanity. Lenin absurdly described Marx's passing reference to a transitional "revolutionary dictatorship of the proletariat"[19] as "the very *essence* of Marx's doctrine,"

meaning quite literally, according to Lenin, "rule based directly
upon force and unrestricted by any laws."[20] Proletarian dictatorship
would be rule not by the masses, but of the masses by the party
leaders:

> large-scale machine industry ... calls for absolute and strict *unity
> of will* ... But how can strict unity of will be ensured? By
> thousands subordinating their will to the will of one. ...
> *unquestioning subordination* to a single will is absolutely
> necessary ... Today ... revolution demands ... that the people
> *unquestioningly obey the single will* of the leaders of labour.[21]

In a word, as Noam Chomsky has said, Leninism was from the
beginning "the exact opposite of socialism."[22]

Merleau-Ponty seems to have come around to this view by the
time of Stalin's death in 1953, for not long thereafter he writes,

> planning from below, "dictatorship propelled from below," in
> short the proletarian society in which proletariat and party are
> one, are phantasms—because there can be no mediation by
> dictatorship, no mediating dictatorship, no authoritarian historical
> creation.
>
> (S 364/291)

> "Direct democracy," "dictatorship propelled from the bottom
> up" ... is a pompous political concept with which one clothes the
> Apocalypse. It is a dream of an "end of politics" out of which one
> wants to make a politics. Like "proletarian power," it is a problem
> that presents itself as a solution, a question that gives itself as an
> answer, a sublation of history in ideas.
>
> (AD 301/218)

What transpired in the years since the Russian Revolution, Merleau-
Ponty now concedes, was a grand failure, the failed convergence of

theory and practice, principle and tactics, progress and violence, past and future—in short, "the liquidation of the revolutionary dialectic" (*AD* 15/7).

Many of Merleau-Ponty's later political writings are an attempt to think through that failure—the failure not just of state communism, but of Marxism itself as an attempt to comprehend history in a definitive and systematic way, an attempt to make sense of the present by explaining past change and forecasting future progress. Marxism's promise to reconcile such opposites and render history intelligible can no longer be taken seriously, for "the Marxist link between philosophy and politics is broken" (*S* 13/8). Marxism has lost credibility as a living creed, a vital, action-guiding view of the world.

To be sure, Marx was a great thinker, and his works are great works, but they now belong to the past among a multitude other great thinkers and great works. They no longer speak to us with any special authority about our own social problems, our political battles, or our economic future. It has become an anachronism, for instance, to ask if someone is or is not a Marxist; it's like asking if someone is or is not a Platonist or a Cartesian. It is, Merleau-Ponty says, "a bad question for which there are only bad answers" (*S* 15/9). Marxism can no longer even be said to be simply true or false, for its very terms and presuppositions, the political and intellectual world it inhabited, are no longer our own. It has instead become a kind of "secondary truth" (*S* 17/11), "a failed truth" (*une verité manquée*) (*S* 16/10), for "Even in the sciences, an outmoded theoretical framework can be reintegrated into the language of the one that replaced it; it remains significant; it keeps *its* truth" (*S* 15/10). Such doctrines "continue to speak to us over and beyond their statements and propositions. These doctrines are *classics*. They are recognizable by the fact that no one takes them literally, and yet new facts are never absolutely beyond their reach" (*S* 16/11). Merleau-Ponty is concerned not to refute or vanquish Marxism, but to resituate it within the humanistic tradition: "a reexamination of

Marx would be a meditation upon a classic" (S 17/11). Like any great work, Marxism "is an immense sedimented field of history and thought where one goes to practice and to learn to think." The idea that it captured and articulated the meaning of history itself, however, was "the height of philosophical arrogance" (S 18/12).

Merleau-Ponty had not become hostile to "dialectical" thinking as such. As we shall see, he criticizes the crude radicalism of Sartre's political thought for failing to take dialectical complexity seriously. But what is dialectic? For Merleau-Ponty, it seem to consist in a kind of holism, an appreciation of the superficiality of familiar dualisms, the mutual dependence of their terms, and the way in which new forms of understanding emerge not by direct confirmation or refutation of considered judgments, but fluidly and unpredictably through transformations in our ways of being in the world. "The dialectic does not, as Sartre claims, provide finality ... but the global, primordial cohesion of a field of experience where each element opens onto the others" (AD 282/204). What dialectic posits is not teleology, but complexity and coherence: "What is obsolete, then, is not the dialectic, but the pretension of terminating it in an end of history, in a permanent revolution" (AD 285/206).

But while Merleau-Ponty's reflections on history and politics remained "dialectical" in this weak sense, the views he attempted to mediate and synthesize had shifted crucially. He now no longer simply rejects the distinction between humanism and terror, or principle and tyranny, in favor of an elusive distinction between progressive and regressive violence. Instead, he moves closer to liberalism by envisioning a middle way between pragmatism and dogmatism, skepticism and rationalism, what Alain called "the politics of understanding," always tentative and conscientious, and "the politics of reason," all too often utopian and unself-critical.

Merleau-Ponty thus writes admiringly of Max Weber: "from Alain to Weber, the understanding has learned to doubt itself. Alain recommended a rather cramped policy: do each day what is just, and don't worry about the consequences." Weber, by contrast, sees that that maxim is empty in times of crisis, that understanding "functions easily only within certain critical limits" (*AD* 40/25). Weber's liberalism is thus both more realistic and more principled than the reactive politics of moral conscience, for it does not just respond to each new situation that presents itself, nor does it "take the formal universe of democracy as absolute; he admits all politics is violence—even, in its own way, democratic politics. His liberalism is militant, even suffering, heroic" (*AD* 41/26). But neither is this realistic political attitude dogmatic, for, contrary to the Marxian faith, we find ourselves "in a history we cannot be sure is finally rational" (*AD* 40/25). More precisely, for Weber, and now for Merleau-Ponty, "history does not have a direction [*sens*] like a river, but meaning [*du sens*]" (*AD* 44/28). There is no teleology inherent in social life, but there is always significance, something to be understood.

Weber, however, did not strike quite the right balance between liberal understanding and revolutionary conviction, Merleau-Ponty argues, for "he emphasizes the opacity of the social as a 'second nature' and thus seems to postpone indefinitely the limiting concept of transparent social relationships" (*RC* 56/106). "Western Marxists"— or as Merleau-Ponty says, "Weberian Marxists"—like Lukács, by contrast, sought to reaffirm a conception of historical meaning or "totality" beyond the opaque and fragmentary world available to conscientious moral understanding. Yet on closer inspection that notion of totality turns out to be little more than the regulative ideal of pulling together and making sense of the dialectical variables history presents us with as best we can. "It is quite superficial to say that Marxism reveals the meaning of history to us: it binds us to our time and its partialities; it does not describe the future for us; it does not stop our questioning; on the contrary, it intensifies it" (*AD* 83/57). The truth Lukács derives from the notion of historical totality is not a substantive theoretical truth, but merely "the incarnation of negativity in history, of the power of doubt and interrogation that Weber calls 'culture'" (*RC* 56/106).

After Lukács, Merleau-Ponty maintains, the revolutionary dialectic fell into crisis and split into two views at once diametrically
opposed and yet bound together by their common unquestioned
loyalties: the increasingly rigid posture of official party doctrine on
the one hand, and Sartre's voluntaristic radicalism on the other. The
crudely deterministic theory of history, for its part, finds no echo
in real events, and "the dialectic in action responds to adversity
either by means of terror exercised in the name of a hidden truth
or by opportunism" (AD 136/95). Communist planning thus
degenerates into cynical social engineering:

> If the social is, as Lukács says, a "second nature," the only thing
> to do is govern it as one governs nature: by a technique that
> permits discussion only among engineers, that is, according to
> criteria of efficiency, not according to criteria of meaning [sens].
>
> (AD 136–37/95)

Communists perpetrate a "fraud" by taking the failure of the dialectic for granted while at the same time cynically deferring it to an
indefinite future, transforming it into an "ideology" (AD 137/96).

Like Merleau-Ponty, Sartre saw through that fraudulent use of
dialectical rhetoric, but embraced communist practice, stripped of
its ideological self-interpretation. What Sartre defended in the early
1950s was not Marxist theory, but practical solidarity with the
working class, whose only effective and reliable advocate in France
in the early 1950s, he not implausibly maintained, was the PCF. Unlike
the communists themselves, however, Sartre tried to make sense of
communist action, as Merleau-Ponty puts it, "by making history, to
the extent that it is intelligible, the immediate result of our voli-
tions, and otherwise an impenetrable opacity" (AD 139/97–98).

Like many seemingly opposed dialectical pairs, however, the crude
objectivism of official party doctrine and Sartre's subjectivism are
equally problematic, and for many of the same reasons. The communists maintain that a revolutionary proletariat is already objectively

real, historical appearances to the contrary notwithstanding, while Sartre imagines it creating itself *ex nihilo* at any moment. Either way, communism finds no support in the concrete complexity and indeterminacy of social life. The two views are theoretical opposites, but practical allies, thanks to their shared contempt for, and refusal to engage with, that complexity and indeterminacy: "The philosophy of pure object and the philosophy of pure subject are equally terroristic, but they agree only about the consequences" (*AD* 139/98).

Merleau-Ponty complains moreover that Sartre's subjectivist interpretation of communism—"reasoning from my principles and not from *theirs*," as Sartre says he is doing[23]—is pathetically idiosyncratic:

> If he "understands" communism correctly, then communist
> ideology is deceitful, and we can ask the nature of the regime that
> hides itself in the philosophy it teaches instead of expressing
> itself there. ... Ultimately, if Sartre is right, Sartre is wrong. Such
> is the situation of the loner who incorporates communism into his
> universe and thinks of it with no regard for what it thinks of itself.
> (*AD* 141/99)

This extreme pragmatism, this "desperate justification of communism" (*AD* 143/100), this utter disregard for the account it gives of itself, is what Merleau-Ponty calls Sartre's "ultrabolshevism." The problem of reconciling communist theory and practice, Merleau-Ponty observes, "is comparable to Christian philosophies confronted with historical Christianity" (*AD* 143/100), and Sartre's commitment to the cause is equivalent to a Kierkegaardian leap of faith (*AD* 148/104). In the end, "ultrabolshevism throws off its cover: truth and reason are for tomorrow, and today's action must be pure" (*AD* 228/164).

Merleau-Ponty concludes *Adventures of the Dialectic* with a critique of revolutionary theory and an attempt to conceive a non-Marxist left, "a new liberalism" akin to "Weber's heroic liberalism" (*AD* 312/ 225–26). He also offers an explicit criticism and disavowal of his own former views as set out in *Humanism and Terror*. It is no accident, he now argues, that revolutionary movements regularly degenerate into oppressive regimes, for once they establish themselves as regimes, they cease to be disruptive, risky, and transformative. A regime that regards itself as the incarnation of revolutionary spirit is incapable of acknowledging its own contingency, its limits, its fallibility:

> Revolutions are true as movements and false as regimes. Thus the question arises whether there is not more future in a regime that does not intend to remake history from the ground up, but only to change it, and whether this is not the regime one must look for, instead of once again entering the circle of revolution.
> (*AD* 287/207)

A theory of history can rationalize the incoherent concept of a revolutionary regime only by deceiving itself (and others) about its own contingent and problematic status as a theory. Thus, "Inside revolutionary thought we find not dialectic, but equivocation" (*AD* 287/207).

More specifically, the "double game of Marxist thought" (*AD* 292/211) equivocates between two concepts of revolution: revolution as what Trotsky called an "incidental cost" or culminating side effect of historical development, and revolution as constant ongoing historical transformation. Marxism tries but fails to combine the two concepts. At some ideal future point, "History as maturation and history as continual rupture would coincide: it would be the course of things that would produce, as its most perfect fruit, the negation of all historical inertia" (*AD* 290/209). In this unstable blend of historical inevitability and radical transformation, "in this certitude of an already present future, Marxism believes it has found the synthesis of its optimism and its pessimism" (*AD* 290/210). But the synthesis remains both a fantasy and a dogma.

In place of revolutionary thought and politics, Merleau-Ponty now advocates a kind of liberalism, not the aggressive anticommunism he attacked in *Humanism and Terror*, but an attitude of tolerance, healthy skepticism, and openness to criticism. Above all, the noncommunist left must be tolerant of communism, not as a desirable regime, but as a critical gadfly:

> If we speak of liberalism, it is in the sense that communist action and other revolutionary movements are accepted only as a useful menace, as a continual call to order, that we do not believe in the solution of the social problem through the power of the proletarian class or its representatives.
>
> *(AD* 312/226)

The liberal left must be open to revolutionary agitation, yet critical of Marxism: "For us, a noncommunist left is this double position, posing social problems in terms of struggle and refusing the dictatorship of the proletariat" (*AD* 313/226).

Merleau-Ponty therefore renounces the "Marxist wait-and-see attitude" (*attentisme marxiste*) he had embraced after the war (*AD* 316/228). In *Humanism and Terror* he was, like other fellow travelers, a sympathetic nonadherent to communism, holding out hope "that Soviet politics might thereby be brought back to the ways of Marxist politics" (*AD* 316/228). If the USSR threatened to invade Europe, he conceded, communism would have to be critically reassessed: "a different question would arise and have to be examined" (HT 202/185). There was no such threat in the late 1940s, however, so the point was moot. In 1950, though, there was: "The USSR did not invade Europe, but the Korean War raised this 'different question,' which was not posed in 1947; and it is with this question that we are now dealing" (*AD* 317/229). In light of North Korean aggression, "our attitude of sympathy was obsolete. ... Marxist wait and see became communist action" (*AD* 317/229).

Merleau-Ponty now more firmly declares himself noncommunist, free even of his earlier "cryptocommunism." Wait-and-see Marxism was "nothing more than a dream, and a dubious dream" (AD 318/230). Nor can Marxist theory be rescued from communist practice, for Soviet aggression confirms their de facto inseparability. To cling to an alluring theory that insists on identifying itself with an untenable practice is to render the theoretical commitment politically inert: "To say, as we did, that Marxism remains true as critique or negation without being true as action or positively was to place ourselves outside of history, and in particular outside of Marxism" (AD 319/231). To try to be Marxist in this way, drawing a sharp distinction between theory and practice, was to relinquish one's Marxism.

In Humanism and Terror Merleau-Ponty had written that to renounce Marxism would be "to dig the grave of historical Reason" (HT 165/153), or as he now puts it, "the failure of Marxism would be the failure of philosophy of history." Such a declaration, he confesses, "shows well enough that we were not on the terrain of history (and of Marxism), but on that of the a priori and of morality" (AD 321/232). Marxism had never been, for him, an empirical theory of history or even one political point of view among others, but a moral imperative. Such an approach, however, cannot claim to be an approach to history itself in all its complexity, plurality, and indeterminacy. In short, "This Marxism that remains true whatever it does, which does without proofs and verifications, is not a philosophy of history" (AD 321/232). A genuine philosophy of history—which Merleau-Ponty never developed—would have to be something beyond the transposition of phenomenological insights into the realm of society and politics that Merleau-Ponty initially attempted.

SUMMARY

Merleau-Ponty emerged from World War II a committed "fellow traveler" of the French Communist Party and the Soviet Union. His early essays, published in 1947 as *Humanism and Terror*, helped to radicalize Sartre, with whom founded the journal *Les Temps modernes*. But as Sartre moved closer to communism in the early 1950s, Merleau-Ponty lost faith in Marxism and revolutionary politics, partly in light of revelations about the wide-scale atrocities in the Soviet labor camps, partly in the wake of Russian aggression in the Korean War. Marx's ideas are no longer simply true or false, he suggests, but are instead "failed truths," deep and important insights articulated in works that endure not as part of a living political creed, but as classics in a humanistic tradition.

Merleau-Ponty's early political writings are guided by an analogy between what he saw as phenomenology's discovery of the sense and direction (*sens*) of perceptual experience and Marx's discovery of the sense and direction of history. That analogy is flawed, however, since the coherence of perceptual awareness is grounded in the unity of the body, whereas the putative coherence of history is not grounded in a subject or agent. Merleau-Ponty's political writing was always guided more by abstract philosophical considerations than by concrete political problems. His account of the Moscow Trials in *Humanism and Terror* is exceedingly naïve about the sheer brutality of Stalin's show trials and purges of the 1930s. In his novel *Darkness at Noon* Koestler was wrong to portray Bukharin as driven by suicidal loyalty to the communist cause. Merleau-Ponty, however, was equally wrong to suggest that Bukharin sincerely believed in his own "objective guilt," contrary to his intentions. In *Humanism and Terror* Merleau-Ponty rejects liberalism as an "ideology of war," but this charge confuses liberalism's commitment to individual liberty and the rule of law with the *de facto* hypocrisy and brutality of Western capitalism and colonial oppression.

Adventures of the Dialectic (1955) contains Merleau-Ponty's account of the decline and death of Marxism, both as theory and as revolutionary politics. Since the Russian Revolution in 1917, Marxist doctrine had become increasingly dogmatic and intolerant—rigidly mechanistic in its account of historical change, blindly optimistic and intolerant of dissent in the face of evidently diminishing prospects of revolutionary social transformation.

FURTHER READING

Aronson, R. *Camus and Sartre: The Story of a Friendship and the Quarrel that Ended It.* The story of Sartre's and Camus's relationship, with reference to their works, the evolution of their ideas, and the divergence of their politics, culminating in their sensational public breakup in 1952.

Kruks, S. *The Political Philosophy of Merleau-Ponty.* An account of his political thought in the context of his philosophy at large. Kruks dismisses *Adventures of the Dialectic* as inferior to Merleau-Ponty's earlier Marxist writings.

Lefort, C. "Thinking Politics." Discussion of the motivation and evolution of Merleau-Ponty's reflections on history and politics.

———. "The French Communist Party After World War II." Mentions Merleau-Ponty in the context of a discussion of the PCF in the 1940s and 1950s.

Sartre, J.-P. "Reply to Camus." Sartre's denunciation of Camus, in particular what he saw as Camus's bad faith in putting himself above history and politics.

———. "Merleau-Ponty *vivant*." Sartre's eulogy of Merleau-Ponty, moving and insightful.

Six

Vision and Style

Merleau-Ponty's principal contributions to aesthetics and the philosophy of art can be found in three core essays, spanning fifteen years: "Cézanne's Doubt" (1945), "Indirect Language and the Voices of Silence" (1952), and "Eye and Mind" (1960). The art form Merleau-Ponty mostly concerns himself with is painting, often in explicit contrast with literature. He also says fascinating things about the philosophical significance of cinema in the essay "Film and the New Psychology" (1945), taking the occasion to explain the advances Gestalt psychology made beyond classical theories of perception. Likewise, in his aesthetic writings generally, Merleau-Ponty revisits, elaborates, and applies the arguments of *Phenomenology of Perception* while advancing original ideas concerning the relation between painting and perception, and between literature and painting. Vision and visual art, he insists, are both forms of stylized *expression*, not just passive registration of sensory input. Moreover, like perception itself, painting is not just directed *toward* but embedded in the world. Merleau-Ponty wants to "put the painter back in touch with his world" (S 72/57/94).

The three core essays on painting can be read together as pursuing three main lines of thought. The first has to do with what Merleau-Ponty calls the *depth* or *thickness* of the perceptual world, its intimation of *reality*, as opposed to mere outward surface and appearance. We do not just see colors and shapes, but *things*, indeed things we see to *be* hard, soft, wet, dry, warm, cold, heavy, dense, light, and so on. How does that peculiar sense of solidity and reality manifest itself in perception? Merleau-Ponty believes it is in virtue of our bodily continuity with the world. What emerges—most fully in the late essay "Eye and Mind," but also already in "Cézanne's Doubt," well before it appears explicitly in his final works—is Merleau-Ponty's notion of our unconscious communion with the world in the form of flesh. "Flesh," as we have seen, is Merleau-Ponty's term for the stuff common to ourselves and the world, a reminder of the essential *reversibility* of perception, that only something perceptible can perceive. Flesh is thus more ontologically fundamental than the conscious experience we have of ourselves as bodily subjects inhabiting a world of objects distinct from us—a world we are in but not of.

The second line of thought concerns the nature of expression, that distinctly recognizable character or stylization that art shares with experience and behavior generally, hence the ambiguous relation between visual and linguistic meaning, and so between art and literature. "All perception, all action," Merleau-Ponty writes, "in short, every human use of the body is already *primordial expression*" (S 84/67/104). Consequently, even in the most mundane circumstances, "perception already stylizes" (S 67/54/91). Both in ordinary experience and in works of art, visual meaning always bears the stamp of a recognizable character, a gestural significance, a communicative import, however inarticulate. Painting shares this expressive character with language and literature, but speaks to us without the system of signs that marks the difference between our symbolic *grasp* of concepts and our more primitive perceptual *grip* on the world: "Perception, history, expression—it is only by bringing together these three problems that ... we shall be able to see why it is legitimate to treat painting as a language" (S 94/75/112). Merleau-Ponty treats expression and its dependence on the world at length in the essay "Indirect Language and the Voices of Silence."

The third line of thought, unique to "Cézanne's Doubt" and more directly continuous with *Phenomenology of Perception*, which he wrote at about the same time, is bound up with the first two, though it goes beyond the scope of aesthetics and the philosophy of art. Simply put, it concerns the question of freedom. We are conditioned by, indeed of a piece with, a world that goes beyond our knowledge and will. How then should we understand our apparent capacity to wrench ourselves free, step back and define ourselves, direct our actions and our lives, and so become something more than a mere effect or product of a deterministic environment? How did Cézanne become Cézanne—not just this particular anxious and disturbed person, but the artist whose work touches so powerfully on perception, perspective, color, reality, and life? How does the style of Cézanne's work manage to open us onto that strange depth and solidity of the perceptual world, which we might forget or evade momentarily in ordinary experience, but which is so unmistakable once we see it made manifest in his canvases?

"Cézanne's Doubt" is virtually two essays in one, for in addition to offering an account of the phenomenological content, indeed the metaphysical implications, of the artist's work, it is also a meditation on human freedom, on the relation between the contingency and conditionedness of life on the one hand, and its seemingly miraculous capacity to surpass itself and define itself in free creative expression on the other. How is it possible for a human being to be thoroughly in—and of—the world, and yet stand apart from it in such a way as to see it, to describe and refer to it in language, to paint it?

1. THE DEPTH OF THE VISIBLE

Cézanne's artistic achievement is best appreciated by contrasting it with the effort of the Impressionists to capture our immediate optical sensitivity to light and color: "Impressionism was trying to capture in the painting the very way in which objects strike our eyes and attack our senses. Objects were depicted as they appear to instantaneous perception" (SNS 16/11/61). The results were often beautiful and fascinating, but the project was epistemologically confused, for we do not in fact *see* the light and the detached colors the Impressionists were trying to paint; we see things—trees, houses, pathways, empty spaces, other people, not to mention what we might call situational objects like threats, obstacles, and opportunities. Like empiricist philosophers and psychologists, the Impressionists were motivated more by theoretical considerations than by our actual experience of seeing things. Perception, they reasoned, is a product of sensory stimulation, an effect of our receptivity to discrete bits of light and color. To paint the stimuli as such, one ought to use the colors of the rainbow rather than, say, the browns and blacks of solid objects.

Like the theory of vision accompanying it, the aesthetic effect of Impressionist technique also turned out to be wrong, in unexpected ways. For shifting visual attention from the world to the proximal lighting conditions made things look less rather than more real: "depicting the atmosphere and breaking up the tones submerged the object and caused it to lose its proper weight," whereas "Cézanne wants to represent the object, to find it again behind the atmosphere" (SNS 16/12/62). Here Cézanne was not simply retreating to the styles and techniques of earlier masters; like the Impressionists, he wanted to paint our *perception* of things, but precisely in and by painting the things themselves. His work might therefore seem paradoxical, for "he was pursuing reality without giving up the sensuous surface" (SNS 17/12/63).

He did this, in part, by posing a radical challenge to received notions of visual perspective. In Merleau-Ponty's view, Cézanne discovered intuitively and aesthetically what the Gestalt psychologists would later articulate in theory, namely, that "lived perspective, that of our perception, is not geometric or photographic perspective" (SNS 19/14/64). For one thing, photographic representation abolishes the size constancy built into real perception: the train on the movie screen gets suddenly bigger as it gets closer, until the picture frame can no longer contain it, whereas in real life the train comes gradually into view until it is simply *here*. There is no *here* in the visual experience of cinema, for as viewers we stand outside the picture we see in a way we cannot stand outside the world we perceive. So too, "To say that a circle seen obliquely is seen as an ellipse is to substitute for our actual perception what we would see if we were cameras" (SNS 19/14/64). Cézanne therefore does not paint the glasses and plates on a table setting as perfect ellipses, but instead lets them bulge outward to evoke their real presence as things one could approach and look at or touch.

What Cézanne manages to paint is not the light at our eyes, which, after all, we never (or hardly ever) see in its own right, but a world perceptually organized by our bodily involvement in it. As a result, his "perspectival distortions ... contribute, as they do in natural vision, to the impression of an emerging order, an object in the act of appearing, organizing itself before our eyes" (SNS 19–20/14/64–65). In this way, Cézanne's paintings attain a sense of reality beyond what the impressionists could achieve in their attempt to paint light and appearance as such. In Cézanne we find that "insurpassable plenitude, which is for us the definition of the real" (SNS 21/15/65).

Merleau-Ponty revisits that sense of plenitude and reality in his last published work, the essay "Eye and Mind," attributing it once again to the deep—though in a sense obvious—fact that painting is a *bodily* act. The painter "'takes his body with him,' says Valéry. Indeed, we cannot imagine how a *mind* could paint" (Œ 16/162/123). The body in question is "not the body as a chunk of space or a bundle of functions, but the body that is an intertwining [*entrelacs*] of vision and movement" (Œ 16/162/124).

As we have seen, by the late 1950s Merleau-Ponty conceived of the body (and the world itself) as "flesh," unconsciously homogeneous with the perceptible world to which it is sensitive: "My mobile body makes a difference to the world, being part of it" (Œ 16/162/124). It is therefore misleading to draw a sharp distinction between the sensing subject and the sensible world, for "the world is made of the same stuff as the body" (Œ 19/163/125).

The body is on neither side of that putative divide, for only something perceptible can perceive: the body "sees itself seeing, it touches itself touching, it is visible and sensitive for itself" (Œ 18/162/124). The perceiver is neither an invisible center of consciousness nor an exposed surface. Instead, the body straddles the boundary between subject and object, visible and invisible, conscious and unconscious. Flesh is itself tangible in touching, visible in seeing, sensible in sensing; it is, in a word, "the reflexivity of the sensible" (Œ 33/168/129). The bodily self is "a self caught up in things" (Œ 19/163/124), and there are distinctively human bodies only in the "blending" (*recroisement*) of perceiving and the perceived.

Vision and movement are also essentially intertwined, according to Merleau-Ponty, so that visible phenomena are always permeated with motor significance. What I see is defined for me in relation to what I can and cannot do. The visible world is a domain of obstacles and opportunities, a field of possible behaviors and actions. This constitutive connection with bodily movement means that no purely cognitive account of visual perception can capture its concrete intuitive motor significance: "This extraordinary overlapping" of perception and movement "precludes conceiving of vision as a function of thought" (Œ 17/162/124). The mind does not move the body, as Descartes supposed; instead, what we call the mind is just an aspect of our bodily intelligence, which is constantly at grips with its environment: "My movement is not a decision made by the mind," rather "my body moves itself, my movement deploys itself" (Œ 18/162/124).

The visual world is saturated with motor sense in virtue of our bodily continuity with the world we perceive. The enigma of painting, Merleau-Ponty maintains, is of a piece with the mystery of bodily existence as such: "since things and my body are made of the same stuff, vision must somehow take place in them; their manifest visibility must be repeated in the body by a secret visibility" (Œ 21–22/164/125). The visible world does not stand over against us as a mere object or appearance, for there is a bond between us and it, in virtue of which we are in a position to perceive it. Objects are not alien and external to us: "things have an internal equivalent in me" (Œ 22/164/126). To get a visual grip on things is not to apprehend their surface appearance, but to sense their bodily affinity with us, to commune with them, to inhabit them. As Cézanne put it, "The landscape thinks itself in me, and I am its consciousness" (SNS 23/17/67). What we see does not just occur, appear, or strike us from without, but invades us, speaks and makes sense to us: "All flesh, even that of the world, radiates beyond itself" (Œ 81/186/145)

Our visual relation to paintings is consequently elusive, for they are on the one hand things in our environment, yet they both emulate and comment on our visual relation to the world. They are perceptibles that speak of perception and perceptibility. They never merely mimic or duplicate visual experience; they are neither objects nor transparent windows onto imaginary worlds. When I look at a painting, *what* exactly am I seeing? Merleau-Ponty remarks,

> I would be hard pressed to say *where* the painting is that I'm looking at. For I do not look at it as I do at a thing, I do not fix it in its place. My gaze wanders in it as in the halos of Being. It is more accurate to say that I see according to it, or with it, than that I *see it.*
>
> (Œ 23/164/126)

A painting is never simply an inert object, since like all forms of meaningful expression, it surpasses itself toward the world. "The accomplished work," Merleau-Ponty says, "is not the work that exists in itself like a thing, but the work that reaches its viewer and invites him to take up the gesture that created it" (S 64/51/88). The work discloses a world for us, precisely because it is a gesture we can identify with. We do not merely observe paintings, we visually participate in them; we do not just see them, we see *with* them. The work of art "teaches us to see" (S 97/77/114). A work of art is thus never complete and finished, for "perception itself is never finished" (S 65/52/89).

A painting is not a mere object, but an *image*, something that organizes our perception both of it and of the world. Recall that an "image," in the relevant sense of the word, is not a mere copy or derivative, but a construction from a *schema*, a set of bodily capacities that carves out a field of possible actions and perceptions. The body schema anticipates and sketches out in advance motor possibilities in terms of which we perceive the world in its familiar aspects. So, for example, the extent of my reach makes the book appear *high* up on the shelf, just as the size of our bodies makes mountains *tall* and canyons *deep*. The imaginary is not the fictional or the counterfactual, but the depth of possibility in virtue of which we are able to experience things as real. The imaginary "is in my body as a diagram of the life of the actual" and presents vision with "the imaginary texture of the real" (Œ 24/164, 165/126). It is no coincidence that people who can paint can also often draw and sculpt, for their skill resides in a "system of equivalences" that affords them a global bodily *grip* on the world (Œ 71/182/142).

Like perception itself, painting concerns itself with the *visibility* of the visible: "painting celebrates no other enigma but that of visibility" (Œ 26/166/127). Painting does not just duplicate appearances, but neither does it refer discursively or abstractly to nonvisual sensory input, for instance tactile sensations. What painting accomplishes instead is the realization of the visible itself and as such: "It gives visible existence to what profane vision thinks is invisible" (Œ 27/ 166/127). What we see in both painting and perception is "a texture of Being," which we do not merely observe or register, but occupy and inhabit. "The eye lives in this texture as a man lives in his house" (Œ 27/166/127). The painter must therefore think magically, as if objects literally pass into him, or as if, as Malebranche (sarcastically) put it, "the mind goes out through the eyes to wander among objects" (Œ 28/166/128).

Of course, we do not typically see the way painters see: ordinarily we see things, whereas painters see and make visible the visibility of things. Seeing the visibility of the visible requires stepping back from our ordinary naïve immersion in things, just as, conversely, seeing things in the ordinary way requires not doing so: "To see the object, it was necessary *not* to see the play of shadows and light around it. The visible in the profane sense forgets its premises; it rests on a total visibility that is to be recreated and that liberates the phantoms captive in it" (Œ 30/167/128). This deep bodily identification with the world, which is inherent in ordinary perception and visibly manifest in Cézanne's paintings, is evident in our intuitive identification with the bodies of others, and even more so in our identification with our own reflection in a mirror. According to Merleau-Ponty, our experience of others is not an experience of invisible minds concealed behind depersonalized physical organisms. Instead, we experience others as sharing our world by sharing our embodiment: "Other minds are given to us only as incarnate, as belonging to faces and gestures" (SNS 21/16/66). Similarly, my own mirror image is not a mere external presence. To see myself in a mirror is to identify unthinkingly with the body I see, which makes immediate reference to myself. This is how I am able to locate my own bodily feelings in the image itself. It is also why when I look at my reflection I never have the feeling of being looked at, for the eyes staring back at me are my own. I therefore draw no more analogy or inference from my mirror image to myself than I do from other bodies to the other persons. What I see in the mirror is a kind of ghost: it is *me*—not *here* but *there*: "the ghost in the mirror draws my flesh outward, just as the invisibility of my body is able to animate [*investir*] other bodies I see" (Œ 33/168/129–30). Quite literally, "man is a mirror for man" (Œ 34/168/130).[1]

Visibility, in Merleau-Ponty's sense of the word, is neither surface appearance nor sensory stimulation. It is the intuitively felt reality of things disclosed to us as part of a dense, opaque world, the milieu in which things show up, amid other things. It is the mystery I mentioned in Chapter 1, namely, that perception reveals a world; that out of the blind density of brute physical matter, a world opens up to us, and we to it. Visibility and invisibility are not the mere presence and absence of visual input; they are our "absolute proximity" to and "irremediable distance" from things (VI 23/8).

For Merleau-Ponty, "any theory of painting is a metaphysics" (Œ 42/171/132); indeed, "the entire modern history of painting ... has a metaphysical significance" (Œ 61/178/139). Conversely, appreciating the phenomenological significance of paintings like Cézanne's demands a radical rethinking of received categories of thought. Mechanism, for example—the idea that all causality works by the immediate contact of one body on the surface of another— renders the notion of visibility virtually unintelligible, or at best reduces it to something subjective, hence irrelevant to a serious description of reality. In the Optics Descartes "in one swoop removes both action at a distance and that ubiquity that is the very problem of vision" (Œ 37/170/131). Reflections and mirrors accordingly have no special significance for him: "These unreal doubles are a class of things, they are real effects, like the bouncing of a ball" (Œ 38/170/131). Cartesian mechanism and dualism can make no sense of our intuitive experience of identification with others, or indeed with our own mirror images: "A Cartesian does not see himself in the mirror: he sees a mannequin, an 'exterior' ... not flesh. ... The mirror image is no part of him" (Œ 38–39/170/ 131). For Descartes, an image, like a word or a sign, refers to an object not by resembling it, but by prompting the idea of it. As a result, "the entire power of a painting is that of a text to be read, without any promiscuity of the seeing and the seen" (Œ 40/171/ 132). As we saw in Chapter 3, Descartes ascribes vision not to the eyes, but to "the faculty of judgment which is in my mind."[2] For him, vision "is a thinking that strictly deciphers the signs given within the body" (Œ 41/171/132). Since the impact of light on our eyes and brains bears no resemblance to the things we see, it makes no sense to wonder how the bodily visibility of things in painting is communicated to the soul.

For Merleau-Ponty, by contrast, painting is all about the visibility of the world, and since objects are visible only in space, "painting is an art of space" (Œ 77/184/144). But what kind of space? Merleau-Ponty focuses his account on the phenomenon of depth. What is depth? It seems paradoxical. I see it, and yet it is not visible in the way sizes, shapes, and colors are. And where is it, in me or in the world? It is not a property of objective space, which is defined by positions and distances, not here or there, near or far, behind or in front of. Cartesian space is a "space without hiding places" (Œ 47/173/134); unlike the worldly space of human action and experience, it lies "beyond all points of view, all latency and depth, without any real thickness" (Œ 48/174/135). Things are hidden or overlapping only relative to me, after all, owing to "my incomprehensible solidarity with one of them, my body" (Œ 46/173/134). But neither is depth a mere subjective quality coloring experience, like a sensation. For Descartes, what is essential to visual representation are the primary qualities of line and form. Consequently, as it would later be in Berkeley's theory of vision, "Depth is a third dimension derived from the other two" (Œ 45/172/133). But then depth is nothing, or more precisely, nothing but breadth seen sideways on. If we insist on distinguishing exclusively between subjective and objective phenomena, depth literally drops out of the picture.

Not only is there depth in the world as we perceive it, but the very surfaces of paintings cannot help but evoke it, even when, as in the abstract geometric paintings of Piet Mondrian, they strive to be perfectly flat. Depth is not just one of the three dimensions of objective space, arbitrarily marked by one's line of sight: "something in space escapes our attempts to survey it from above" (Œ 50/175/135). Depth is not some "unmysterious interval, as seen from an airplane, between these trees nearby and those farther away" (Œ 64/180/140). For space itself is not external to me: "I live it from the inside, it encompasses me. After all, the world is all around me, not in front of me" (Œ 59/178/138).

What then is depth? It is, of course, relative to perspective, and so dependent on us. Yet it is not simply the radial extension of objective space from the zero point of the observer; first of all because the observer's position is not a zero point, but an organized, spatially extended body, and second of all because mere radial extension, geometrically defined, fails to capture what is essential to depth, namely, its capacity to reveal and conceal, to occlude and disclose.

What Merleau-Ponty is describing is neither an objective property of space nor a subjective experience, but the very fact of our perceptual situatedness in a world. If nothing ever occluded or revealed anything else, if nothing stood behind or in front of anything—in short, if there were no depth—there would be no world we could perceive ourselves as occupying and inhabiting: "the enigma consists in the fact that I see things, each one in its place, precisely because they eclipse one another, and that they are rivals before my sight precisely because each one is in its own place" (Œ 64/180/140).

It is precisely this perspective-relative orientation of embodied perception that allows us to see the world as something separate from us, as independent of our point of view on it, as fully and genuinely real:

> Depth, so understood, is ... the experience of the reversibility of dimensions, of a global "locality" where everything is at once, from which height, breadth, and distance are abstracted, of a voluminousness we express in a word when we say that a thing is *there*.
>
> (Œ 65/180/140)

Moreover, we get a palpable sense of the reality of the perceived world not just from primary qualities of line and form, as Descartes supposed, but from color. This is why painting can evoke aspects of depth or disclosedness that prints, drawings, and black-and-white photographs cannot. To see in color is not just to see discrete color qualities, but to see things in all their robust presence. When Cézanne captures the virtually tangible colors of apples or pears on a table, "the painter's vision is not a view on an *exterior*," but "a kind of concentration or coming to itself of the visible" (Œ 69/181/ 141). The perceptual world speaks to us not just in outline, shape, and motion, but by invading and animating our own sense of bodily presence in the world. It is not surprising that painters sometimes say they feel as if things are looking at them. The idea of inspiration, too, implies being invaded and inhabited by the world, as opposed to acting on it. This sense of bodily communion with the world is crucial to the art of painting: "this internal animation, this radiation of the visible is what the painter seeks under the names of depth, space, color" (Œ 71/182/142).

These constitutive elements of painting cannot be reduced to isolated qualitative presences, bits of paint corresponding to discrete units of sensory data. Consider the lines that painters paint and draftsmen draw. We sometimes think of lines naïvely as real presences in the world, delineating things and individuating them from one another. But of course there are no such lines in the real world, lines are not properties of objects, and modern painters, Impressionists for example, have often tried to do without them altogether. When it reappears, for example in the works of Klee and Matisse, "the line no longer imitates the visible, it 'renders visible'" (Œ 74/183/143). Figurative or nonfigurative, the line functions as a kind of "disequilibrium" that carves out a "constitutive emptiness" in which things can be visible. Moreover, "the distinction between figurative and nonfigurative art is badly drawn" (Œ 87/ 188/147), for visual representations never merely reproduce objects, and even the most abstract art is defined by the world it tries *not* to represent. In either case, a line is neither an objective property nor a subjective *quale*, but a trace of disclosedness, a gesture marking out the visibility of things.

What line, depth, and color evoke is the *visibility* of the visible, the disclosedness of the world, which is always bound to horizons of invisibility, horizons that make up "the immemorial ground [fond] of the visible" (Œ 86/188/147). Everything seen, in order to be seen, must be surrounded by a kind of halo of the unseen: "the hallmark [propre] of the visible is to have a lining of invisibility in the strict sense, which it makes present as a certain absence" (Œ 85/187/147). Effective evocations of bodily action in painting, for example, often require paradoxical juxtapositions of limbs to avoid the effect photographs and slow-motion film often have of freezing, suspending, or obliterating the sense of movement. Echoing Rodin, Merleau-Ponty observes,

> When a horse is photographed at that instant when it is completely off the ground, with its legs almost folded under it—an instant, therefore, when it must be moving—why does it look as if it were leaping in place? And why, by contrast, do Géricault's horses really *run* on canvas, in a posture impossible for a real horse at a gallop?
>
> (Œ 80/18/145)[3]

One could say that photographs reveal too little in capturing a single instant and stripping away the temporal horizons surrounding it, yet one could equally say they reveal too much by exposing what we ordinary never see and forcing it to our attention. As Rodin says, "It is the artist who tells the truth and the photograph that lies. For in reality, time does not stand still."[4] A photograph shows a horse hovering in midair, legs tucked under it. *Epsom Derby,* by contrast, elicits a sense of real weight and movement, the sound and feel of hooves on turf, though what Géricault literally paints is oversized horses in mid-stride, legs extending (impossibly) both forward and back. The photograph thus reveals both too little and too much—or better, it *merely* registers and exposes and as a result dispels the aura of invisibility that renders the horses in the painting visible *as* horses, galloping across a damp field on a cloudy day.

2. THE LANGUAGE OF ART

In characterizing Merleau-Ponty's notion of the bodily *depth* of the visible, and its submersion in and blending with the invisible, I said the world speaks to us in both perception and art and that the line a painter paints is a gesture marking out the visibility of things. This was no accident, for such words are virtually irresistible when we try to describe our perceptual grip on the world, the sense we make of thing things and the sense they make to us. It is hard not to say that in seeing things we grasp them, that the bodily skills guiding us through the world somehow express our familiarity with it, and that artists manage to enact and exhibit those expressive skills in exemplary ways. There is a kind of brute meaning in any coherent perception, and "art, especially painting, draws upon this fabric of brute meaning [*sens*]" (Œ 13/161/123).

Perception and painting are not literally languages, though, so it remains to say what they have in common with speech and what the difference is between the brute meaning grasped in vision and visual art on the one hand, and the semantic meaning articulated in language and literature on the other. This is the theme of "Indirect Language and the Voices of Silence," whose title refers to *The Voices of Silence*, the 1951 edition of André Malraux's four volumes of art history and criticism, originally published together under the title, *The Psychology of Art*. Merleau-Ponty criticizes Malraux for inferring from recent disenchantment with classical conceptions of objective representation that modern art represents a retreat into subjectivity, interiority, and disconnection from the world. That inference, which Malraux borrows from Hegel's account of the increasing subjectivity and abstractness of modern consciousness, as expressed in Romantic art, not only ignores the rich middle ground between objective and subjective, but does so precisely by overestimating the adequacy of the categories of objectivity and subjectivity in making sense of perception, the body, and the world.

As he does with so many of his interlocutors, Merleau-Ponty takes Malraux to task for getting it wrong by *almost* getting it right.

For Malraux, painting and literature, abstracted from the world they represent, are two manifestations of the same phenomenon, namely creative expression:

> miniatures, frescoes, stained glass, tapestries, Scythian plaques, pictures, Greek vase paintings, "details" and even statuary ... the performance of an Aeschylean tragedy ... diverse as they are, all these objects ... speak for the same endeavor; it is as though an unseen presence, the spirit of art, were urging all on the same quest ... Nothing conveys more vividly and compellingly the notion of a destiny shaping human ends than do the great styles, whose evolutions and transformations seem like long scars that Fate has left, in passing, on the face of the earth.[5]

But this can only be half right, at best, for although it is true that all art forms are expressive, visual and linguistic expression differ profoundly, and not just in the means or materials available to them, but in relation to the world itself. Malraux criticizes the "objectivist prejudice" according to which meaning simply adheres to things, awaiting reflection or imitation in art or language. He is right that meaning is not an objective property, but neither does it lie solely in the subjective moment of creative expression. Perhaps, Merleau-Ponty suggests, Malraux "has not measured how deeply the prejudice is rooted. Perhaps he was too quick to concede the domain of the visible world to it" (S 59/47/84).

To get clear about the similarities and differences between perception and language, and so between art and literature, we need to draw some distinctions that Merleau-Ponty himself tends to blur, or at least gloss over. In particular, we need to distinguish between two distinctions that cut across each other: one between the visual and the linguistic, another between the ordinariness of life and the refinement of art. On the one hand, vision and painting are nonlinguistic phenomena, in contrast to speech and literature. On the other hand, vision and speech are everyday occurrences, in contrast to painting and literature, which are specialized cultural products.

There are accordingly two different questions regarding the relation between painting and language. First, how is the art of painting rooted in the mute, nonsymbolic, inarticulate world of ordinary visual experience? Second, how does painting nevertheless acquire at least some of the symbolic expressiveness of language and literature? These two questions can be collapsed into a single question, implicit in all of Merleau-Ponty's essays on painting, namely, how does *visual* art manage to *speak* to us? Merleau-Ponty says, "language speaks, and the voices of painting are the voices of silence" (S 101/81/117). Is the phrase "voices of silence" more than an oxymoron?

To frame the question in these terms is not to deny that there is a fundamental difference between visual and symbolic content. As J. J. Gibson has written,

> the essence of a picture is just that its information is *not* explicit. The invariants *cannot be put into words or symbols*. ... There is no way of describing the awareness of being in the environment at a certain place. Novelists attempt it, of course, but they cannot put you in the picture in anything like the way the painter can.[6]

There is surely a difference between the nonsymbolic content of visual experience and the symbolic content of linguistic signs. Yet Gibson's remark about the unique expressive capacity of painting raises our question again: how are visual works of art able to capture our concrete sense of *being* somewhere, given that they are neither full-fledged experiences nor mere signs?

I think Merleau-Ponty would agree with Gibson that there is an irreducible difference between perceptual and semantic meaning, for while language relies on general and abstract terms, perception and painting are bound to the concrete scenes they apprehend or depict. Language does not just reveal, it *refers*: "a statement purports to reveal the thing itself, it goes beyond itself toward what it signifies" (S 101/81/117). Language has something in common with "mute forms of expression such as gestures or paintings" (S 101/81/118), yet it differs from them in allowing (at least approximate) synonymy, "the substitution of equivalent meanings [*sens*]" (S 102/81/118). Painting and perception, by contrast, are inarticulate, for they admit of neither reference nor the substitutivity of terms.

Yet, as Merleau-Ponty insists, painting does have a kind of voice, somehow akin to language and literature, and he is more interested in what the three have in common than in how they differ. What they have in common is what he calls "the phenomenon of expression" (SNS 27/20/71). In exploring their rootedness in perception, he wants to rescue them from the false dichotomy we have seen looming in all his work, namely between the supposedly bare givens of sense experience and the supposedly pure abstractions of the intellect. Perception is not a dumb confrontation with sensory input, and "no thought ever detaches itself entirely from a support" in our concrete relation to the world (Œ 91/189/149). To see the wrongness of those distorted images of perception and cognition, we need to appreciate the primitive expressive intelligence at work in both vision and language, and in both art and literature. We need to look beneath the difference between perceptual and semantic content to see their common origins in expression and style.

Consider language. Language is not just an abstract system of signs. According to the structural linguist Ferdinand de Saussure, signifiers signify only in virtue of the system of differences among them, never by directly expressing some discrete semantic content. And yet, Merleau-Ponty insists, our experience of speaking and listening testifies to "the power speaking subjects have of going beyond signs toward their meaning [*sens*]. Signs do not simply evoke other signs for us, on and on without end, nor is language like a prison we are locked up in" (S 101/81/118). We experience and understand language as opening us onto a world, and no theory of syntax or semantics should tempt us to dismiss that experience as an illusion.

Putting words together in speech is thus not just a matter of manipulating symbols according to an algorithm, but is more like painting. For both speaking and painting are ways of evoking, ways of rendering things freshly visible. The writer's task, Merleau-Ponty says, is to apprehend and make the world manifest through language, and in this sense, "his procedure is not so different from the painter's" (S 56/45/82). We might suppose that a painting is mere color and line and cannot literally say anything, unlike a poem or a novel, which is composed of an established system of signs. Yet language is meaningful not just as a function of the combination of signifiers, but thanks to such quasiperceptual effects as mood, inflection, and silence. Speech emerges against "a background of silence that does not cease to surround it and without which it would say nothing" (S 58/46/83). Spoken language is "simply the highest point of a tacit and implicit accumulation of the same sort as painting. ... Like a painting, a novel expresses tacitly" (S 95/76/113). The silent significance of Julien's actions in The Red and the Black, for example, is "not in the words at all: it is between them, in the hollows of space, time, and signification they mark out, just as movement at the cinema is between the stationary images that follow one another" (S 95/76/113). Literary language has a "halo of signification" comparable to "the mute radiance of painting" (S 97/78/114–15). In addition to the explicit, articulate language of words and sentences, Merleau-Ponty therefore maintains, "there is a tacit language, and painting speaks in this way" (S 59/47/84).

"Indirect Language and the Voices of Silence" is dedicated to Sartre and can also be read as a reply to his essay, "What Is Literature?" There Sartre draws a sharp distinction between art and writing, poetry and prose. The artist is concerned only with appearances. "He is therefore as far as he can be from considering colors and signs as a *language*."[7] Like Merleau-Ponty, Sartre observes that linguistic

meaning permits the synonymy of different expressions: "the significance of a melody—if one can still speak of significance—is
nothing outside the melody itself, unlike ideas, which can be adequately
rendered in several ways."[8] Language is an instrument for disclosing
facts, truths about the way the world is, whereas painting merely
uncovers the appearance of concrete particulars: "The writer can
guide you and, if he describes a hovel, make it seem the symbol of
social injustice and provoke your indignation. The painter is mute.
He presents you with a hovel, that's all."[9] Sartre's distinction, however, is not between linguistic and visual representation as such,
but between significative and aesthetic uses of representation,
between denotation and decoration, prose and poetry: "The empire
of signs is prose; poetry is on the side of painting, sculpture, and
music. ... Poets are men who refuse to utilize language," for the
poetic attitude "considers words as things and not as signs."[10]

Merleau-Ponty rejects Sartre's distinction by insisting, first, that
visual arts like painting and sculpture do have a kind of voice of
their own, a kind of language, that they never merely display, but
also (so to speak) *speak* of the things they show; and second, that no
use of language, not matter how artless or prosaic, is literally
without style, a mere transparent signifying instrument. What
vision and painting, art and literature, poetry and prose all share is
a way of seeing, a character, a style.

Even our normal ways of seeing and hearing, not to mention
watching and listening, are imbued with a certain character. Again,
prior to any special effort, "perception already stylizes" (S 67/54/
91). How? By means of an "inner schema" (S 66/53/90), a
"system of equivalences" (S 68/54/91) that coordinates one's grip
on things and allows the world to reveal itself as coherent and
intelligible. The body schema, as we saw in Chapter 3, is a bundle
of flexible but enduring dispositions that organize ordinary perception and behavior. Likewise, there are more refined acquired
schemas that generate the styles immediately recognizable in artistic works. So, for example,

> Our handwriting is recognizable whether we trace letters on
> paper with three fingers of our hand or in chalk on the
> blackboard at arm's length, for it is not a purely mechanical
> movement of our body ... but a general power of motor
> formulation capable of the transpositions that make up the
> constancy of style.
>
> (S 82/65/102).

Expression—affective, linguistic, or artistic—presupposes a world given in perception, yet perception itself always already has expressive significance of its own, for the body brings a distinct style of comportment to its apprehension of what it perceives: "if expression recreates and transforms, the same was already true ... of our perception of the world before painting, since that perception already marked things with the trace of human elaboration" (S 74/59/96). We each find ourselves with subtly unique and individually recognizable ways of walking, talking, and seeing things, and the creative expression of artists is a further deliberate refinement of those characteristic dispositions: "For each painter, style is the system of equivalences that he sets up for himself" (S 68/54/91).

Creative artistic expression does not take place in some inner mental sanctum, but in the artist's concrete engagement with the world:

> The work is not brought to fulfillment far from things and in some
> intimate laboratory to which the painter and the painter alone has
> the key. ... he always goes back to *his* world, as if the principle of
> the equivalences by means of which he is going to manifest it had
> been buried there since the beginning of time.
>
> (S 68/55/92)

The cultivated body schema of the artist is a kind of second nature, a set of acquired yet spontaneous skills, skills that come to feel natural though they are in fact products of years of effort and practice. Carving out a unique artistic style worthy of the name, over and beyond one's everyday personal style of moving and speaking, is like learning a second language. Merleau-Ponty therefore refers to "the painter's labor and study, that effort that is so like an effort of thought and that allows us to speak of a language of painting" (S 69/55/92). If painting is a language, it is a language learned with reference to the more primitive means of expression inherent in ordinary perceptual behavior.

Vision is itself already essentially expressive, for it always has its own bodily character, its own style. It is no more a brutely given natural fact than any (so-called) "natural" language, no more fixed and surveyable in all its possible forms and purposes. Like speech, vision "moves itself, a means that invents its own ends" (Œ 26/ 165/127). This is why painting can never simply duplicate the structure and content of visual experience. Even Renaissance painters knew that their *perspectiva artificialis* was not simply a copy of perception, "that no technique of perspective is an exact solution," that linear perspective is not a uniquely correct mode of representation, but rather "opened several pathways for painting" (Œ 50/174/135). Painting is a mode of creative expression, not a means of technically reproducing what we see in our actual bodily engagement with the world: "Geometrical perspective is no more the only way of looking at the sensible world than the classical portrait is the only view of man" (PM 75/53).

Another reason painting never simply mirrors perception, however, has once again to do with the fundamental difference between visual and symbolic meaning. Since painting always acquires and generates symbolic content of some kind, it can never fully recapture or express the nonsymbolic content of visual perception. Painting is not just a duplication of vision, for it is language-like in a way vision is not. Images and icons are bound up with discourse in such a way that they never merely reveal the world, but also always allude, refer, indicate, and comment. Perception, by contrast, lies beyond symbolic discourse and remains inarticulate in relation to it. Consequently, "no means of expression, once mastered, resolves the problems of painting or transforms it into a technique, for no symbolic form ever functions as a stimulus" (Œ 50–51/175/135).

Malraux is therefore right to deny that meaning somehow simply inheres in the world itself, that there is a kind of natural language of things, which the arts merely echo or reflect. Unfortunately, he counters that crude objectivist prejudice, which he thinks defined classical art, with an equally crude subjectivist interpretation of modern art as withdrawing from all concrete engagement with the world and retreating into the inner sanctum of subjectivity, into "a secret life outside the world" (S 59/47/84).

Merleau-Ponty considers that dialectical reversal not just internally incoherent, but wrong even as a description of the works of art Malraux discusses. The difference between classical and modern painting cannot be understood simply as a difference between objective and subjective. Not surprisingly, Malraux's flawed notion of the putative subjectivity of modern art is parasitic on a correspondingly flawed notion of the putative objectivity of classical styles. Malraux assumes that sensory input as such has remained more or less constant through history and accordingly conceives of the classical ideal as an effort to reflect and reproduce that input. As we have seen, however, the very idea of determinately given sense data is confused, for it is meant to satisfy two competing, often conflicting, identity criteria, namely sensory stimulus and phenomenal appearance. The moon looks bigger on the horizon than at its zenith, though its angular diameter, hence stimulus value, remains constant. So, how big *does* it look?[11]

Classical painters cannot simply have been trying to mimic or duplicate the world, even if they said they were. Instead, "classical perspective is just one of the ways man has invented for projecting the perceived world before him, it is not the copy of that world. It is an optional interpretation of spontaneous vision" (S 61/48–9/86). Granted, some paintings approximate the formal and material properties of natural vision more closely than others. But this is like saying that some particular pieces of music express emotion better than others. That is true, but it does not imply that there is a single musical form or tradition best suited to the expression of emotion. And neither is there a single aesthetic style best suited to the evocation of visual experience. Given some artistic techniques and resources, one can always do better or worse, but nature does not —indeed cannot—prefer one style over others *a priori*.

Nor is modern nonfigurative painting in any sense merely subjective or unworldly. Even the most painstakingly realistic portraits and still lifes are always saturated with culturally specific style and significance, just as the most abstract art inevitably makes reference to a world, however flattened or distorted its aspect. How could it be otherwise? If human being just is being in the world, what could a retreat from the world amount to? The very idea is incoherent: "How would the painter or poet express anything other than his encounter with the world? What does abstract art itself speak of, if not a negation or refusal of the world? ... the painting always says something" (S 70–71/56/93).

The evolution from classical to modern art, from representation to abstraction, is not a retreat from the outer to the inner, from objectivity to subjectivity, but an evolution from an emphasis on objects and their properties to a meditation on the mystery of visibility as such: "what replaces the object is not the subject, it is the allusive logic of the perceived world" (S 71/57/94). In identifying modern art with subjectivity, Malraux loses sight of the artist's essential embeddedness and entanglement in the world and in effect "makes painters divine" (S 73/58/95). In part, this is because his attitude is that of the admiring spectator, the connoisseur, not the working artist. The artist sees his own work not as transcending the world and history, but as constantly caught up in and responding to the world: "In his eyes, his work is never completed; it is always in progress, so that no one can prevail against the world" (S 73/58/95).

3. CÉZANNE AND HIS WORLD

If all painting is essentially worldly, as Merleau-Ponty insists, then to understand a work of art is to understand its involvement in the world, not its transcendence of historical and psychological conditions or its inclusion in an ideal "imaginary museum" of great works, each embodying the same "unseen presence, the spirit of art," as Malraux says.[12]

This is not to say that the meaning of a work of art can be reduced to the accidents and idiosyncrasies of the artist's personality and circumstances, for no amount of psychological and biographical information can dispel the undeniable manifestation of meaning that tempts critics like Malraux to speak, all too vaguely, following Hegel, of a universal, superhistorical spirit of art. Still, Merleau-Ponty rejects Malraux's appeal to timeless values and transcendent sources of inspiration: "the devotion to artists that precludes our knowing anything about their lives and places their work beyond private or public history and outside the world like a miracle, hides their true greatness from us" (S 80/64/101).

How then should we understand the surplus meaning that surfaces in works of art and cannot be reduced to the psychological and historical accidents that produced them? On Merleau-Ponty's account, the convergence and coherence of artistic styles—on a small scale in miniatures and coins and on a large scale in painting and sculpture, for example, or in distant parts of the world between which there could be no lines of influence—is a reflection of the convergence and coherence of bodily styles that characterize human perception and action generally. One can choose to view the constancy of style as a kind of miracle, but there is nothing literally extraordinary about it, for it is ubiquitous in human life. If it is a miracle, it is a mundane miracle characteristic of all behavior: "Here, the spirit of the world is ourselves, as soon as we know how to move and look. These simple acts already contain the secret of expressive action" (S 82–83/66/103); "the presence of style ... is bound up with the fact of our corporeity and does not call for any occult explanation" (S 84/67/104). And phenomenology helps us to see this: "the theory of perception reinstalls the painter in the visible world and rediscovers the body as spontaneous expression" (S 81/65/102).

Merleau-Ponty's account of the generality of perceptual and artistic style forges a middle way between relativism and universalism, more specifically between psychologism and Platonism. There are no forms or archetypes guiding artistic expression *a priori*, yet neither are the styles and works of one culture wholly idiosyncratic, hence opaque and unintelligible to others: "We must understand why what one culture produces makes sense to another culture, even if not its original sense" (S 84/68/104).

The meaning that emerges in historical and intercultural interpretation is not a meaning already fully formed in the acts or intentions of artists, for there is always a "significance the work has in excess of the painter's deliberate intentions" (S 85/68/105). That significance is at once a product and a condition of the relative unity of the world of human works. As a result, the diversity of artistic traditions is not a mere chaos of differences, but constitutes *one* history, "*one* universe of painting" (S 84/68/104). This is because human expression is in principle intelligible and interpretable: "every gesture is *comparable* to every other, they all arise from a single syntax" (S 85/68/105).

What gets lost both in glib universal narratives of the history of art and in highly particularized psychological profiles of the lives of artists is the essential intertwining of individual style and publicly available meaning. That combination sounds paradoxical only if we cling to artificially polarized categories of particular and universal, concrete and abstract. It looks less problematic if we remind ourselves that every person is just such a blend of individual character and generic recognizability, for

> the body is capable of gathering itself into a gesture that ... puts a
> stamp on everything it does. In the same way, we may speak of a

unity of human style that transcends temporal and spatial
distances to bring the gestures of all painters together in a single
effort, and their works in a single cumulative history, a single art.

(S 86/68–69/105)

In both art and literature, "the continued attempt at expression
constitutes a single history—just as the grip [prise] our body has
on every possible object constitutes a single space" (S 87/70/107).
Perceived space is not the idealized manifold of Euclidean geometry or Newtonian mechanics, but a roughly unified field of
possible situations and actions. Likewise, the history of art is not
Malraux's imaginary museum, but a roughly unified field of
expressive possibilities, held together by the structure of our shared
body schema.

"Cézanne's Doubt" is an attempt to illustrate this point with
reference to a particular artist's life and work. Cézanne was by all
accounts an anxious, insecure, and unsociable person.[13] It is of
course possible to regard Cézanne's (or anyone's) paintings as
symptoms, as reflections of his idiosyncrasies rather than as
speaking to us about the world and perception. And yet his style
was not just an emanation of his inner feelings and attitudes.
Indeed, works of art are never mere reflections of the actions and
attitudes of artists. Art history and criticism are not psychology:
"Admitting that the painter likes to handle colors (the sculptor,
clay) because he is 'anal'—this does not always tell us what it is to
pain or sculpt" (S 80/64/100–1). What Cézanne painted was not
his own mind, but the world he saw:

The meaning Cézanne gave to objects and faces in his paintings
presented itself to him in the world as it appeared to him.
Cézanne simply released this meaning: it was the objects and the
faces themselves as he saw them that demanded to be painted,
and Cézanne simply expressed what they *wanted* to say.

(SNS 27/21/71)

Generated from within or from without, were his paintings merely effects of his encounter with the world? Did he not freely create them? If they sprang uniquely from his innate character and arbitrarily given circumstances, "How ... can any freedom be involved?" (SNS 27/21/71).

Sartre, for his part, insists that freedom is metaphysically primitive. Every human life, he argues, involves a free project or primal choice that cannot be squared with any form of biological, historical, or psychological determinism. Consciousness is a metaphysical gratuity, a floating bubble in reality, incommensurable with empirically observable causes and effects.

Merleau-Ponty rejects Sartre's account of freedom as, at best, a distorted and abstract image of just one aspect of a richer, more complex, more ambiguous phenomenon. More precisely, for Merleau-Ponty, free action would be impossible without the inertia imposed on us by our bodies and our environments: "Will presupposes a field of possibilities among which I choose" (PP 189/162/188). If consciousness were as frictionless as Sartre imagines, there could be no behavior, no action, no choice:

> our life always has the form of a project or choice, and therefore seems to us spontaneous. But to say that we are from the start the way we aim at our future would be to say that our project has already stopped with our first ways of being, that the choice has already been made for us with our first breath.
>
> (SNS 27/21/71)

Freedom presupposes a world of constrained and conditioned opportunities given in perception and practical life, again a "clearly articulated field of possibilities" (SNS 27/21/71). Within that field, we are free, but to be free is not to wrench ourselves out of the natural or social world altogether. Sartre's notion of freedom is as incoherent as Kant's image of the dove striving to fly out of the atmosphere: "existence never outruns anything entirely, for then the tension that is essential to it would disappear" (PP 197/169/ 196). We are free not by escaping the constraints of the world, but precisely by being in their grip: "freedom dawns on us without breaking our bonds with the world" (SNS 28/21/72); "our freedom rests on being in a situation, and is itself a situation" (PP 191/164/190).

Unlike Cézanne, Leonardo da Vinci was by all accounts a placid, detached, intellectualized, sexually indifferent—or perhaps, as Freud suspected, thoroughly sublimated—individual.[14] Perhaps he only ever loved his mother, perhaps he never really grew up, perhaps his many unfinished works and bizarre experiments were the products of some form of psychosexual frustration. However arbitrary such hypotheses may be, Merleau-Ponty insists that insight can be gained from what he calls "*psychoanalytic intuition*" (SNS 31/ 24/74) and "the psychoanalyst's hermeneutic musing" (SNS 32/ 25/75). What psychoanalysis reveals is a "relations of motivation" (SNS 31/24/74). Such relations can occur piecemeal, but they can also constitute a more general schema of interpretation, a recognizable character or style: "in every life, one's birth and one's past define categories or basic dimensions that do not impose any particular act, but can be found in all" (SNS 31–32/24/75). Such a style is intelligible only in the context of a world, in the concrete situations in which it is implicated: "the very decisions that transform us are always made in reference to a factual situation" (SNS 32/25/75).

No amount of psychoanalytic insight or interpretation should tempt us to dismiss such a style as the mere effect of a cause, for it is the behavior itself qua free that poses the questions psychoanalysis tries to answer, and we take freedom for granted when we ask for a psychoanalytic account. What might look like reductive causal explanation, in Freudian metapsychology for example, is in fact intelligible explication of the motivations and circumstances that gave rise to the action, precisely by conditioning and constraining it: "Psychoanalysis does not make freedom impossible, it teaches us to think of this freedom concretely" (SNS 32/25/75). It does this by extending ordinary psychological explanation into domains in which it was not previously considered applicable:

> It would be a mistake to imagine that even with Freud psychoanalysis rules out the description of psychological motives and is opposed to the phenomenological method; it has on the contrary (albeit unwittingly) helped to develop it by affirming, in Freud's words, that every human action "has a sense" [sens][15] and making every effort to understand the event, short of relating it to mechanical conditions.
>
> (PP 184–85/158/183)

Sexuality, for example, which figures so centrally and pervasively in Freudian theory, is not a purely physiological function, but a complex system of affects, desires, wishes, fantasies, and pleasures. Nor is it merely an isolated element in our psychic lives, but a global aspect of our being in the world. Finding sexual significance in seemingly nonsexual contexts is thus not the crudely reductive maneuver it might appear to be. On the contrary, if anything, it is almost trivial, assigning as it does a new, broader sense to the term "sexual," as opposed to preserving the older, narrower sense and thus reconstruing human behavior in crudely erotic terms:

> Since sexual life can no longer be circumscribed, since it is no longer a separate function definable in terms of the causality proper to a set of organs, there is now no sense in saying that all existence is understood through sexual life, or rather this statement becomes a tautology.
>
> (PP 185/159/184)

Human biological phenomena in general cannot be understood in mechanical terms, for "biological existence is geared to [embrayée sur] human existence and is never indifferent to its distinctive

rhythm" (PP 186/160/185). Bodily and mental events are intertwined, they express one another, and so are never just meaningless
occurrences: "the life of the body, or the carnal, and the life of the
psyche are involved in a relation of reciprocal *expression*," so that
"the bodily event always has a psychic significance" (PP 186–87/
160/185).

The psychoanalytic patient who loses her voice, for example,
neither suffers actual paralysis nor merely chooses to remain silent.
Likewise, she "will recover her voice, not by an intellectual effort
or by an abstract decree of the will, but through a conversion in
which the whole of her body makes a concentrated effort in the
form of a genuine gesture" (PP 192/165/191). The human body is
always an expression of human existence, for "existence realizes
itself in the body. This incarnate significance is the central phenomenon of which body and mind, sign and significance are
abstract moments" (PP 193/166/192). Meaning emerges in our
taking up situations, responding to them, and letting them in turn
shape us:

> Human existence ... is the transformation of contingency into
> necessity by an act of repossession [*reprise*]. All that we are, we
> are on the basis of a *de facto* situation that we appropriate to
> ourselves and that we ceaselessly transform by a sort of *escape*
> that is never an unconditioned freedom.
>
> (*PP* 199/170–71/198)

Mechanical determinism and Sartrean freedom are two false abstractions
that miss, on either side, the complex intertwining of world and
behavior, situation and action, circumstance and spontaneity.

This general account of conditioned freedom might strike the
reader as a mere digression or tangent leading away from the other
line of argument, which "Cézanne's Doubt" shares with "Eye and
Mind," the more narrowly focused discussion of depth, visibility,
and the capacity of painting to capture them by exploiting and

refining the expressivity always already at work in perception itself. Yet the two lines of thought converge in the idea we have found at the center of Merleau-Ponty's work from the outset, namely, that perception and action are two sides of the same coin, two aspects of a single phenomenon. Human freedom, whether manifest in ordinary everyday behavior or in the extraordinary achievement of a creative artist, can be understood only in its concrete perceptual setting, which is to say our bodily encounter with and immersion in a world that reveals itself to us as at once thickly visible, solidly real, and inexhaustibly deep. Likewise, the visibility, reality, and depth of the world must in turn be as revealed to a subject receptive to it neither purely passively in sensation nor purely spontaneously in thought, but in virtue of a bodily being in the world that is always already expressive and free, even in its most basic sensitivities and comportments. "Cézanne's Doubt" looks like two separate lines of argument, two essays in one, only if we forget the moral of Merleau-Ponty's phenomenological story, namely, that perception and freedom are inseparable, that every perceiving is a doing, and every doing stands in relation to a world disclosed in perception.

SUMMARY

Merleau-Ponty's writings on the philosophy of art concentrate on three main themes. The first has to do with the depth or thickness of things, both in sense experience and in Cézanne's paintings, which somehow seem to capture the perceptual weight of the world. We do not perceive discrete properties or surface appearances, but whole things, and we do so not just with our eyes or ears or brains, but with our whole bodies.

The second theme concerns the nature of meaning and expression. Linguistic meaning differs fundamentally from perceptual meaning, not because perception is simply lacking expressive and stylistic significance, but because it discloses forms of significance different from and irreducible to the articulated content of symbolic expressions. Our perceptual *grip* on things is not the same as our conceptual *grasp* of concepts. Malraux, in *The Voices of Silence*, too casually construes the visual arts as constituting their own kind of "language" and wrongly imagines, with Hegel, that modern art has withdrawn from the sensible world altogether into the subjective interior of self-consciousness.

Third, in the essay "Cézanne's Doubt" Merleau-Ponty reflects on the intertwining of the historical and social conditionedness of our lives and our capacity for free and creative self-definition. Cézanne was a disturbed and depressed person, but from out of his anxiety he was able to seize on that weight and solidity of the visible world, from which we can never extricate ourselves. Psychoanalysis, at its best, offers hermeneutical insight into the life and work of artists like Leonardo and Cézanne without trivializing their achievements as a mere effect of neurosis. Like perception itself, Cézanne's paintings make manifest the necessarily constrained disclosure of the world, the confluence of our subjugation to it and its openness to our gaze and grip.

FURTHER READING

Baldwin, T. "Speaking and Spoken Speech." A critical discussion of Merleau-Ponty's distinction between two aspects of language: spontaneous expressive behavior ("speaking speech") and sedimented or codified systems of signs ("spoken speech").

Gilmore, J. "Between Philosophy and Art." An overview of Merleau-Ponty's writings on art. Gilmore observes, correctly, that Merleau-Ponty does not offer a general theory of art, but a phenomenological interpretation of select works at a particular moment in the history of art.

Panofsky, E. *Perspective as Symbolic Form.* Highly influential theory of Renaissance perspective as one element of a culturally specific form of intelligibility, as opposed to a uniquely correct copy of perceptual representation. Merleau-Ponty refers approvingly to this essay in "Eye and Mind" (Œ 49, 90/174, 189/135, 148).

Seven

Legacy and Relevance

Merleau-Ponty's influence on intellectual life in the near half-century since his death has been solid and steady, yet somewhat less spectacular than one might expect, considering the power of his ideas and their increasing relevance to contemporary philosophy, psychology, and neuroscience. His reputation in philosophy proper has tended to be overshadowed by the other major figures in phenomenology: Husserl, Heidegger, and Sartre. Husserl and Heidegger were of course the pioneers of phenomenology, while Sartre's literary brilliance and versatility made him a more charismatic intellectual celebrity in the heyday of existentialism. Unlike Merleau-Ponty, Sartre also had the good fortune of surviving into the 1960s and 1970s to see a younger generation of readers take renewed interest in his work. Later, with the rise of structuralism in France and the United States, Merleau-Ponty was all too often dismissed as belonging to a bygone era marked by naïve philosophical earnestness, in contrast to the more thoroughly critical—indeed, often ironic and evasive—styles of discourse that became fashionable in the meantime, especially in literary theory and cultural studies.

Yet Merleau-Ponty's work is arguably more topical and urgent now than ever. And far from being a philosophical throwback rendered quaint by the rise of structuralism, Merleau-Ponty played a vital role in the emergence of structuralist discourse in the 1950s. The philosophical significance of his work has also become clearer with the passage of time, thanks in part to developments in analytical philosophy of mind and language, psychology, neuroscience, and sociology.

1. STRUCTURALISM AND THE *HABITUS*

Merleau-Ponty often describes perceptual and bodily phenomena in terms of what he calls their "structures," as for example in the title of his first book, The Structure of Behavior. The "behavior" (comportement) Merleau-Ponty had in mind was not the objectively measurable bodily movement into which behaviorists once supposed all mental phenomena could in principle be analyzed, but the meaningful actions and activities familiar to ordinary understanding. Nor was Merleau-Ponty's notion of structure a wholly objective concept, for it referred not to impersonal, invariant, and unconscious patterns in nature, culture, and language, but to intuitively intelligible configurations and ensembles grasped from a concrete situated perspective. Structure for Merleau-Ponty was, in short, not the structure posited in what later came to be known as structuralism, but rather the form or "shape" (Gestalt) of Gestalt psychology.

Merleau-Ponty did, however, happen to be a close friend of Claude Lévi-Strauss, who was elected to the Collège de France in 1959 on Merleau-Ponty's recommendation. In 1962 Lévi-Strauss dedicated his book The Savage Mind to his deceased friend, and Merleau-Ponty's picture always sat on his desk.[1] On the face of it, their respective philosophical outlooks and intellectual values seem worlds apart. Lévi-Strauss, for his part, apparently had little interest in bridging the gulf between experience and the formal structures he claimed to have discovered in kinship, myth, and cuisine. In his 1955 memoir, Tristes Tropiques, his writes, "Phenomenology I found objectionable in that it postulated a kind of continuity between experience and reality. ... but I had learned ... that the transition between one order and the other is discontinuous." For Lévi-Strauss, serious inquiry should not busy itself with "the illusions of subjectivity." Rather, "the mission incumbent on philosophy until science becomes strong enough to replace it" is "to understand being in relationship to itself and not in relationship to myself."[2]

And yet Lévi-Strauss concedes that his conception of scientific knowledge is not as dispassionate and indifferent to human interests as he sometimes suggests. Like Merleau-Ponty, and in spite of his insistence on the gap between experience and reality, he takes for granted a kind of continuity between ourselves and the world as described by the sciences. Knowledge consists, he says,

> in selecting *true* aspects, that is, those coinciding with the properties of my thought. Not, as the Neo-Kantians claimed, because my thought exercises an inevitable influence over things, but because it is itself an object. Being "of this world," it partakes of the same nature as the world.[3]

There must, after all, be some kind of metaphysical and epistemological affinity or continuity between ourselves and the world, otherwise things would be forever alien and opaque to us. Lévi-Strauss was anxious to avoid idealism, the notion that objective reality is somehow answerable in principle to conditions peculiar to the subject. Being an anthropologist rather than a philosopher, he was of course under no compulsion to explain how knowledge itself is possible. And yet his passing observation that thought "partakes of the same nature as the world" is strikingly similar to Merleau-Ponty's concept of flesh. Perhaps this is no accident, for he wrote those words when he knew Merleau-Ponty, indeed just when Merleau-Ponty was beginning to formulate his account of our unconscious continuity with the world we inhabit and know.

Still, Merleau-Ponty was a philosopher, Lévi-Strauss was an anthropologist, and their differences were emblematic of the relative decline of philosophy and the rise of the human sciences in French intellectual life in the middle of the century. As Lévi-Strauss put it some 30 years later, "I asked him what existentialism was. He answered: an attempt to reestablish great philosophy in the tradition of Descartes and Kant. ... Merleau-Ponty believed in philosophic thought."[4] More precisely, what Merleau-Ponty believed in was the *relative* autonomy of philosophic thought, which both science-minded structuralists like Lévi-Strauss and literary-minded theorists like Jacques Derrida would deny.

Like Sartre, and unlike many younger structuralists and poststructuralists, Merleau-Ponty believed in philosophy. Unlike Sartre, however, whose nonphilosophical interests lay primarily in literature and politics, he also read widely and lectured enthusiastically on structural linguistics and anthropology to a generation of future social and literary theorists. Although he was not a structuralist, he expressed sympathy for a concept of structure that is no longer just the intuitive *Gestalt* (shape or form) of Gestalt psychology. In a short essay entitled "From Mauss to Lévi-Strauss," for example, he writes,

> This notion of structure, whose present good fortune in all domains responds to an intellectual need, establishes a whole system of thought. For the philosopher, the presence of structure outside us in natural and social systems and within us as symbolic function points to a way beyond the subject–object correlation that has dominated philosophy from Descartes to Hegel. By showing us that man is eccentric to himself and that the social finds its center only in man, structure particularly enables us to understand how we are in a sort of circuit with the sociohistorical world.
>
> (S 155/123)

These are the words not of someone trying nostalgically "to reestablish great philosophy in the tradition of Descartes and Kant," but of someone attentive to an important new research program. Merleau-Ponty knew full well that structuralism did not sit well with phenomenology, the concrete description of (more or less) manifest forms and contents of experience. Yet he was eager to avail himself of insights that theorists like Saussure and Lévi-Strauss might have to offer into our complex reciprocal relation to the world, the "circuit" in which we stand to patterns that transcend consciousness and subjectivity.

Merleau-Ponty thus played a vital pedagogical role in the emergence of structuralism, as the linguist Michel Arrivé recalls: "Merleau-Ponty was an eminent mediator; it is very certainly thanks to him that Lacan read Saussure." Similarly, Jean-Marie Benoist remarks, "Merleau-Ponty acted like a precursor phase conditioning the reception of the richness of structuralist work."[5] Unlike many of his younger listeners, however, Merleau-Ponty remained committed to the philosophical relevance of ordinary experience and understanding. Vincent Descombes says, "I remember his course on Lévi-Strauss, where he presented him as the algebra of kinship in need of completion by the meaning of the familial for humans: paternity, filiation."[6]

Although phenomenology came to be considered *passé* in the 1960s and 1970s, many of Merleau-Ponty's central insights meanwhile found a voice in the work of sociologist Pierre Bourdieu. Though trained in the structuralist tradition, Bourdieu insists on the essential role of concrete bodily skills in the ongoing configuration and reconfiguration of social reality. Like Merleau-Ponty, Bourdieu maintains that the *social field* is always conceptually interdefined and causally interconnected with what he calls the *habitus*, the bodily capacities and "systems of durable, transposable dispositions" that both structure and are structured by the social environment.[7]

The *habitus* is, in essence, the socially conditioned *body schema*. It is not a mental state, a conscious or cognitive attitude, nor even a network of such attitudes, but a set of bodily habits produced and stabilized by the social world, which they in turn reproduce and restabilize. It is this reciprocal intermeshing of intuitive bodily skills and structured social field that generates the appearance— indeed, Bourdieu sometimes says, the *illusion*—of a fixed, determined, objective social order, "the continuity and regularity which objectivism sees in social practices without being able to account for it."[8] Social practices and institutions are indeed relatively continuous and regular, but this is due precisely to their absorption and anchoring in the *habitus*, which continually projects and perpetuates the forms we ordinarily regard as simply natural and inevitable, right and proper. Virtually paraphrasing Merleau-Ponty, Bourdieu writes, "Nothing is more misleading than the illusion created by hindsight in which all the traces of a life, such as the works of an artist or the events of a biography, appear as the realization of an essence that seems to preexist them."[9]

The *habitus* is not a conceptual capacity, but a kind of schematizing bodily intelligence, a "practical sense" (*sens pratique*), which is neither fully available to consciousness nor fully subject to rational deliberation. Yet neither is it merely a causal system of socially conditioned physiological capacities. This is what distinguishes Bourdieu's notion from John Searle's otherwise similar-sounding theory of "the Background." As Searle conceives it, the Background is "the capacities, abilities, and general know-how that enable our mental states to function."[10] Crucially, for Searle, the Background is *not* intentional; it has no *content* specifying or describing the world toward which it directs our actions and attitudes. It is instead "the set of nonintentional or preintentional capacities that enable intentional states of [sic] function." And indeed, "By *capacities* I mean," Searle writes, "*causal structures.*"[11] Yet he also describes the Background as "an inductively based set of expectations."[12] But *expectations* are intentional attitudes; they have *content*: I expect *that I will be applauded*, or more simply, *I expect applause*. Searle wants the Background to play the role of Bourdieu's *habitus*, not just causally supporting but *normatively guiding* our behavior. But this is an intermediary role that his own metaphysical categories will not allow it to play, for doing so would require acknowledging another kind of intentional content in addition to the descriptive content of self-conscious mental states, namely the *motor intentional* content of bodily skills.[13]

Moreover, unlike Bourdieu, Searle maintains that the normativity of social institutions is *exhausted* by the rules that a detached observer could in principle articulate in *describing* them: "the institutional structure is a structure of rules, and the actual rules that we specify in *describing* the institution will *determine* those aspects under which the system is normative."[14] This methodological privileging of the observer's point of view is just the opposite of Bourdieu's conception of the essentially prearticulate normativity of bodily practices, as distinct from the explicit articulation of rules from the conventionally authoritative standpoint of sociological observation. For Bourdieu, although it has its own rhythm and inertia as a kind of second nature, the *habitus*—indeed, precisely because it exceeds and resists cognition and reflection—is the concrete source of conventional propriety, the ground of social normativity·

> being the *product* of a particular class of objective regularities, the *habitus* tends to engender all the "reasonable," "common-sense" behaviors, and only those, that are possible within the limits of these regularities ... and which are likely to be positively sanctioned because they are objectively adjusted to the logic characteristic of a particular field, whose objective future they anticipate. At the same time, "without violence, art, or argument," it tends to exclude all "foolishness" [*folies*] ("it's not for us"), that is, all the behaviors that would be negatively sanctioned because they are incompatible with the objective conditions.[15]

The *habitus* is thus a dovetailing of normative and nonnormative aspects of practical behavior, a blend of conditionedness and spontaneity that is constitutive of concrete freedom. Bourdieu's conception and application of the idea in sociology have been one of the most fruitful and important legacies of Merleau-Ponty's thought.

2. BEHAVIORISM, COGNITIVISM, AND ARTIFICIAL INTELLIGENCE

Merleau-Ponty's phenomenology has also played a significant role in contemporary philosophy of mind, psychology, and cognitive science, not only in theories of perception, but in critical engagements with cognitivism, artificial intelligence, and conceptualist theories of intentional content.

Charles Taylor was one of the first and best Anglo-American readers of the existential phenomenologists, and his systematic work, *The Explanation of Behaviour*, owes much to Merleau-Ponty in particular.[16] In that book, drawing on both *The Structure of Behavior* and *Phenomenology of Perception*, Taylor defends the coherence and plausibility of the kind of teleological explanation we rely on in understanding animal behavior and human action, insists on the intentional character of action, and makes a powerful case for the sterility of behaviorist attempts to reduce action and behavior to observable movements and dispositions to move. According to Taylor, the conflict between mechanical and teleological theories of behavior must be decided not *a priori* on purely conceptual grounds, but in terms of their empirical plausibility and fruitfulness. Subsequent developments in philosophy and psychology appear to have confirmed Taylor's claim that behaviorism was indeed a scientific dead end.

Taylor also indirectly sparked a lively debate in the philosophy of mind concerning the nature of perceptual content, specifically whether experience can be intentional but nonconceptual. In an essay on "Demonstrative Identification," Gareth Evans argued that a kind of nonconceptual content must underlie and inform our basic judgments about the world, for example in those states that allow animals to sense their own bodily position and orientation. Thus, "When we hear a sound as coming from a certain direction, we do not have to *think* or *calculate* which way to turn our heads (say) in order to look for the source of the sound."[17] It is no accident that Evans appeals to Taylor, who was in turn drawing on Merleau-Ponty. Yet Evans seems to miss something crucial in stressing only the factual information contained in such states, at the expense of what Taylor and Merleau-Ponty insist is their normative aspect. Evans thus elides some of the most important remarks in the passage he quotes from Taylor, for although he recognizes the essential links between perception and movement, he says nothing of the bodily sense of *rightness* and *wrongness* arguably inherent in the perceptual field. It is worth quoting Taylor's original comments more fully than Evans does:

> Our perceptual field has an orientational structure ... In those rare moments where we lose orientation, we don't know where we are; and we don't know where or what things are either; we lose the thread of the world, and our perceptual field is no longer our access to the world, but rather the confused debris into which our normal grasp on things crumbles. ... It is not just that the field's perspective centers on where I am bodily this by itself doesn't show that I am essentially agent. But take the up-down directionality of the field. What is it based on? Up and down are not simply related to my body; up is not just where my head is and down where my feet are. For I can be lying down, or bending over, or upside down ... I have to maintain myself upright to act, or in some way align my posture with gravity. Without a sense of "which way is up," I falter into confusion.[18]

To be *oriented* in the relevant sense is not just to be here or there, in front of, behind, or to the right or left of something, but to be *guided* by "the thread of the world." Conversely, to lose our orientation is to get lost, to be thrown into confusion, to lose our grip.

The nonconceptual content informing our ordinary behavior does not just inform us in a blandly factual way about our bodily position relative to objects in the environment, nor do my bodily movements appear to me as mere physical events. Rather, I experience my behavior as subject to the demands of the situation: my body does what it must do in order to get me where I need to be, to do what needs to be done. So too, I am not merely accustomed to the fact that if I turn my head, I *will* see the tree. Rather, I know that in *order* to see the tree, I *need* to turn my head. Seeing the tree requires that I turn to look at it. It is not just that the environment presents me with sensory input that I know as a matter of fact to be correlated in various ways with the movements of my body, even granting that I somehow grasp that fact without calculating or thinking about it. My environment is also a world and so confronts me with both options and demands. A world is not just what is the case, but also always affords, tempts, facilitates, obtrudes, resists, thwarts, eludes, and coerces. Things present themselves to me with positive and negative valence of all kinds, primordially and inextricably fused with my own bodily needs and capacities.[19]

Nonconceptual content remains a controversial notion among philosophers of mind and theorists of perception. John McDowell's influential Mind and World challenges the idea by equating conceptuality with normativity: if content is normative, he argues, as it must be to justify rather than merely trigger our beliefs, then it must also be conceptual, even if the concept in question is demonstrative, as in that shade of red.[20] In any case, as he points out, Evans's account gives no comfort to those who maintain that perception has conscious nonconceptual content, for Evans believed that perceptual awareness requires concepts. Replying to McDowell, Christopher Peacocke has defended the notion of nonconceptual content on the grounds that concepts are either too crude or too refined to capture the qualities presented in perception. For whereas a concept like red is too coarse-grained to specify precisely what I see when I see something red, a demonstrative concept such as this shade of red imports a notion of shade that need not play any role in my sensory experience as such.[21] Sean Kelly, again appealing explicitly to Merleau-Ponty, has argued that the nonconceptual content of perception is due not only to the context-dependence of the appearance of objects, but also to the object-dependence of the appearance of qualities. Not only do the same things look different in different situations, but generically similar properties differ phenomenally depending on the kinds of objects they are properties of.[22] As Sartre says, and as Merleau-Ponty reiterates, when Matisse paints a red carpet, he manages to evoke the color not as an abstract property, but as a concrete feature of a genuinely tactile object: what he paints is not just *red*, but "a *woolly* red."[23]

With the early Heidegger and the later Wittgenstein, Merleau-Ponty is one of the main sources of inspiration behind the critique of cognitivism, conceptualism, and artificial intelligence (AI) that Hubert Dreyfus has been pursuing since the mid-1960s. First in a controversial report written for the RAND Corporation in 1964, entitled "Alchemy and Artificial Intelligence," and then more fully in *What Computers Can't Do* and *Mind over Machine* (written with his brother, Stuart), Dreyfus has argued that early efforts at "cognitive simulation," then mainstream AI, and finally the design of more specialized "expert systems" have all been from the outset phenomenologically misguided, conceptually confused, and—perhaps most importantly—chronically unsupported by empirical evidence and experimental success. Such programmed systems have consistently failed to exhibit characteristic features of commonsense understanding, namely fringe or horizonal awareness, or tacit sensitivity to "background" elements in the perceptual or cognitive field; ambiguity tolerance and context sensitivity; discrimination between essential and inessential, or relevant and irrelevant features of objects and situations; and the recognition of patterns and "typical" cases and the ability to group things bearing only loosely overlapping "family resemblances," as Wittgenstein called them, as opposed to discrete shared properties involved in explicit classificatory schemes.[24]

Unlike Searle, who claims to have shown that thought cannot in principle be defined by computational states and operations, Dreyfus's case against AI, like Taylor's critique of behaviorism, rests on its phenomenological and conceptual implausibility and its *de facto* empirical failure. Phenomenology is thus vital to Dreyfus's critique in a way it is not to Searle's, for whereas Searle (rightly or wrongly) claims to have proven that computation is not sufficient for thought, Dreyfus merely insists that there is no reason, conceptual or empirical, to believe that it is.[25]

Although Heidegger is the figure to whom Drefyus most frequently appeals, his argument frequently draws more directly from *Phenomenology of Perception* than from *Being and Time*. Heidegger's existential analytic of Dasein challenges all forms of mental representationalism, not just Cartesian dualism, but all mentalist, internalist, and intellectualist theories of understanding, including modern cognitivism and computationalism. If, as Heidegger maintains, human being is essentially being-in-the-world, then the very idea of a mind related to the world through internal representations is already a gross misdescription of the phenomena that a theory of action and intelligence ought to explain. Dreyfus's critique of AI proceeds from that basic Heideggerian insight, yet it relies in detail on Merleau-Ponty's phenomenology of the body and perception, which are at best only implicit in Heidegger, who said little about other animals and almost nothing about the body. It is Merleau-Ponty, not Heidegger, who insists that *bodily skills* are constitutive of intelligence, from which Dreyfus infers that the disembodied symbol manipulation performed by computers has no realistic hope of reproducing the concrete, flexible, intuitive, and nuanced competent behavior we share with many (not all) other animals. As Dreyfus says,

> If the body turns out to be indispensable for intelligent behavior, then we shall have to ask whether the body can be simulated on a heuristically programmed digital computer. If not, then the project of artificial intelligence is doomed from the start.[26]

Dreyfus's objections to AI were never merely theoretical, but ethical and existential as well. From the beginning, his recognition of the sterility of AI as a research program was part of a wider critique of an entire culture enamored of the idea of man-made machine intelligence, an idea frequently exploited to justify massive funding of dubious research projects, utopian hype, and an increasingly distorted and nihilistic image of human life. Dreyfus has thus enlisted Merleau-Ponty's phenomenology, along with Kierkegaard's critique of modernity and Heidegger's later essays, in making a case for the practical dangers lurking in our increasingly technological understanding of ourselves.[27]

With Taylor and Dreyfus, Samuel Todes was among the first Anglo-American philosophers to appreciate Merleau-Ponty's importance. The dissertation he wrote at Harvard in 1963, *The Human Body as Material Subject of the World*, was republished posthumously under the title *Body and World*—a critical allusion to McDowell's *Mind and World* (at Dreyfus's suggestion). In it Todes applies, but also extends and enriches, Merleau-Ponty's phenomenology, first by enlisting it in a detailed critique of early modern metaphysics and epistemology, then by further specifying the ways in which the formal structure of the world is correlated with the concrete material structures and capacities of the body. Whereas Merleau-Ponty says little about the contingent corporeal forms peculiar to human beings, over and beyond perspectival orientation and figure/ground contrast, Todes ingeniously notes the crucial importance of facts such as that we stand upright in a gravitational field, that we face— hence look and move—forward rather than backward, and that we must therefore turn *around* to survey what are quite literally our given "circumstances."[28]

3. EMBODIED COGNITION, EXTENDED MIND, ENACTIVISM

Finally, it should be noted that Merleau-Ponty's work has recently been cited by theorists of perception whose views in fact have little in common with his. At the intersection of philosophy, psychology, and neuroscience, for example, a cluster of so-called "enactive" theorists of mind and perception have identified Merleau-Ponty's phenomenology as a friendly precursor, if not a positive inspiration.

The late neurobiologist Francisco Varela, for example, conceived his theory of *embodied cognition* as an elaboration of (and improvement on) Merleau-Ponty's phenomenology. Many of Varela's claims, however, are drawn from brain science and Buddhist meditation practices and so, in either case, have little to do with ordinary lived experience. He argues, for example, that consciousness is not really continuous and unified, as it seems to be, but fragmentary and parceled out in discrete bursts corresponding to synchronous firings of clusters of brain cells, roughly once every second.[29] Buddhism is supposed to help us see the relevance of this to our lives: "An examination of experience with mindfulness/awareness reveals that one's experience is discontinuous—a moment of consciousness arises, appears to dwell for an instant, and then vanishes, to be replaced by the next moment."[30]

Merleau-Ponty, I think, would never dismiss the testimony of ordinary experience in this way in favor of such dubious conclusions gleaned from neurophysiology, let alone artificial effects induced by meditation. If brain activity is discontinuous second by second, then it remains to account for our ordinary sense of enduring bodily and personal identity. Confronted with that challenge, Merleau-Ponty would draw attention to those aspects of the body schema that ground our intuitive sense of personal unity and continuity, notwithstanding whatever patterns of electrical activity may be going on at the neuronal level. By itself, the mere fact that brain activity is discontinuous on that smaller scale is arguably no more (or less) interesting than the fact that solid objects like Sir Arthur Eddington's desk turn out to be composed of atoms separated by relatively vast stretches of empty space. The empty space between atoms says nothing against the solidity of Eddington's desk, and neither does discontinuity in the firing of neurons say anything against the phenomenological continuity of conscious experience.[31]

In a somewhat different vein, Andy Clark and David Chalmers have suggested that the mind is not confined to the head or even the whole body of the organism, but is literally "extended" into the surrounding physical environment. For example, although we often perform calculations or consult memories with no apparent external

support, we also sometimes use devices to assist with those operations. So, why not say that we think, believe, and remember not
just with our brains, but with our fingers, or even with pencil and
paper? Echoing Hilary Putnam's memorable slogan about linguistic
meaning, they write, "Cognitive processes ain't (all) in the head!"[32]
Clark has elaborated this theory in his book, Being There.

In spite of that Heideggerian-sounding title and the occasional
friendly quotations from Merleau-Ponty that find their way into the
text, Clark's argument in fact has very little in common with the
phenomenological sources he would like to enlist in his cause, and
for two reasons. First, what Clark is interested in is the mind, or
cognition. As we have seen, Merleau-Ponty, following Heidegger, is
concerned with perception not as a purely mental or cognitive
operation, but as an aspect of human existence that conditions and
situates thought. The question for them is not, How (or where) is cognition implemented in the physical world? but, How does cognition manifest itself as
intelligible to us in the wider context of our experience and behavior? Like so
much of the rest of contemporary philosophy of mind, Clark's
project focuses so exclusively and uncritically on the mind, that it
ignores the many noncognitive attitudes and competences that
condition and inform our understanding of the mental in the first
place.

The second reason Clark's program has so little to do with phenomenology is that the main issue he is addressing, namely the
(so-called) mind–body problem, is one the phenomenologists say
almost nothing about. Why not? Because it is not a phenomenological
question at all, but a metaphysical problem, posed from a naïvely
unsituated point of view, whose possible solutions have no direct
echo in experience. Phenomenology cannot tell us whether a
person is one substance or two, whether mental properties are
identical with physical properties, or how large a chunk of the
physical world functions as the substratum or vehicle of cognitive
process, whether it is the brain alone, the nervous system as a
whole, the entire organism, or perhaps the organism plus some its

favorite paraphernalia. What phenomenology can do instead is deny such questions their spurious metaphysical urgency by exposing them as, at best, empirical questions concerning causal mechanisms of perception and action, and then further deflate the problem by exposing its own phenomenological premises as distortions of actual lived experience. Do we experience ourselves as mind-body pairs? No. Do we experience ourselves as substances with properties? No. Phenomenology is descriptive, critical philosophy, not dogmatic metaphysics.

Finally, although he cites *Phenomenology of Perception* as one of several inspirations for his own version of enactivism in his book *Action in Perception*, Alva Noë likewise departs crucially from Merleau-Ponty by insisting that sensory *appearance* is more basic than full-fledged perception of the world. Perception, he says, is a "two-step process"; "perceiving is a way of finding out how things are from how they look or sound or, more generally, appear."[33] Noë's "appearances" are not sensations or sense data exactly, and yet the concept is arguably incoherent for the same reason, namely, the demand that it play two incompatible roles in the theory: first, to describe our objective relation to sensory *stimuli*; and second, to capture our experience of how things actually *seem*. So, for example, according to Noë, "there is a single apparent size of an object—namely, the unique way that an object looks with respect to size from a particular position. This is secured by phenomenology."[34] What, one wonders, is the "single apparent size" of the moon on the horizon? Is it the same as its "single apparent size" at its zenith? On Noë's criterion—which is geometrical, not phenomenological—it must be. And yet that's not how it *looks*.

So, are sensory appearances, or "P-properties" as Noë calls them, phenomenally manifest, perceptually conscious, or not? He insists that "P-properties are themselves *objects of sight*, things that we see. They are visible. From where you stand, you can see the P-shape of the plate, and you can distinguish this from the actual shape." Moreover, although "In normal life we tend to pay little attention to P-properties ...

This does not mean that we are not perceptually sensitive to them, even when we fail to attend to them." On the other hand, he believes, "One of the results of change blindness [experiments] is that we only see, we only experience, that to which we attend."[35] So, are we *seeing* P-properties even when we don't notice or attend to them, when we are not *aware* of them? And what is the evidence for that claim? It appears to be a mere theoretical stipulation. Noë's theory requires as a matter of principle that we see appearances as well as things; phenomenology does not.

Finally, and more fundamentally, Merleau-Ponty's phenomenology is, after all, an attempt to understand perception as a concrete bodily encounter with the world in which things are genuinely given—not merely conceived, imagined, remembered, entertained, anticipated, or surmised. On Noë's account, by contrast, the distinction between what is perceptually given and what is not turns out to be an illusion of naïve common sense. Although it seems as if some things and sides or aspects of things are given directly while others are hidden, horizonal, or "amodally" present, Noë concludes that "perceptual content is *thoroughly* virtual," or as he says, virtual "*all the way in.*"[36] But this not only threatens the distinction on which his theory rests, namely between given sensory appearances and the full-blown perceptual content constituted by its association with bodily movement it also in effect repudiates the very phenomenon a theory of perception ought to address, namely the *givenness* of the things to our senses, as distinct from the way we construe them in our thoughts, judgments, memories, wishes, expectations, and fantasies.

SUMMARY

Although Merleau-Ponty has not had the same impact on philosophy as the other major phenomenologists, his influence has been widely felt in French intellectual life and contemporary Anglo-American philosophy of mind. He played a vital role in the rise of structuralism in the 1950s by lecturing on Saussure and promoting the work of Lévi-Strauss. More recently, Bourdieu's account of social reality

230 **Merleau-Ponty**

as an interconnection of the bodily *habitus* and social field is indebted to Merleau-Ponty's notions of the body schema, motor intentionality, and the phenomenal field.

In Anglo-American philosophy, Merleau-Ponty has influenced Charles Taylor's critique of behaviorism and, through Taylor and Evans, contemporary debates about the nonconceptual content of perceptual experience. Merleau-Ponty is also arguably the chief source for Dreyfus's critique of AI, in some ways even more crucial than Heidegger, who says almost nothing about the body's role in intelligent behavior.

Not all recent enthusiasm about the significance of the body for intelligence and intentionality should be credited to (or blamed on) Merleau-Ponty, however. Varela's and Noë's "enactive" theories of embodied cognition and Clark's "extended mind" hypothesis, for example, remain embroiled in traditional epistemological and metaphysical problems, and so fail to appreciate Merleau-Ponty's effort to describe our ordinary intuitive understanding of ourselves and our place in the world.

FURTHER READING

Bourdieu, P. *The Logic of Practice*. Drawing tacitly on Merleau-Ponty, Bourdieu describes the social world as an interdependence of bodily *habitus* and social field. See especially chapters 3 and 4.

Carman, T. "On the Inescapability of Phenomenology." A Merleau-Pontyan argument against eliminativist theories of intentionality and consciousness, especially Dennett's, and "enactive" theories of perception, especially Noë's.

Dreyfus, H. L. *What Computers Still Can't Do*. A critique of artificial intelligence research from the 1950s to the 1990s, inspired by Merleau-Ponty's phenomenology, as well as Heidegger's *Being and Time*. See especially chapter 7.

————. *On the Internet*. A critique of the distorted and nihilistic image of human life fostered by computer technology and the World-Wide Web. Argues that our Cartesian conception of ourselves as detached, disembodied observers promotes actual disengagement and inauthenticity. See especially chapter 3.

Kelly, S. D. "The Non-Conceptual Content of Perceptual Experience." A Merleau-Pontyan intervention in the debate between John McDowell and Christopher Peacocke concerning perceptual content.

Aphasia   Loss of ability to speak, write, or understand language.

Apperception   Awareness of oneself.

Being-in-the-World   Heidegger's term for human existence, in contrast to the objective occurrence of mere things.

Body Schema   The set of enduring dispositions and capacities responsible for our intuitive sense of bodily position and possibility (not to be confused with *body image*).

Chiasm   Crisscrossing, overlapping, intertwining (*entrelacs*).

Cognitivism   The equations of experience generally with thought (see Intellectualism).

Constancy Hypothesis   The traditional assumption, criticized by Köhler, of a strict correlation between sensory stimulus and perceptual experience.

Dasein   Heidegger's term for human being (not to be confused with *mind*).

Eidetic Reduction   In Husserl's theory of intentionality, the turn of attention from particulars to ideal or general features of things, for example, in the case of consciousness, from the *noesis* to the *noema* (cf. Transcendental Reduction).

Empiricism   The view that sensations or impressions constitute the most basic form of experience (contrasted with Intellectualism).

Facticity   The concrete givenness of situations, in contrast to what we can voluntarily control or grasp in thought.

Flesh (chair)   Merleau-Ponty's term for the identity of perception and the perceptible.

Gestalt   German word for *shape* or *form*.

Habitus   Bourdieu's term for the bodily skills and dispositions that allow us to inhabit a particular social field (see Body Schema).

Hyletic   From the Greek *hulê* (material or stuff); Husserl's term for sensation, as distinct from the intentional content of perception.

Intellectualism   The view that judgment is, or is necessary for, the most basic form of experience (contrasted with Empiricism).

Intentionality   The directedness, of-ness, or "aboutness" of attitudes.

Intertwining (entrelacs)   See Chiasm.

Motor Intentionality   Concrete bodily awareness of oneself and one's environment, manifest not in thought or consciousness, but the ability to move and interact with things skillfully.

Noema   Husserl's term for the intentional *content* of consciousness, as distinct from its object.

Noesis   Husserl's term for a concrete mental state, as distinct from its intentional content.

Ontology   The study of being.

Phenomenology   For Husserl, the study of conscious experience, or appearance as opposed to reality (to be contrasted with Ontology); for Heidegger, the study of how things "show up" or manifest themselves (*not* to be contrasted with Ontology).

Proprioception   Immediate, non observational perception of one's own body.

Schema   General, but open-ended, conceptually unarticulated sketch, prefiguration, or anticipation of concrete objects or images.

Semantic Paradigm   The attempt to model intentional content on linguistic meaning, the assimilation of intentionality (with a t) to intensionality (with an s).

Structuralism   In linguistics, anthropology, and literary theory, the view that language, society, or texts, respectively, are governed by objective, universal, invariant forms or patterns ordinarily unavailable to consciousness or subjectivity.

Teleology   Purposiveness, end-directedness.

Transcendental Reduction   In Husserl's theory of intentionality, the turn of attention from the *external objects* to the *internal contents* (*noesis* and *noema*) of consciousness (cf. Eidetic Reduction).

Ultrabolshevism   Merleau-Ponty's term for Sartre's radical, unorthodox defense of communism in the early 1950s as the only viable political position for the working class.

Notes

ONE LIFE AND WORKS

1 I have relied for the preceding on Robinet, *Merleau-Ponty: Sa vie, son œvre.*

2 For more on the history of theories of visual perception, see Wade, *A Natural History of Vision.*

3 *Phenomenology of Spirit,* ¶73.

4 Hence Wittgenstein's remark, "If someone says, 'I have a body,' he can be asked, 'Who is speaking here with this mouth?'" *On Certainty,* §244.

5 Of course, the distinction between description and explanation is neither sharp nor exclusive, for some descriptions, precisely by describing as they do, also explain. The difference remains, however, since it is possible to describe *without* explaining.

6 For a recent spirited defense of the theory of ideas and its livelihood in cognitive science, see Fodor's *Hume Variations.*

7 *An Essay concerning Human Understanding,* 47–48.

8 Alexius Meinong, another student of Brentano's, tried to solve this problem by positing both existent *and* nonexistent objects. But in what sense can there be nonexistent objects? And what could constitute an intentional relation *to* such things?

9 Frege, "On Sense and Meaning." Confusingly, Frege's term *Bedeutung* is sometimes translated "reference," sometimes "meaning." It should be kept in mind, however, as others, including Husserl, have observed, that Frege's usage is idiosyncratic; in ordinary German *Sinn* and *Bedeutung* are virtually synonymous. So, for example, when Husserl himself uses the word *Bedeutung,* he means something more like what Frege means by *Sinn.*

10 Dagfinn Føllesdal was the first to recognize this analogy with Fregean semantics and its importance for understanding Husserl's phenomenology. See Føllesdal, "Husserl's Notion of *Noema.*"

11 The semantic model of mental representation is alive and well among philosophers as otherwise different as John Searle, whose theory of intentionality rests on the concept of "conditions of satisfaction" or "conditions of success," which is also central to his theory of speech acts, and Jerry Fodor, who argues that thought, owing to its compositional structure, must take place in a kind of mental language. See Searle's *Intentionality* and Fodor's *Language of Thought*. As Fodor says elsewhere, tracing his own view back to its early modern sources, "the idea that there are mental representations is the idea that there are Ideas minus the idea that Ideas are images." *Concepts*, 8.

12 See Gurwitsch's 1936 essay, "Some Aspects and Developments of Gestalt Psychology," which was based on his lectures of 1933–34, and in which he thanks Merleau-Ponty in a footnote for having read it prior to its publication. Although Merleau-Ponty never gave him proper credit for it, it is clear that Gurwitsch first introduced him to Gestalt theory and the work of Gelb and Goldstein.

13 See Ash, *Gestalt Psychology in German Culture*, chapter 3.

14 Köhler, "On Unnoticed Sensations and Errors of Judgment."

15 See *The Organism*, chapter 8.

16 See the epigraph to the "Temporality" chapter of *Phenomenology*, in which Merleau-Ponty quotes Paul Claudel likening the meaning of life to the direction of a river, the meaning of a phrase, the grain or weave of a fabric, and the sense of smell: "*Le temps et le sens de la vie (sens: comme on dit le sens d'un cours d'eau, le sens d'une phrase, le sens d'une étoffe, le sens de l'odorat)*" (PP 469/410/476).

17 Saussure, *Course in General Linguistics*, 13–15.

18 Colin Smith misleadingly translates *expression seconde* as "second-order expression," and *parole sur des paroles* as "speech about speech," which gives the false impression that what Merleau-Ponty has in mind is the linguistic description of language, or words referring to words. In fact, what he means is speech based on prior speech, speech parasitic on established, customary, or previously articulated expressions.

19 Wittgenstein, *Culture and Value*, 31.

TWO INTENTIONALITY AND PERCEPTION

1 *On the Trinity: Books 8–15*, 61, 62. Victor Caston identifies these ancient sources in article "Intentionality in Ancient Greek Philosophy."

2 "The Intentionality of Sensation," 4.

3 *Theaetetus*, 194a.

4 Knudsen, "Intentions and Impositions," 479. The latter clause is from al-Fārābī's commentary on *De interpretatione*, also quoted in Gyekye, "The Terms 'Prima Intentio' and 'Secunda Intentio' in Arabic Logic," 35.

5 *Psychology from an Empirical Standpoint*, 88.

6 Ibid., 89.

7 Ibid., 89.

8 J. L. Austin makes this point, too dogmatically I think, in *Sense and Sensibilia*, 94–96. We ought to say only that seeing *ordinarily* implies success, for we do sometimes use the verb in simply reporting a visual experience, veridical or not. That derivative, noncommittal sense of the word may be parasitic on the factive sense, but it's neither an abuse of language nor a philosopher's invention, as Austin suggests.

9 *The Principle of Reason*, 123–24/71.

10 *Parcours*, 54; *Texts and Dialogues*, 113.

11 *Basic Problems of Phenomenology*, 91/65, 93/66. "Dasein" (literally *being-there*) is ordinarily just the German word for *existence*. Heidegger uses it to refer specifically to the individual human being. See my *Heidegger's Analytic*, 35–43.

12 According to Köhler, the *"experience error* ... occurs when certain characteristics of sensory experience are inadvertently attributed to the mosaic of stimuli," as when, for example, one says "the shape of a pencil or of a circle is projected upon the retina." For, "In the mosaic of all retinal stimuli, the particular areas which correspond to the pencil or the circle are not in any way singled out and unified." *Gestalt Psychology*, 160, 180.

13 See Köhler, "On Unnoticed Sensations and Errors of Judgment."

14 "And so," Descartes writes, "something which I thought I was seeing with my eyes is in fact grasped solely by the faculty of judgment which is in my mind." *Meditations*, AT VII 32. Similarly, Kant writes, "all synthesis, through which even perception itself becomes possible, stands under the categories, and since experience is cognition through connected perceptions, the categories are conditions of the possibility of experience." *Critique of Pure Reason*, B161.

15 *Meditations*, AT VII 31 (emphasis added).

16 Dennett calls this view "first-person operationalism." *Consciousness Explained*, 132.

17 Here Merleau-Ponty quotes the Sixth Meditation: "These and other judgments that I made concerning sensory objects, I was apparently taught to make by nature; for I had already made up my mind that this was how things were, before working out any arguments to prove it." *Meditations*, AT VII 76.

18 Dennett, *Consciousness Explained*, 354–55. Cf. J. K. O'Regan, R. A. Rensink, and J. J. Clark, "Change-Blindness as a Result of "Mudsplashes." *Nature* 398 (1997): 34; and S. J. Blackmore, G. Brelstaff, K. Nelson, and T. Troscianko, "Is the Richness of our Visual World an Illusion? Transsaccadic Memory for Complex Scenes." *Perception* 24 (1995): 1075–1081.

19 *Essay* II.ix.8.

20 *The Philosophy of the Enlightenment*, 108.

21 In essay on "Molyneux's Question," for example, Gareth Evans points out that the debate was confused by misguided qualms about whether the blind have any understanding of space *at all*, whereas the philosophically interesting question is how normal visual experience of space is coordinated with tactual-kinaesthetic perception. Evans argues, and I think Merleau-Ponty would agree, that Berkeley's negative answer to Molyneux's question rests on the untenable assumption that the visual field has its own spatiality, distinct from the "behavioral space" in which we move our bodies and touch things.

22 J. J. Gibson found that subjects wearing goggles made of bisected ping-pong balls, which diffuse light into an undifferentiated array, don't see white, as you might expect. What they see is *nothing*. *The Ecological Approach to Visual Perception*, 151–52.

23 Merleau-Ponty is quoting Lèjean, *Étude psychologique de la "Distance" dans la vision*.

24 In its original incarnation as his 1963 doctoral dissertation, Todes's *Body and World* was entitled *The Human Body as Material Subject of the World*.

THREE BODY AND WORLD

1 *Principles of Philosophy*, AT VIIIA 22; *Meditations*, AT VII 32.

2 *Meditations*, AT VII 81.

3 *The Passions of the Soul*, AT XI 330.

4 See, for example, his description of hunger in the Sixth Meditation as "that curious tugging in the stomach" (AT VII 76). Similarly, "when I feel a pain in my foot, physiology tells me that this happens by means of nerves distributed throughout the foot, and that these nerves are like cords which go from the foot right up to the brain. When the nerves are pulled in the foot, they in turn pull on inner parts of the brain to which they are attached, and produce a certain motion in them" (AT VII 87).

5 "The Reflex Arc Concept in Psychology," 97.

6 Ibid., 99.

7 Ibid., 101.

8 Ibid., 102.

9 Ibid., 105.

10 *The Organism*, 71.

11 *Treatise on Man*, AT XI 176–77, and *Passions of the Soul*, AT XI 351ff. Actually, Descartes at times retains the holistic image, in the Sixth Meditation for example, where he says, "I am very closely joined and, as it were, inter-mingled with" my body, "so that I and the body form a unit" (AT VII 81). Nevertheless, there is still a crucial difference from the scholastic conception.

On Descartes's view, since the soul has no physical location, and so as he says, "no relation to extension," it cannot literally be closer to the pineal gland than to anything else. Consequently, "the soul is really joined to the whole body, and ... we cannot properly say that it exists in any one part of the body to the exclusion of the others" (AT XI 351). Unfortunately, this cuts both ways, for while the soul may be as much in the heart as in the brain, there is a sense in which it is no less in the sky than in the heart: "it is no more necessary that our soul should exercise its functions directly in the heart in order to feel its passions there, than that it should be in the sky in order to see the stars there" (AT XI 354).

12 Ryle, *The Concept of Mind*, 27, 19.

13 See for example Dennett, *The Intentional Stance*, 5.

14 Merleau-Ponty's *on* is as it were the sensorimotor analogue of *das Man*, Heidegger's term for the anonymous normative authority governing our everyday practices, in terms of which we understand ourselves, but which we regard as neither me nor you nor anyone in particular, but rather *anyone*. See my *Heidegger's Analytic*, 138–42. See also Merleau-Ponty, *VI* 244/190: "I don't perceive any more than I speak—Perception has me as language does—And just as I must be there all the same to speak, I must be there to perceive—But in what sense? As *one*."

15 *Concept of Mind*, 196.

16 Some such ontological exaltation of the third-person standpoint is what guides eliminative theories of consciousness and intentionality, like those of Daniel Dennett, who was a student of Ryle's. Dennett's "heterophenomenology" is not really phenomenology at all, but instead a policy of countenancing first-person phenomena *only* in the form of testimony regarded as observable verbal *behavior*. See Dennett's *Consciousness Explained*, chapter 4.

17 J. J. Gibson argues similarly that the classical notion of proprioception as a distinct sensory channel rests on thinking of perception generally as based on discrete inputs and separate sensation pathways. For Gibson, on the contrary, as for Merleau-Ponty, perception is not *based on* sensation at all: "the experiencing of facts about the body is not the basis of experiencing facts about the world. ... We do not perceive stimuli." *The Ecological Approach to Visual Perception*, 55. Perception is a function not of discrete *senses*, but of organized perceptual *systems*. "Proprioception or self-sensitivity is ... an overall function, common to all systems, not a special sense." *The Senses Considered as Perceptual Systems*, 320. Consequently, "all the perceptual systems are propriosensitive as well as exterosensitive"; "self-perception and environment perception go together." *Ecological Approach*, 115, 116. Cf. *Senses Considered as Perceptual Systems*, 1–6, 33–38, 47–58.

18 For an accessible account of recent work on phantom limbs, see Ramachandran and Blakeslee, *Phantoms in the Brain*, chapters 2 and 3, and Chapter 6 below.

19 As I explain briefly in Chapter 6, Pierre Bourdieu has elaborated Merleau-Ponty's notion of bodily understanding in his account of the essential inter-connectedness of the *habitus* and the social field. See Bourdieu, *The Logic of Practice*, chapters 3 and 4.

20 Facts about the poverty of parafoveal vision have recently generated debate over the absurd proposal that our perception of a seemingly richly detailed world is in fact a kind of hallucination. See Noë's *Is the Visual World a Grand Illusion?* The fact that such a proposal could inspire debate at all shows how far some theorists are willing to go in throwing their intuitions overboard in the face of phenomenologically undigested empirical data. The debate serves as a reminder, however, that sensory *stimulation*, which is discrete and local, is neither necessary nor sufficient for *perception*, which is holistic and environmental. See my paper, "On the Inescapability of Phenomenology."

21 Unfortunately, the Colin Smith translation of *Phenomenology of Perception* (almost always) originally had "body image" for *schéma corporel*, which is exactly wrong. Merleau-Ponty inherits the term from Henry Head, who makes a point of distinguishing the body *schema* from an *image of* the body. See Gallagher, "Body Schema and Intentionality," 226–29.

22 References to the *Critique of Pure Reason* are to the A and B page numbers given in the *Akademie* edition.

23 *On Dreams* 460b20; *Metaphysics* 1011a33.

24 For more on the concept of motivation in Merleau-Ponty, see Wrathall, "Motives, Reasons, and Causes," and also my paper, "The Body in Husserl and Merleau-Ponty," from which parts of this chapter have been adapted.

25 For a more thorough account of this kind of perceptual normativity, see Kelly, "What Do We See (When We Do)?" 119–20, and "Seeing Things in Merleau-Ponty," 90–94.

26 Goodale and Milner, *Sight Unseen*, 15–18.

27 The difference between vision for perception and vision for action, that is, can be understood as a difference between the "what" (object-identification) and the "how" (motor-interaction) content of visual perception. Goodale and Milner describe a woman with visual form agnosia due to brain damage resulting from carbon monoxide poisoning, whose symptoms in many ways resemble Schneider's. See *Sight Unseen*, Chapters 1 and 2, and Ramachandran and Blakeslee, *Phantoms in the Brain*, Chapter 4. See also Kelly, "Grasping at Straws."

28 The priority of the available to the occurrent is not for Heidegger a *metaphysical* priority of one kind of entity to another, but a *hermeneutical* priority of one form of understanding to another. See my *Heidegger's Analytic*, 190–99.

29 Goldstein's own view was structurally speaking something like this, only less plausible, for he thought Schneider had retained tactile perception in its "pure" state, stripped of the usual "qualitative coloring" of visual data. What Goldstein apparently failed to recognize is the unconscious visual processing that guides fine motor action. Merleau-Ponty, by contrast, sees that Schneider's motor skills are guided not just by touch, but by vision. He therefore points out that if Goldstein's account is right, it implies "that the word 'touch' does not have the same sense applied to the normal and to the impaired subject, that the 'pure tactile' is a pathological phenomenon that does not enter as a component into normal experience" (PP 138/119). But in that case we literally don't know what we're saying when we say that Schneider has "pure tactile" sensations.

30 Here too, Merleau-Ponty objects all too discreetly in passing (PP 125n/108n) to Goldstein's conjecture that normal persons are able to identify which parts of their bodies are being touched only because they have "kinesthetic residua," that is, memory traces of relevant bodily movements, whereas Schneider must actually carry out the movements himself. This not only radically understates the extent of Schneider's impairment, it also gets the phenomenology wrong, for "Nonetheless, in every case, without any movement, the normal person can distinguish a stimulus applied to his head from a stimulus applied to his body" (PP 125/108).

31 Schneider, for example, cannot recognize his own handwriting as his own (PP 153n/132n). Similarly, when he hears and retells a story, "he doesn't emphasize anything," nor can he comprehend the story as a whole, but feeds it back "bit by bit" (PP 154/133). Generally speaking, Schneider cannot "grasp simultaneous wholes" or "take a bird's-eye view [survoler]" of his own movements (PP 147/126–27).

32 Talk of the "projection" of a given world might sound contradictory. Remember, though, that "given" in phenomenology does not mean what it means in the empiricist tradition—for example in Wilfrid Sellars's famous attack on what he calls "The Myth of the Given"—namely raw sense data. What is "given" in the phenomenological sense of the word is not inferred from anything more basic or immediate, but neither is it just raw, meaningless data. It is instead the coherent configuration of things we find in a perceptual situation, as opposed to what we initiate or will or judge by our own effort.

33 I think Sean Kelly is wrong to equate Schneider's concrete movements with normal "unreflective motor actions like grasping an object," and to describe Goldstein's distinction between pointing and grasping as a "phenomenological distinction." Kelly, "Grasping at Straws," 166, 169. If concrete movement or

dorsal-stream processing is unconscious, as both Goldstein and Milner and Goodale maintain, it is hard to see how the neurobehavioral distinction as such can be a phenomenological distinction. The distinction Merleau-Ponty draws, which is in any case what Kelly describes, is instead a distinction between motor intentionality and thought, both of which are (or can be) conscious. Separating the manifest phenomena from the brain functions in this way leaves Kelly's argument intact; moreover I believe it has methodological implications for how to coordinate empirical research with phenomenological description generally.

34 Scientists often present their discoveries to the public with a kind of naïve hyperbole that makes philosophers squirm. V. S. Ramachandran, for example, suggests that to understand syndromes like visual form agnosia, "we need to abandon *all* our commonsense notions about what seeing really is." *Phantoms in the Brain*, 65 (emphasis added). *All?*

35 *Sight Unseen*, 2–3.

36 There are, after all, other visual pathways and modules in the brain in addition to the two at issue in accounts of visual form agnosia. See *Phantoms in the Brain*, chapter 4.

37 Noam Chomsky has made this point about the widening, hence emptying, of the concept of the physical. See *On Nature and Language*, 53.

38 In *The Being of the Phenomenon*, Renaud Barbaras lays great stress on the later "ontological" phase of Merleau-Ponty's thought, but regards it not as a radical change of direction, but as a vital but ultimately unfulfilled promise of improvement on what he considers the overly "reflective" (xxix), "dualistic" (3–18), "idealistic" (14–18, cf. 40) orientation of *Phenomenology of Perception*. Barbaras may be right that "Merleau-Ponty's thought is profoundly unified" (xxx), but I am much less confident that, within that unity, his increasingly "ontological" line of thought was moving in a very promising direction. For example, Barbaras speaks of "the necessity of passing from a phenomenology of perception—open to the reproach of being nothing other than a psychology of perception—to a *philosophy* of perception, discovering in perception a mode of being that holds good for every possible being" (xxi). But the search for something "that holds good for every possible being" strikes me as the mark of just the kind of outmoded metaphysics many of us would like to think phenomenology helped to render obsolete.

39 Barbaras thinks Merleau-Ponty never went far enough in this direction. Hence, "the famous notes on the necessity of leaving behind the consciousness–object duality should be read as the expression of an exigency rather than as a final report." *Being of the Phenomenon*, xxiv.

40 This phrase is a reference to Canguilhem's claim that illness is itself an aspect or "mode of living" (*allure de la vie*). See *The Normal and the Pathological*, 228.

41 *Ecological Approach*, 116.

42 *Ideas II*, §37. I can, of course, feel *pain* in my eyes if the light is very bright, or in my ears if the sound is very loud. But pain is a tactile sensation: "the eye is *also* a field of localization, but *only for touch sensations.*" *Id II* 148.

43 *Cartesian Meditations*, 128.

44 In fact, it is not hard to generate the effect. See Ramachandran and Blakeslee, *Phantoms in the Brain*, 58–62.

45 See *Id I* 86, 109–10, 150, 160–61, 192, 253; *Id II*, §§22–29; *Cartesian Meditations*, §§8, 11, 16, and Fourth Meditation.

46 *Meditations*, AT VII 32.

47 See Smith, "The Flesh of Perception," for an argument to the contrary.

FOUR   SELF AND OTHERS

1 *Being and Time*, 202/246–7.

2 *Cartesian Meditations*, 140.

3 ibid., 141

4 ibid., 142.

5 Rizzolatti et al., "Mirrors of the Mind."

6 Merleau-Ponty cites no source for this remark, but he is presumably referring to Scheler's book, *The Nature of Sympathy*, the French translation of which he includes in the bibliography of *Phenomenology*. Of course, Scheler's remark cannot itself have been a response to Husserl, since Scheler died in 1928, three years before the publication of *Cartesian Meditations* (in French) in 1931. The first edition of Scheler's book appeared in 1913, the second, with additional material, in 1923.

7 *Being and Nothingness*, 387/315.

8 *Being and Nothingness*, 345/281 (translation modified).

9 *A Theory of Moral Sentiments*, 11–12. To his credit, although Smith believed that empathy rests on our imaginative transposition with the other, his example of immediate, seemingly unthinking motor mimicry is meant to show precisely that such an explanation is not obvious. Recent psychological and neurological research suggests it might well be false.

10 See the studies of Meltzoff and Moore cited in the bibliography.

11 From these recent studies, Meltzoff and Gopnik themselves draw precisely the intellectualist conclusion that Merleau-Ponty rejects, namely, that neonatal imitations must be "the product of inferencelike processes," which are in effect "nature's way of solving both the problem of other minds and the mind-body problem at one fell swoop." Otherwise, they suppose, such primitive

capacities would have to be "merely reflexive." Gopnik and Meltzoff, *Words, Thoughts, and Theories*, 130–31. But is there nothing midway between reflex and inference? One might fairly ask how the problem of other minds and the mind-body problem could ever become problems for a baby less than an hour old. It would be better, I think, to say that spontaneous infantile mimicry and empathy are nature's way not of solving but of avoiding such problems.

12 Piaget writes, "So long as thought has not become conscious of self, it is a prey to perpetual confusions between objective and subjective, between the real and the ostensible; it values the entire content of consciousness on a single plane in which ostensible realities and the unconscious interventions of the self are inextricably mixed." *The Child's Conception of the World*, 34.

13 Ibid., 92, 48.

14 It is this transcendental twist in Merleau-Ponty's argument that it seems to me Renaud Barbaras misses when he concludes that Merleau-Ponty's account in *Phenomenology of Perception* fails, since there "the problem of the other is posed, but it is not genuinely resolved"; that he "cannot get beyond Husserl's perspective"; that in *Phenomenology of Perception* "solipsism is not overcome." *Being of the Phenomenon*, 36, 38. But solipsism need not be "overcome" by argument, for it is inherently self-defeating. Solipsism, that is, withers away as soon as we realize that what it asks us to imagine, namely the absence of others, is intelligible thanks precisely to what renders it false, namely the primitively felt sociality of the world in light of which questions concerning the *de facto* presence or absence of others can even make sense. What is it, we ought to ask skeptics, the presence or absence of which you're worried about? If they can answer us at all, then we have made our point. Merleau-Ponty's deep insight on this subject, it seems to me, is that the (so-called) "problem of the other" is not an epistemological problem at all, not a question with an answer, but a permanent source of existential tension and mystery, the appropriate philosophical response to which is not demonstrative argument, but demystifying phenomenological description and hermeneutical insight. The existence of others poses a philosophical problem only for bad philosophical accounts of our relation to them (and of theirs to us).

15 *Tractatus Logico-Philosophicus*, 5.631ff. Wittgenstein refers to death, too, as a structural limit at 6.4311 and 6.4312.

FIVE HISTORY AND POLITICS

1 Aronson, *Camus and Sartre*, 104.

2 Sartre, "Merleau-Ponty vivant," 580.

3 Ibid., 601 (translation modified).

4 *Camus and Sartre,* 169.

5 "Merleau-Ponty *vivant,*" 601.

6 See Sartre's harshly polemical essays of 1953, *The Communists and Peace.*

7 See Hegel's accounts of the "knight of virtue" and the "beautiful soul," *Phenomenology of Spirit,* ¶¶381–93, ¶¶632–71. Each represents a kind of practical inertia, and in the end hypocrisy, entailed by ill-conceived notions of moral purity.

8 Bukharin, quoted in Cohen, *Bukharin and the Bolshevik Revolution,* 291, 299, 286.

9 Ibid., 335.

10 Ibid., 349.

11 Ibid., 350, 354.

12 Ibid., 366.

13 Ibid., 348, 351.

14 Conquest, *The Great Terror: A Reassessment,* 20.

15 Ibid., 485–86. Conquest stresses rightly that all these figures can only be rough approximations.

16 Bukharin, 375.

17 Aron, *Memoirs: Fifty Years of Political Reflection,* 215.

18 Bukharin, 377.

19 "Critique of the Gotha Program." *The Marx-Engels Reader,* 538.

20 "The Renegade Kautsky." *The Lenin Anthology,* 463, 466.

21 "The Immediate Tasks of Soviet Government." Ibid., 454–55.

22 *Language and Politics,* 537.

23 *The Communists and Peace,* 68.

SIX VISION AND STYLE

1 Here, again, Merleau-Ponty's observations can be seen to anticipate recent studies concerning the neurological foundations of identification and empathy in the activation of mirror neurons. See Rizzolatti et al., "Mirrors of the Mind."

2 *Meditations,* AT VII 32.

3 This passage is a paraphrase of Rodin's remarks in *Art,* 32–33.

4 Œ 80/185–86/145. *Art,* 32.

5 *The Voices of Silence,* 45–46.

6 *The Ecological Approach to Visual Perception,* 285.

7 *"What Is Literature?" and Other Essays,* 26.

8 Ibid., 27.

9 Ibid., 27.

10 Ibid., 28–29. In an exchange with the composer and music theorist René Leibowitz, shortly after writing "What Is Literature?" Sartre modified his view somewhat by conceding that although music is a *nonreferring* medium,

it can nevertheless have a kind of political significance by subverting and sur-passing dominant musical forms, styles, techniques, and idioms, thus mani-festing and anticipating future freedom. See Sartre, "The Artist and His Conscience."

11 You might think the moon looks about the size of a coin held at arm's length, but in fact its angular diameter is much smaller—more like the size of a pea, small enough to fit (easily) in one of the holes punched in the margin of a piece of notebook paper. Should we then say that it looks smaller than you thought it did? Were you seeing it incorrectly before you knew its equivalence to the pea or the hole punch at arm's length? The truth is, we ordinarily have no opinion at all regarding the angular diameter of the moon; instead, the size the moon normally appears to be is just the size of the moon, though we do probably underestimate its distance from us, and consequently also its actual size.

12 *Voices of Silence*, 46. The first volume, or part I of the later edition, is entitled "Museum Without Walls" (*Musée imaginaire*).

13 Merleau-Ponty even refers to a "schizoid disorder" (*schizoïdie*) (SNS 15/10/71), though the behaviors and traits he describes would nowadays more likely be diagnosed as autism. Psychological jargon changes with every generation, so labels can be very misleading. In 1944, when Hans Asperger first described the condition that would eventually bear his name, for example, he called it "autistic psychopathy."

14 *Leonardo da Vinci and a Memory of His Childhood.*

15 Freud, *Introductory Lectures on Psycho-Analysis*, 41.

SEVEN LEGACY AND RELEVANCE

1 Dosse, *History of Structuralism*, 1.39.

2 *Tristes Tropiques*, 58.

3 Ibid., 56.

4 Lévi-Strauss and Eribon, *Conversations with Claude Lévi-Strauss*, 46, 119. Lévi-Strauss also speaks touchingly of Merleau-Ponty's tireless support for his election to the Collège: "despite the generosity he displayed on my behalf, he had a hard time combating the fear that he had laid a goose egg. He thought me capable of the most outrageous inventions." *Conversations*, 61.

5 *History of Structuralism*, 1:41 (translation modified).

6 Ibid., 1:39.

7 *The Logic of Practice*, 53.

8 Ibid., 54.

9 Ibid., 55.

10 *The Rediscovery of the Mind*, 175. Cf. *Intentionality*, chapter 5.

11 *Construction*, 129.

12 *Rediscovery*, 182.

13 For a more detailed critique of Searle, see my *Heidegger's Analytic*, 115–21. Concerning Merleau-Ponty's relevance to problems of rule following, including Searle's theory, see Wrathall, "The Phenomenology of Social Rules."

14 *Construction*, 146–47, emphasis added.

15 *Logic of Practice*, 55–56 (translation modified).

16 For early critical discussions of Merleau-Ponty's project, see Kullman and Taylor's "The Pre-Objective World," and Dreyfus and Todes's reply, "The Three Worlds of Merleau-Ponty."

17 Evans, *Varieties of Reference*, 155, cf. 227, 156.

18 Taylor, "The Validity of Transcendental Arguments," *Philosophical Arguments*, 23.

19 Sean Kelly also makes a convincing case for the bodily normativity of perception, arguing for example that the privileged context for *seeing* is, as he says, "the distance one *ought* to stand from the object, the orientation in which the object *ought* to be with respect to the viewer, the amount of surrounding illumination that *ought* to be present." Kelly, "What Do We See (When We Do)?" 120.

20 *Mind and World*, 57.

21 Peacocke, "Perceptual Content" and "Nonconceptual Content Defended."

22 Kelly, "The Non-Conceptual Content of Perceptual Experience."

23 *The Imaginary*, 364–65/190. See also Merleau-Ponty, PP 10/4–5/5. For "woolly blue," see PP 361/313/365. For more on the contemporary debate, see the papers collected in Gunther, *Essays on Nonconceptual Content*.

24 Dreyfus, *What Computers Still Can't Do*, 100–28.

25 See Searle, *Mind, Brains and Science*, chapter 2 and 3, and *Rediscovery*, chapter 9.

26 *What Computers Still Can't Do*, 235. For a discussion of Merleau-Ponty's continuing relevance to current research, see Dreyfus, "Merleau-Ponty and Recent Cognitive Science."

27 See Dreyfus, *On the Internet*.

28 *Body and World*, 49ff. In Merleau-Ponty, as Todes points out, "The body proper is not further characterized and fleshed out as we have done." *Body and World*, 265.

29 Varela, "The Specious Present."

30 Varela et al., *The Embodied Mind*, 69, 73.

31 Daniel Dennett makes the same bad argument against phenomenology in *Consciousness Explained* when he appeals to experiments concerning virtually instantaneous perceptual effects such as phi movement. See my paper, "On the

Inescapability of Phenomenology." See also Dreyfus's review of Varela et al., *The Embodied Mind*.
32 Clark and Chalmers, "The Extended Mind."
33 *Action in Perception*, 82, 81.
34 Ibid., 82, 83, 84.
35 Ibid., 83, 59.
36 Ibid., 215, 134, 193.

Bibliography

WORKS BY MERLEAU-PONTY

La Structure du comportement. Paris: Presses Universitaires de France, 1942 / *The Structure of Behavior*. A. Fisher, trans. Boston, MA: Beacon Press, 1963.

Phénoménologie de la perception. Paris: Gallimard, 1945 / *Phenomenology of Perception*. C. Smith, trans. London: Routledge & Kegan Paul, 1962; 1981 / London and New York: Routledge, 2002.

Humanisme et terreur. Essai sur le problème communiste. Paris: Gallimard, 1947 / *Humanism and Terror: An Essay on the Communist Problem*. J. O'Neill, trans. Boston, MA: Beacon Press, 1969.

Sens et non-sens. Paris: Nagel, 1948 / *Sense and Non-Sense*. H. L. Dreyfus and P. Dreyfus, trans. Evanston, IL: Northwestern University Press, 1964.

"La Doute de Cézanne." *Sens et non-sens*. Paris: Nagel, 1948 / "Cézanne's Doubt." *Sense and Non-Sense*. H. L. Dreyfus and P. Dreyfus, trans. Evanston, IL: Northwestern University Press, 1964.

"Le cinéma et la psychologie moderne." *Sens et non-sens*. Paris: Nagel, 1948 / "Film and the New Psychology." *Sense and Non-Sense*. H. L. Dreyfus and P. Dreyfus, trans. Evanston, IL: Northwestern University Press, 1964.

Éloge de la philosophie. Paris: Gallimard, 1953; *Éloge de la philosophie et autres essais*. Paris: Gallimard, 1960 (folio essais) / *In Praise of Philosophy and Other Essays*. J. Wild, J. Edie, J. O'Neill, trans. Evanston, IL: Northwestern University Press, 1988.

Les Aventures de la dialectique. Paris: Gallimard, 1955 (folio essais) / *Adventures of the Dialectic*. J. Bien, trans. Evanston, IL: Northwestern University Press, 1973.

Signes. Paris: Gallimard, 1960 / *Signs*. R. McCleary, trans. Evanston, IL: Northwestern University Press, 1964.

"Le Langage indirect et les voix du silence." *Signes*. Paris: Gallimard, 1960 / "Indirect Language and the Voices of Silence." *Signs*. R. McCleary, trans. Evanston, IL: Northwestern University Press, 1964.

Le Visible et l'invisible. C. Lefort, ed. Paris: Gallimard, 1964 / *The Visible and the Invisible*. A. Lingis, trans. Evanston, IL: Northwestern University Press, 1968.

L'Œil et l'esprit. Paris: Gallimard, 1964 (folio essais) / "Eye and Mind." *The Primacy of Perception and Other Essays on Phenomenological Psychology, the Philosophy of Art, History and Politics*. J. M. Edie, ed. Evanston, IL: Northwestern University Press, 1964 / "Eye and Mind." *The Merleau-Ponty Aesthetics Reader: Philosophy and Painting*. G. A. Johnson and M. B. Smith, eds. Evanston, IL: Northwestern University Press, 1993.

Résumés de cours, Collège de France 1952–1960. Paris: Gallimard, 1968 / "Themes from the Lectures at the Collège de France, 1952–1960." In *Praise of Philosophy and Other Essays*. J. Wild, J. Edie, J. O'Neill, trans. Evanston, IL: Northwestern University Press, 1988.

La Prose du monde. C. Lefort, ed. Paris: Gallimard, 1969 / *The Prose of the World*. J. O'Neill, trans. Evanston, IL: Northwestern University Press, 1973.

Texts and Dialogues. H. J. Silverman and J. Barry, Jr., eds. M. B. Smith et al., trans. New Jersey: Humanities Press International, Inc. 1992.

La Nature: Notes, Cours du Collège de France. D. Séglard, ed. Paris: Seuil, 1994 / *Nature: Course Notes from the Collège de France*. R. Vallier, trans. Evanston, IL: Northwestern University Press, 2003.

The Merleau-Ponty Aesthetics Reader: Philosophy and Painting. G. A. Johnson and M. B. Smith, eds. Evanston, IL: Northwestern University Press, 1993.

Notes des Cours au Collège de France: 1958–1959 et 1960–1961. Paris: Gallimard, 1996.

Le Primat de la perception et ses conséquences philosophiques. Paris: Verdier, 1996 / *The Primacy of Perception and Other Essays on Phenomenological Psychology, the Philosophy of Art, History and Politics*. J. M. Edie, ed. Evanston, IL: Northwestern University Press, 1964.

Parcours, 1935–1951. J. Prunair, ed. Paris: Verdier, 1997.

Psychologie et pédagogie de l'enfant. Cours de Sorbonne 1949–1952. J. Prunair, ed. Paris: Verdier, 2001 / *Consciousness and the Acquisition of Language*. H. J. Silverman, trans. Evanston, IL: Northwestern University Press, 1973.

Parcours deux, 1951–1961. J. Prunair, ed. Paris: Verdier, 2001.

Causeries 1948. S. Ménasé, ed. Paris: Seuil, 2002.

L'Union de l'âme et du corps chez Malebranche, Biran et Bergson. 2nd ed. J. DePrun, ed. Paris: Vrin, 2002. First edition pagination / *The Incarnate Subject: Malebranche, Biran, and Bergson on the Union of Body and Soul*. A. G. Bjelland and P. Burke. P. B. Milan, trans. Amherst, NY: Humanities Books, 2001.

Husserl at the Limits of Phenomenology. L. Lawlor and B. Bergo, eds. Evanston, IL: Northwestern University Press, 2002.

OTHER WORKS

Anscombe, G. E. M. "The Intentionality of Sensation: A Grammatical Feature." *Metaphysics and the Philosophy of Mind: Collected Philosophical Papers, Vol. 2*. Oxford: Blackwell, 1981.

Aristotle, *The Basic Works of Aristotle.* R. McKeon, ed. New York: Random House, 1941.

Aron, R. *Memoirs: Fifty Years of Political Reflection.* G. Holoch, trans. New York: Homes & Meier, 1990.

Aronson, R. *Camus and Sartre: The Story of a Friendship and the Quarrel that Ended It.* Chicago: University of Chicago Press, 2004.

Ash, M. G. *Gestalt Psychology in German Culture, 1890–1967: Holism and the Quest for Objectivity.* Cambridge: Cambridge University Press, 1998.

Augustine, St. *On the Trinity: Books 8–15.* G. B. Matthews, ed. S. McKenna, trans. Cambridge: Cambridge University Press, 2002.

Austin, J. L. *Sense and Sensibilia.* G. J. Warnock, ed. Oxford: Oxford University Press, 1962.

Baldwin, T. "Speaking and Spoken Speech." *Reading Merleau-Ponty: On "Phenomenology of Perception."* T. Baldwin, ed. London and New York: Routledge, 2007.

Barbaras, R. *The Being of the Phenomenon: Merleau-Ponty's Ontology.* T. Toadvine and L. Lawlor, trans. Bloomington and Indianapolis: Indiana University Press, 2004.

Beauvoir, S. de, "Merleau-Ponty and Pseudo-Sartreanism." *The Debate between Sartre and Merleau-Ponty.* J. Stewart, ed. Evanston, IL: Northwestern University Press, 1998.

Bourdieu, P. *The Logic of Practice.* R. Nice, trans. Stanford, CA: Stanford University Press, 1990.

Brentano, F. *Psychology from an Empirical Standpoint.* 2nd ed. London: Routledge, 1995.

Canguilhem, G. *The Normal and the Pathological.* C. R. Fawcett and R. S. Cohen, trans. New York: Zone Books, 1991.

Carman, T. "The Body in Husserl and Merleau-Ponty." *Philosophical Topics* 27 (fall 1999): 205–26.

——. *Heidegger's Analytic: Interpretation, Discourse, and Authenticity in "Being and Time."* Cambridge: Cambridge University Press, 2003.

——. "Husserl and Heidegger." *The Blackwell Companion to Philosophy.* N. Bunnin and E. P. Tsui-James, eds. Oxford: Blackwell, 2003.

——. "Sensation, Judgment, and the Phenomenal Field." *The Cambridge Companion to Merleau-Ponty.* T. Carman and M. B. N. Hansen, eds. Cambridge: Cambridge University Press, 2005.

——. "On the Inescapability of Phenomenology." *Phenomenology and the Philosophy of Mind.* A. Thomasson and D. W. Smith, eds. Oxford: Oxford University Press, 2005.

Cassirer, E. *The Philosophy of the Enlightenment.* C. A. Koelln and J. P. Pettegrove, trans. Princeton, NJ: Princeton University Press, 1951.

Caston, V. "Intentionality in Ancient Greek Philosophy." *The Stanford Encyclopedia of Philosophy* (Winter 2003 Edition), E. Zalta, ed. http://plato.stanford.edu/archives/win2003/entries/intentionality-ancient/

Chomsky, N. *On Nature and Language*. Cambridge: Cambridge University Press, 2002.
———. *Language and Politics*. Expanded 2nd ed. C. P. Otero, ed. Oakland, CA: AK Press, 2004.

Churchland, P. "Eliminative Materialism and the Propositional Attitudes." *Journal of Philosophy* 78 (1981): 67–90. Reprinted in Churchland, *A Neurocomputational Perspective: The Nature of Mind and the Structure of Science*. Cambridge, MA: MIT Press, 1989.

Clark, A. *Being There: Putting Brain, Body, and World Together Again*. Cambridge, MA: MIT Press, 1997.

Clark, A. and D. Chalmers, "The Extended Mind." *Analysis* 58 (1998): 10–23.

Cohen, S. F. *Bukharin and the Bolshevik Revolution: A Political Biography, 1888–1938*. Oxford: Oxford University Press, 1980.

Conquest, R. *The Great Terror: A Reassessment*. New York: Oxford University Press, 1990.

Déjean, M. R. *Étude psychologique de la "Distance" dans la vision*. Paris: Presses Universitaire de France, 1926.

Dennett, D. C. *The Intentional Stance*. Cambridge, MA: MIT Press, 1987.
———. *Consciousness Explained*. Boston, MA: Little, Brown & Co., 1991.

Descartes, R. *The Philosophical Writings of Descartes*. 3 vols. J. Cottingham, R. Stoothoff and D. Murdoch, eds. Cambridge: Cambridge University Press, 1984, 1985, 1991. References are to volume and page numbers of the Adam and Tannery edition (AT).

Dewey, J. "The Reflex Arc Concept in Psychology." *The Early Works, 1882–1898; Volume 5: 1895–1898*. Carbondale: Southern Illinois University Press, 1972.

Dosse, F. *History of Structuralism*. 2 vols. D. Glassman, trans. Minneapolis: University of Minnesota Press, 1997.

Dreyfus, H. L. "Alternative Philosophical Conceptualizations of Psychopathology." *Phenomenology and Beyond: The Self and Its Language*. H. A. Durfee and D. F. T. Rodier, eds. Dordrecht, The Netherlands: Kluwer Academic Publishers, 1989.
———. *What Computers Still Can't Do*. Cambridge, MA: MIT Press, 1992.
———. Review of Varela, Thompson and Rosch, *The Embodied Mind*. *Mind* 102 (July 1993): 542–46.
———. "Merleau-Ponty's Critique of Husserl's (and Searle's) Concept of Intentionality." *Rereading Merleau-Ponty*. L. Hass and D. Olkowski, eds. Amherst, MA: Humanity Books, 2000.
———. *On the Internet*. London and New York: Routledge, 2001.
———. "Merleau-Ponty and Recent Cognitive Science." *The Cambridge Companion to Merleau-Ponty*. T. Carman and M. B. N. Hansen, eds. Cambridge: Cambridge University Press, 2005.
———. "Reply to Romdenh-Romluc." *Reading Merleau-Ponty: On "Phenomenology of Perception."* T. Baldwin, ed. London and New York: Routledge, 2007.

Dreyfus, H. L. and S. E. Dreyfus. *Mind over Machine: The Power of Human Intuition and Expertise in the Era of the Computer.* New York: The Free Press, 1986.

Dreyfus, H. L. and S. Todes. "The Three Worlds of Merleau-Ponty." *Philosophy and Phenomenological Research* 22 (1962): 559–65.

Eilan, N. "Consciousness, Self-Consciousness and Communication." *Reading Merleau-Ponty: On "Phenomenology of Perception."* T. Baldwin, ed. London and New York: Routledge, 2007.

Evans, G. *Varieties of Reference.* J. McDowell, ed. Oxford: Clarendon Press, 1982.

———. "Molyneux's Question." *Collected Papers.* J. McDowell, ed. Oxford: Oxford University Press, 1985.

Fodor, J. A. *The Language of Thought.* Cambridge, MA: Harvard University Press, 1975.

———. *Concepts: Where Cognitive Science Went Wrong.* Oxford: Clarendon Press, 1998.

———. *Hume Variations.* Oxford: Clarendon Press, 2003.

Føllesdal, D. "Husserl's Notion of Noema." *Journal of Philosophy* 66 (1969): 680–87. Reprinted in *Husserl, Intentionality, and Cognitive Science.* H. L. Dreyfus and H. Hall, eds. Cambridge, MA: MIT Press, 1982.

Frege, G. "On Sense and Meaning." *Collected Papers on Mathematics, Logic, and Philosophy.* B. McGuiness, ed. Oxford: Blackwell, 1984.

Freud, S. *Introductory Lectures on Psycho-Analysis.* J. Strachey, trans. New York: Norton, 1966.

———. *Leonardo da Vinci and a Memory of His Childhood.* J. Strachey, trans. New York: Norton, 1961.

Fried, M. *Art and Objecthood.* New ed. Chicago: University of Chicago Press, 1998.

Gallagher, S. "Body Schema and Intentionality." *The Body and the Self.* J. Bermúdez, A. Marcel and N. Eilan, eds. Cambridge, MA: MIT Press, 1995.

Gibson, J. J. *The Senses Considered as Perceptual Systems.* Boston, MA: Houghton Mifflin, 1966.

———. *The Ecological Approach to Visual Perception.* Boston, MA: Houghton Mifflin, 1979.

———. "A Theory of Direct Visual Perception." *The Psychology of Knowing.* J. R. Royce and W. W. Rozeboom, eds. New York: Gordon & Breach, 1972. Reprinted in *Vision and Mind: Selected Readings in the Philosophy of Perception.* A. Noë and E. Thompson, eds. Cambridge, MA: MIT Press, 2002.

Gilmore, J. "Between Philosophy and Art." *The Cambridge Companion to Merleau-Ponty.* T. Carman and M. B. N. Hansen, eds. Cambridge: Cambridge University Press, 2005.

Goldstein, K. *The Organism: A Holistic Approach to Biology Derived from Pathological Data in Man.* New York: Zone Books, 2000.

Goodale, M. A. and A. D. Milner. *Sight Unseen.* Oxford: Oxford University Press, 2005.

Gopnik, A. and A. N. Meltzoff. *Words, Thoughts, and Theories.* Cambridge, MA: MIT Press, 1997.

Gunther, Y. ed. *Essays on Nonconceptual Content.* Cambridge, MA: MIT Press, 2003.

Gurwitsch, A. "Some Aspects and Developments of Gestalt Psychology." *Studies in Phenomenology and Psychology.* Evanston, IL: Northwestern University Press, 1966.

Gyekye, K. "The Terms 'Prima Intentio' and 'Secunda Intentio' in Arabic Logic." *Speculum* 46: 1 (1971): 32–38.

Hegel, G. W. F. *Phenomenology of Spirit.* A. V. Miller, trans. Oxford: Oxford University Press, 1977.

Heidegger, M. *Being and Time,* J. Macquarrie and E. Robinson, trans. New York: Harper & Row, 1962 / *Sein und Zeit.* Tübingen, Germany: Niemeyer, 1927; 15th ed. 1979.

————. *The Basic Problems of Phenomenology,* A. Hofstadter, trans. Bloomington: Indiana University Press, 1982; rev. ed., 1988 / *Grundprobleme der Phänomenologie. Gesamtausgabe* 24. Marburg lectures, summer 1927. F.-W. von Herrmann, ed. Frankfurt, Germany: Klostermann, 1975.

————. *The Principle of Reason.* R. Lilly, trans. Bloomington: Indiana University Press, 1991 / *Der Satz vom Grund.* Stuttgart: Neske, 1957.

Husserl, E. *Ideas Pertaining to a Pure Phenomenology and to a Phenomenological Philosophy. First Book.* F. Kersten, trans. The Hague: Nijhoff, 1983 / *Ideen zu einer reinen Phänomenologie und phänomenologischen Philosophie, Erstes Buch: Allgemeine Einführung in die reine Phänomenologie.* K. Schumann, ed. *Husserliana* III. The Hague: Nijhoff, 1976.

————. *Ideas Pertaining to a Pure Phenomenology and to a Phenomenological Philosophy. Second Book.* R. Rojcewicz and A. Schuwer, trans. Dordrecht, The Netherlands: Kluwer, 1989 / *Ideen zu einer reinen Phänomenologie und phänomenologischen Philosophie. Zweites Buch: Phänomenologische Untersuchungen zur Konstitution.* W. Biemel, ed. *Husserliana* IV. The Hague: Nijhoff, 1952.

————. *Ideas Pertaining to a Pure Phenomenology and Phenomenological Philosophy.Third Book. Phenomenology and the Foundations of the Sciences.* T. E. Klein and W. E. Pohl, trans. The Hague: Nijhoff, 1980 / *Ideen zu einer reinen Phänomenologie und phänomenologischen Philosophie. Drittes Buch: Die Phänomenologie und die Fundamente der Wissenschaften.* M. Biemel, ed. *Husserliana* V. The Hague: Nijhoff, 1952.

————. *Cartesian Meditations: An Introduction to Phenomenology.* D. Cairns, trans. The Hague: Nijhoff, 1960. *Cartesianische Meditationen und Pariser Vorträge.* 2nd ed. S. Strasser, ed. *Husserliana* I. Dordrecht, The Netherlands: Kluwer, 1963.

Kant, I. *Critique of Pure Reason.* ed. and trans. P. Guyer and A. W. Wood. Cambridge: Cambridge University Press, 1997.

Kelly, S. D. "What Do We See (When We Do)?" *Philosophical Topics* 27 (fall 1999): 107–28. Reprinted in *Reading Merleau-Ponty: On "Phenomenology of Perception."* T. Baldwin, ed. London and New York: Routledge, 2007.

————. "Grasping at Straws: Motor Intentionality and the Cognitive Science of Skilled Behavior." *Heidegger, Coping, and Cognitive Science.* M. Wrathall and J. Malpas, eds. Cambridge, MA: MIT Press, 2000.

————. "The Non-Conceptual Content of Perceptual Experience: Situation Dependence and Fineness of Grain." *Philosophy and Phenomenological Research* 62 (2001): 601–8. Reprinted in *Essays on Nonconceptual Content*, Y. Gunther, ed. Cambridge, MA: MIT Press, 2003.

————. "Seeing Things in Merleau-Ponty." *The Cambridge Companion to Merleau-Ponty.* T. Carman and M. B. N. Hansen, eds. Cambridge: Cambridge University Press, 2005.

Knudsen, C. "Intentions and Impositions." *The Cambridge History of Later Medieval Philosophy: From the Rediscovery of Aristotle to the Disintegration of Scholasticism*, 1100–1600. N. Kretzmann, A. Kenny, J. Pinborg and E. Stump, eds. Cambridge: Cambridge University Press, 1982.

Koestler, A. *Darkness at Noon.* D. Hardy, trans. New York: Scribner, 1941.

————. *The Yogi and the Commissar and Other Essays.* New York: Collier Books, 1961.

Köhler, W. *Gestalt Psychology: An Introduction to New Concepts in ModernPsychology.* New York: Liveright, 1947.

————. "On Unnoticed Sensations and Errors of Judgment." *The Selected Papers of Wolfgang Köhler.* M. Henle, ed. New York: Liveright, 1971.

Kravchenko, V. *I Chose Freedom: The Personal and Political Life of a Soviet Official.* New York: Charles Scribner's and Sons, 1946.

Kruks, S. *The Political Philosophy of Merleau-Ponty.* Sussex, U.K.: Harvester, 1981.

Kullman, M. and C. Taylor. "The Pre-Objective World." *Review of Metaphysics* 12 (1958/9): 108–32.

Lefort, C. "Thinking Politics." *The Cambridge Companion to Merleau-Ponty.* T. Carman and M. B. N. Hansen, eds. Cambridge: Cambridge University Press, 2005.

————. "The French Communist Party After World War II." *Complications: Communism and the Dilemmas of Democracy.* J. Bourg, trans. New York: Columbia University Press, 2007.

Lenin, V. I. *The Lenin Anthology.* R. C. Tucker, ed. New York: Norton, 1975.

Lévi-Strauss, C. *Tristes Tropiques.* J. and D. Weightman, trans. New York: Penguin, 1992.

Lévi-Strauss, C. and D. Eribon. *Conversations with Claude Lévi-Strauss.* Chicago: University of Chicago Press, 1991.

Locke, J. *An Essay concerning Human Understanding.* P. H. Nidditch, ed. Oxford: Clarendon Press, 1975.

Malraux, A. *The Voices of Silence.* S. Gilbert, trans. Princeton, NJ: Princeton University Press, 1978.

Marx, K. *The Marx-Engels Reader.* 2nd ed. R. C. Tucker, ed. New York: Norton, 1978.

Matthews, E. *The Philosophy of Merleau-Ponty.* Montreal: McGill-Queens University, 2002.

McDowell, J. *Mind and World*. Cambridge, MA: Harvard University Press, 1993.

Meltzoff, A. N. and M. K. Moore. "Imitation of Facial and Manual Gestures by Human Neonates." *Science* 198: 4312 (October 1977): 75–78.

———. "Newborn Infants Imitate Adult Facial Gestures." *Child Development* 54 (1983): 702–9.

Milner, D. A. and M. A. Goodale. *The Visual Brain in Action*. Oxford: Oxford Univsity Press, 1996.

Nagel, T. "What Is It Like to Be a Bat?" *Philosophical Review* 83 (1974): 435–50. Reprinted in *Mortal Questions*. Cambridge: Cambridge University Press, 1979.

Noë, A. "Is the Visual World a Grand Illusion?" *Is the Visual World a Grand Illusion?* ed. A. Noë. Charlottesville, VA: Imprint Academic, 2002.

———. *Action in Perception*. Cambridge, MA: MIT Press, 2004.

Noë, A., Pessoa, L., and Thompson, E. "Beyond the Grand Illusion: What Change Blindness Really Teaches Us About Vision." *Visual Cognition* 7 (2000): 93–106.

Panofsky, E. *Perspective as Symbolic Form*. New York: Zone Books, 1997.

Peacocke, C. "Perceptual Content." *Themes from Kaplan*. J. Almog, J. Perry and H. Wettstein, eds. New York: Oxford University Press, 1989.

———. "Nonconceptual Content Defended." *Philosophy and Phenomenological Research* 58 (1998): 381–88.

Piaget, J. *The Child's Conception of the World*. J. Tomlinson and A. Tomlinson, trans. Totowa, NJ: Rowman & Allanheld, 1960.

Plato, *Theaetetus*. J. McDowell, trans. Oxford: Clarendon Press, 1973.

Ramachandran, V. S. and S. Blakeslee. *Phantoms in the Brain: Probing the Mysteries of the Human Mind*. New York: HarperCollins, 1998.

Rizzolatti, G., L. Fogassi, and V. Gallese. "Mirrors of the Mind." *Scientific American* 295: 5 (November 2006): 54–61.

Robinet, A. *Merleau-Ponty: Sa vie, son œvre avec un exposé de sa philosophie*. Paris: Presses Universitaires de France, 1963.

Rodin, A. *Art: Conversations with Paul Gsell*. J. de Caso and P. B. Sanders, trans. Berkeley: University of California Press, 1984.

Romdenh-Romluc, K. "Merleau-Ponty and the Power to Reckon with the Possible." *Reading Merleau-Ponty: On "Phenomenology of Perception."* T. Baldwin, ed. London and New York: Routledge, 2007.

Rousset, D. *Coercion of the Worker in the Soviet Union*. Prepared by the International Commission Against Concentrationist Regimes. Boston, MA: Beacon Press, 1953.

———. *Police-State Methods in the Soviet Union*. Prepared by the International Commission Against Concentrationist Regimes. Boston, MA: Beacon Press, 1953.

Ryle, G. *The Concept of Mind*. New York: Harper & Row, 1949.

Sartre, J.-P. "The Artist and His Conscience." *Situations*. B. Eisler, trans. Greenwich, CT: Fawcett, 1965.

———. "Reply to Albert Camus." *Situations*. B. Eisler, trans. New York: Fawcett, 1966.

———. *Being and Nothingness: A Phenomenological Essay on Ontology*. H. Barnes, trans. New York: Washington Square Press, 1966; London and New York: Routledge, 2003. Page references are to these two editions.

———. "Merleau-Ponty vivant." *Situations*. B. Eisler, trans. New York: Fawcett, 1966.

———. *The Communists and Peace, With a Reply to Claude Lefort*. M. H. Fletcher, trans. New York: George Braziller, 1968.

———. *"What Is Literature?" and Other Essays*. S. Ungar, ed. Cambridge, MA: Harvard University Press, 1988.

———. *The Imaginary*. J. Webber, trans. London and New York: Routledge, 2004.

Sartre, J. P. and Merleau-Ponty, M. *The Debate between Sartre and Merleau-Ponty*. J. Stewart, ed. Evanston, IL: Northwestern University Press, 1998.

Saussure, F. de, *Course in General Linguistics*. W. Baskin, trans. New York: McGraw-Hill, 1959; R. Harris, trans. Chicago and La Salle, IL: Open Court, 1986.

Scheler, M. *The Nature of Sympathy*. P. Heath, trans. New Haven, CT: Yale University Press, 1954.

Searle, J. R. *Intentionality: An Essay in the Philosophy of Mind*. Cambridge: Cambridge University Press, 1983.

———. *Minds, Brains and Science*. Cambridge, MA: Harvard University Press, 1984.

———. *The Rediscovery of the Mind*. Cambridge, MA: MIT Press, 1992.

———. *The Construction of Social Reality*. New York: Free Press, 1995.

Seebohm, T. M. "The Phenomenological Movement: A Tradition Without Method? Merleau-Ponty and Husserl." *Merleau-Ponty's Reading of Husserl*. T. Toadvine and L. Embree, eds. Dordrecht, The Netherlands: Kluwer, 2002.

Smith, A. *A Theory of Moral Sentiments*. K. Haadonssen, ed. Cambridge: Cambridge University Press, 2002.

Smith, A. D. "The Flesh of Perception." *Reading Merleau-Ponty: On "Phenomenology of Perception."* T. Baldwin, ed. London and New York: Routledge, 2007.

Stewart, J. ed. *The Debate between Sartre and Merleau-Ponty*. Evanston, IL: Northwestern University Press, 1998.

Taylor, C. *The Explanation of Behaviour*. London: Routledge, 1964.

———. "The Validity of Transcendental Arguments." *Proceedings of the Aristotelian Society* 79 (1978/9): 151–65. Reprinted in *Philosophical Arguments*. Cambridge, MA: Harvard University Press, 1995.

———. "Merleau-Ponty and the Epistemological Picture." *The Cambridge Companion to Merleau-Ponty*. T. Carman and M. B. N. Hansen, eds. Cambridge: Cambridge University Press, 2005.

Todes, S. *Body and World.* Cambridge, MA: MIT Press, 2001.

Varela, F. J. "The Specious Present." *Naturalizing Phenomenology: Issues in Contemporary Phenomenology and Cognitive Science.* J. Petitot, F. J. Varela, B. Pachoud and J.-M. Roy, eds. Stanford, CA: Stanford University Press, 1999.

Varela, F. J., E. Thompson, and E. Rosch. *The Embodied Mind: Cognitive Science and Human Experience.* Cambridge, MA: MIT Press, 1991.

Wade, N. J. *A Natural History of Vision.* Cambridge, MA: MIT Press, 1998.

White, M. "The Effect of the Nature of the Surround on the Perceived Lightness of Grey Bars within Square-Wave Test Gratings." *Perception* 10 (1981): 215–30.

Wittgenstein, L. *On Certainty.* G. E. M. Anscombe and G. H. von Wright, eds. New York: Harper & Row, 1972.

———. *Tractatus Logico-Philosophicus.* D. Pears and B. F. McGuinness, trans. London and New York: Routledge, 1974.

———. *Philosophical Remarks.* R. Rhees, ed. R. Hargreaves and R. White, trans. Chicago: University of Chicago Press, 1975.

———. *Culture and Value.* G. H. von Wright, ed. P. Winch, trans. Chicago: University of Chicago Press, 1980.

Wrathall, M. "Motives, Reasons, and Causes." *The Cambridge Companion to Merleau-Ponty.* T. Carman and M. B. N. Hansen, eds. Cambridge: Cambridge University Press, 2005.

———. "The Phenomenology of Social Rules." *Reading Merleau-Ponty: On "Phenomenology of Perception."* T. Baldwin, ed. London and New York: Routledge, 2007.

Index

Alain, 171
Al-Fārābī, 31
anosognosia, 98, 100–1
Anscombe, E., 31
aphasia, 21, 231
apperception, 137, 149, 231
Aristotle, 8, 31, 106
Aron, R., 5, 161
Arrivé, M., 217
artificial intelligence (AI), 219–20, 223–4, 230
Asperger, H., 245 n13
Augustine, St., 31
Austin, J. L., 236 n8

Barbaras, R., 134, 150, 241 n38, 241 n39, 243 n12
Barthes, R., 5
Beauvoir, S. de, x, 4–5, 151–2, 155, 157
behaviorism, 214, 219–20, 223, 230
Benoist, J.-M., 217
Berkeley, G., 67, 190, 237 n21
Bergson, H., 5
body schema, 79, 102, 105–7, 110, 121, 132–3, 144, 149–50, 187, 199–200, 206, 217, 226, 230, 231, 232, 239 n21
Bourdieu, P., 5, 217–19, 229–30, 232, 239 n19

Brentano, F., 14, 31–3, 75, 234 n8
Breton, A., 151
Buddhism, 226
Bukharin, N., 158–61, 166, 178

Camus, A., 151–2, 179
Canguilhem, G., 242 n40
Carman, T., 29, 76, 230
Caston, V., 235 n1
Cézanne, P., 6, 23–4, 124, 180–4, 186, 188–9, 192, 204, 206, 208, 210–12
Chalmers, D., 226
change blindness, 229
Cheselden, W., 67
chiasm, 80, 120, 124–6, 131–3, 231, 232
Chomsky, N., 169, 241 n37
Chrysippus, 31
CIA, 151
Clark, A., 226–7, 230
Claudel, P., 235 n16
Coghill, G. E., 125
cognitivism, 12, 27, 53, 55–6, 219–20, 223–4, 231
constancy (size and color), 20, 76, 183
constancy hypothesis, 20, 21, 28, 49–50, 52, 54, 59–60, 231
Copernicus, N., 118

Davidson, D., 77, 134
Democritus, 8
Dennett, D., 53, 55–7, 230, 236
  n16, 238 n16, 246 n31
Derrida, J., 216
Descartes, R., 12, 15, 26, 27, 34, 44,
  53–4, 59, 75, 80, 83–5, 90, 92,
  130, 134, 154, 185, 189–91, 216,
  236 n14, 237–8 n11
Descombes, V., 217
Dewey, J., 86, 91
dialectic, 25, 154, 166, 170–3, 175
Dreyfus, H., 29, 76, 134, 223–5, 230
Dreyfus, S., 223
dualism, 15, 79, 84–5, 92–3, 96,
  109, 119, 130, 134, 171, 189,
  224, 241 n38

Eddington, A., 226
eidetic reduction, 39–40, 132, 231,
  232
empiricism, 5, 28, 50, 53–5, 59, 75–
  6, 231, 232
Epicurus, 8
epochê, 39–41
equilibrium, 22, 51, 72, 86, 109–10,
  114, 126, 140, 163–4, 192
Euclid, 7
Euclidean geometry, 206
Evans, G., 76, 220–2, 230, 237 n21
existentialism, 161, 213, 215
externalism, 75

Fink, E., 41
flesh (chair), 2, 79–80, 120, 123–5,
  132–3, 181, 184–6, 188–9, 215
Fodor, J., 235 n11
Føllesdal, D., 234 n10
Foucault, M., 5
Frege, G., 16, 27, 234 n9
French Communist Party (PCF), 152,
  177
Freud, S., 208–9

Galileo, 118
Gelb, A., 21, 111, 235 n12
Géricault, T., 193

Gesell, A., 126
Gestalt psychology, x, 4, 6, 19–22,
  25, 27–8, 120–1, 125, 180, 183,
  214, 216
Gibson, J. J., 1, 127, 196, 237 n22,
  238 n17
Gilmore, J., 212
Goethe, W., 24
Goldstein, K., 21–2, 87, 90, 111,
  113, 116–17, 122, 125, 133, 235
  n12, 240 n29, 240 n30, 240–1
  n33
Goodale, M., 111, 117, 133, 239
  n27, 241 n33
Gopnik, A., 242 n9
grasping (Greifen), 111–12, 116–17,
  134, 240 n33
grip (prise), 40, 47, 51, 56, 67, 71,
  80, 109–10, 114, 143, 181, 185–
  7, 194, 199, 206, 212, 221
Gurwitsch, A., x, 4, 20, 235 n12

habit, 98, 106, 111, 217
habitus, 214, 217–19, 230, 232, 239
  n19
Hegel, G. W. F., 10, 25, 139, 158,
  194, 204, 212, 216, 244 n7
Heidegger, M., 1, 6, 11, 14, 25, 26,
  38–40, 42, 74, 75, 112–13, 120,
  136–7, 161, 213, 223–5, 227,
  230, 231, 232, 236 n11, 238 n14,
  239 n28
Helmholtz, H. von, 12
hulê, 40, 44, 129, 232
humanism, 25, 157, 165, 171
Hume, D., 15, 134, 136, 163
Husserl, E., 6, 14–20, 27, 31, 35–43,
  75, 103, 107, 127–32, 137–40,
  149, 213, 234 n9, 234 n10, 239
  n24, 242 n4, 243 n12

ice cream headache, 101
idealism, 134, 150, 153, 215, 241
  n38
impressionism, 182–4
intellectualism, 5, 12, 27, 28, 53–60,
  75–6, 131, 162, 231, 232

internalism, 34, 75, 224
intertwining (*entrelacs*), 80, 120, 125, 133, 142, 231, 232

Kant, I., 12, 15, 27, 53, 65, 105–7, 134, 207, 216, 236 n14
Kelly, S., 76, 134, 222, 230, 240–1 n33, 246 n19
Kepler, J., 8
Khrushchev, N., 161
Klee, P., 192
Koestler, A., 151, 158–61, 178
Koffka, K., 19
Köhler, W., 19, 231, 236 n12
Korean War, 152, 176, 178
Kravchenko, V., 167
Kruks, S., 179
Kullman, M., 20

Lacan, J., 217
Lefort, C., 179
Leibniz, G., 9, 67, 134
Leibowitz, R., 244 n10
Lenin, V., 166–9
Leonardo da Vinci, 8, 208, 212
Les Lettres française, 167–8
Les Temps modernes, x, xi, 5, 24–5, 152, 157, 167, 178
Lévi-Strauss, C., 4, 214–17, 229, 245 n4
liberalism, 29, 154–8, 162–3, 165–6, 171–2, 175–6, 178
lifeworld, 29
Locke, J., 15, 27, 67, 75
logical positivism, 14
Lukács, G., 172–3

Malebranche, N., 59, 187
Malraux, A., 194–5, 202–4, 206, 212
Marx, K., 153, 167–8, 170–1, 178
Marxism, 25, 29, 152–9, 162, 164–5, 170–8
materialism, 57, 109
Matisse, H., 192, 222
Matthews, E., 29
McDowell, J., 134, 222, 225, 230
mechanism, 19, 21, 85, 92–3, 99–100, 126, 189

Meltzoff, A. N., 150, 242 n8, 242 n9
Millner, D., 111, 117, 133, 239 n27, 241 n33
mind blindness (*Seelenblindheit*), 111
mirror neurons, 137, 150, 244 n1
Molyneux, W., 67–8, 72, 74, 76, 237 n21
Mondrian, P., 190
Moore, M. K., 150, 242 n8
Morgenbesser, S., 166
Moscow Trials, 6, 24, 158, 161, 163, 166, 178
motivation, 58, 81, 107–9, 134, 139, 208, 239 n24
motor intentionality, 79, 110, 111, 115–17, 122–3, 133, 150, 230, 232, 241 n33
Müller-Lyer illusion, 48–9
Myth of the Given, 55, 240 n32

Newtonian mechanics, 206
Noë, A., 228–30, 239 n20
noema, 17–18, 27, 31, 35, 39, 42–3, 231, 232, 233
noesis, 17, 39, 231, 232, 233

"one" (*le "on"*), 94, 142
ontology, 29, 74, 79, 84, 232

Panofsky, E., 212
parafoveal vision, 60, 105, 239 n20
phantom limb, 98–102, 238 n18
phenomenal field, 61–8, 71–2, 76, 81–2, 86, 91, 96, 105, 133, 230
phenomenological reductions, 37–43
physicalism, 53, 96, 119
Piaget, J., 144–5, 243 n10
ping-pong ball goggles, 237 n22
Plato, 7, 12, 31, 84, 154, 162, 170
Platonism, 154, 170, 205
pointing (*Zeigen*), 111–12, 116, 134, 240 n33
pragmatism, 14, 166, 171, 174
proprioception, 68, 98, 101, 124, 127, 131, 232, 238 n17
psychoanalysis, 208–9, 212
psychologism, 205

Ptolemy, 7
Putnam, H., 227

quale, 63, 192

RAND Corporation, 223
Rassemblement Démocratique
  Révolutionnaire (RDR), 151
rationalism, 9, 11–13, 27, 53, 62,
  75, 94, 171
reflex, 86–91, 107, 242–3 n9
reflexivity, 128, 185
Rizolatti, G., 150
Rodin, A., 193, 244 n3
Romdenh-Romluc, K., 134
Rousset, D., 151, 167–8
Russian Revolution, 169, 178
Ryle, G., 92, 95, 238 n16

Sartre, J.-P., x, xi, 4–6, 14, 25, 39,
  83, 137–40, 149, 151–7, 167,
  171, 173–4, 178, 179, 198–9,
  207, 210, 213, 216, 222, 233,
  244 n6, 244–5 n10
Saussure, F. de, 24, 197, 216–17, 229
"Schneider" (Goldstein's patient),
  111–17, 122–3, 133, 239 n27,
  240 n29, 240 n30, 240 n31, 240
  n33
Searle, J., 76, 218, 223, 235 n11,
  246 n13
Seebohm, T., 77
Sellars, W., 55, 240 n32
semantic paradigm, 18, 77, 35, 75,
  232
sense data, 19, 28, 45–6, 52, 76,
  202, 228, 240 n32
Slánský, R., 152

Smith, A., 141, 242 n7
Smith, A. D., 134
Smith, C., 235 n18, 239 n21
solipsism, 136, 138, 141, 144, 146–
  8, 150, 243 n12
Spinoza, B., 58
Stalin, J., 152, 158–60, 169, 178
Stalinism, 153, 159–61, 166–7
Stendhal, 155
structuralism, 14, 213–17, 229, 232

Taylor, C., 29, 77, 134, 220–1, 223,
  225, 230
teleology, 65, 164, 171–2, 220, 233
Todes, S., 29, 76, 134, 225, 237
  n24, 246 n28
transcendental ego, 130, 138
transcendental reduction, 39–40, 75,
  231, 232
Trotsky, L., 167, 175

Uexküll, J. von, 126
ultrabolshevism, 5, 174

Varela, F., 225, 230
visual form agnosia, 111, 133, 239
  n27, 241 n34, 241 n36

Weber, M., 156, 171–2, 175
Weil, S., 4
Wertheimer, M., 19
White's illusion, 48–9
Wittgenstein, L., 24, 118, 120, 136–
  7, 148, 223, 234 n4, 243 n13
Wrathall, M. 134
Wundt, W., 12

Zöllner's illusion, 56–7